THAILAND

A CLIMBING GUIDE

THAILAND
A CLIMBING GUIDE

SAM LIGHTNER JR.

THE MOUNTAINEERS BOOKS

THE MOUNTAINEERS BOOKS
*is the nonprofit publishing arm of The Mountaineers Club,
an organization founded in 1906 and dedicated to the exploration,
preservation, and enjoyment of outdoor and wilderness areas.*

1001 SW Klickitat Way, Suite 201, Seattle, WA 98134

Published simultaneously in Great Britain by Cordee, 3a DeMontfort Street, Leicester,
England, LE1 7HD

Manufactured in the United States of America

Acquiring Editor: Christine Hosler
Project Editor: Mary Metz
Copy Editor: Ellen Smithee
Cover and Book Design: The Mountaineers Books
Layout Artist: Marge Mueller, Gray Mouse Graphics
Cartographer: Jennifer Shontz/Red Shoe Design
All photographs by author unless otherwise noted.

Cover photograph: *Dr. Volker Schoeffl pulling into the crux of* Asia's Shadow Play *(8a) above
Tonsai Beach on the Phra Nang Peninsula*
Backcover photo: *The beautiful first pitch of* Fit to be Thai'd *on the Thaiwand, Phra Nang
Peninsula* (Dr. Volker Schoeffl)
Frontispiece: *Gerd Schoeffl with his back to the bay on* Organ Grinder *(6c)*

Library of Congress Cataloging-in-Publication Data

Lightner Jr., Sam, 1967-
 Thailand : a climbing guide / Sam Lightner Jr.—1st ed.
  p. cm.
 Includes bibliographical references and index.
 ISBN 0-89886-750-9
 1. Mountaineering—Thailand—Guidebooks. 2. Thailand—Guidebooks. I. Title.
 GV199.44.T52L54 2005
 796.52'2'09593—dc22
            2005012739

 Printed on recycled paper

DEDICATION

This book is dedicated to everyone who has ever helped out with replacing fixed anchors in Thailand. It's horrible work, and your efforts are keeping this great climbing area open to climbers from all over the world. Thank you very much.

When I say this book is dedicated to you, I truly mean it. All of the profits I generate with this book, 100 percent of the money earned by me, will be donated to the American Safe Climbing Association and earmarked exclusively for use in Thailand. Purchasing this book pays for bolts and anchor material. One hundred percent. This is not "we help rebolt" or "portions of the profits will go to rebolting" but *100 percent*. You have it here in writing.

CONTENTS

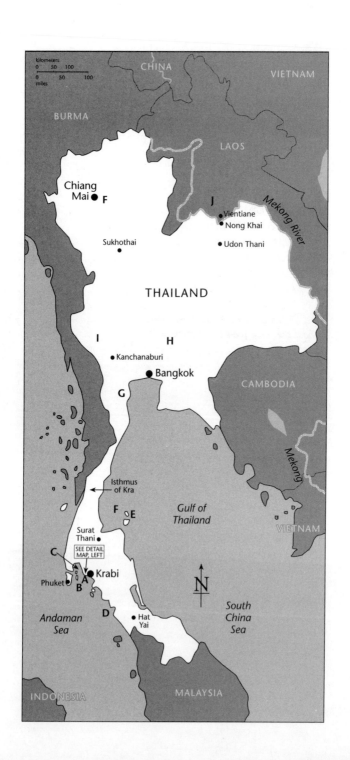

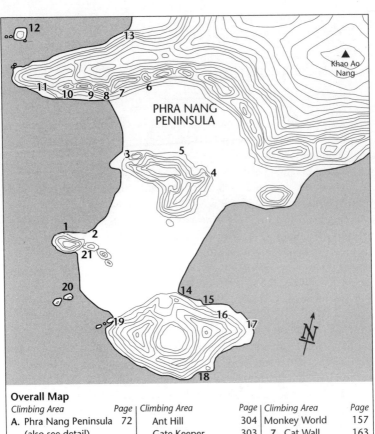

Overall Map

A LETTER TO YOU ALL

A week after I sent this manuscript to The Mountaineers Books, a tsunami ripped across the Indian Ocean Basin, killing hundreds of thousands of people and leaving millions homeless.

In Thailand, on Koh Phi Phi, the event was as devastating as it was anywhere else in the world. At around 10:35 A.M., thousands of people were torn apart or drowned in the massive tidal wave. On the Phra Nang Peninsula, where shallower water and a large reef worked to our advantage, the devastation was less severe. Still, there were many casualties, especially among snorkelers and people out sea kayaking. Fortunately, no climbers were killed while they were climbing off the exposed beaches, but we may never know who was lost while they spent a rest day at Koh Po Da or Chicken Island.

In the immediate aftermath, the Thai government and various locals whose boats had survived the disaster (Luang at Hot Rock, for instance) evacuated all tourists and locals who wanted to leave. One group, by and large, stayed to help: the climbers. Just after the initial wave, there was a warning that another surge might be on the way. Despite this, at least one group of climbers went out in a small boat to search for people who had been swept out to sea. In the days that followed, climbers went about repairing damaged boats, cleaning up the beach, and just helping the locals get back on their feet. More than a few, like Pep Massip, actually flew to Thailand when most tourists were in mass exodus, just to lend a hand in their beloved climbing area. Perhaps most important, the climbers stayed and gave the best assistance there could have been for the area by being patrons to the locals' businesses.

So often I find myself angry at climbers for being self-centered and not lending a hand to their fellow man. But when the chips were really down, we came through. On December 26, 2004, the world ran in fear from southern Thailand, but we stayed and did the right thing. I personally thank you all for that, and I know that you will always get a warm welcome by the locals of southern Thailand, who now clearly know who will stand by their side when they need a helping hand.

Sam Lightner Jr.
January 1, 2005
Railay Beach, Thailand

PREFACE

The lion's share of this book focuses on the Phra Nang Peninsula, the main climbing area in Thailand. That part of this little tome has been a twelve-year project of mine. However, Thailand is perhaps the easiest country in the world for travel, offering a lot more to see and do than just rock climbing in the *Laem* (land of) Phra Nang. For that reason, I have included not only climbing information for other areas, but also various bits of travel information so that you won't *have* to buy separate guidebooks for climbing as well as moving about in the Kingdom. For a climbing guidebook, this little book has a lot of information on the history, culture, and ecology of Thailand. It is limited in scope and thus does not cover every single climb in the country, but instead focuses on those that you are likely to visit and that I feel are worth your efforts.

This book comes from my heart. Laem Phra Nang is the only place I have fallen in love with the sport of climbing over and over again. What I will do with my life, who I will spend it with, and where I will be for many of my years—all of the biggest decisions of my life—have been made between the walls of the Phra Nang Peninsula. I have had moments on these walls, alone above the jungle canopy and turquoise water, where nothing else but *that moment* mattered. It is the only place where I have experienced what I can call true tranquility, and I will spend the rest of my life searching for it and knowing that, if I must, I can find it again on these walls.

I hope that this book can give you at least a fraction of the pleasure I have received during my years of living in paradise.

A NOTE ABOUT SAFETY

Safety is an important concern in all outdoor activities. No guide-book can alert you to every hazard or anticipate the limitations of every reader. Therefore, the descriptions of roads, trails, routes, and natural features in this book are not representations that a particular place or excursion will be safe for your party. When you follow any of the routes described in this book, you assume responsibility for your own safety. Under normal conditions, such excursions require the usual attention to traffic, road and trail conditions, weather, terrain, the capabilities of your party, and other factors. Because many of the lands in this book are subject to development and/or change of ownership, conditions may have changed since this book was written that make your use of some of these routes unwise. Always check for current conditions, obey posted private property signs, and avoid confrontations with property owners or managers. Political conditions may add to the risks of travel in Thailand and Laos in ways that this book cannot predict. When you travel, you assume this risk, and should keep informed of political developments that may make safe travel difficult or impossible. Keeping informed on current conditions and exercising common sense are the keys to a safe, enjoyable outing.

The Mountaineers Books

ACKNOWLEDGMENTS

Before I thank anyone who helped with the book, I thank Princess Nang for letting us climb in her domain. It's her paradise that we are passing through. There are a bunch of people who need to be thanked for helping me. First, I must thank Bobby Model for graciously donating the best photos in this book. The brilliant, devilishly handsome, witty, and charming Viking, Magnus Wiklund, is thanked for helping out with the information on Koh Phi Phi. Shamick Byszewski needs my thanks, as well as yours, for his continuing efforts on rebolting southern Thailand. King, aka Somporn Suebhait, needs to be thanked for his help with this book, as well as for many untold hours of belay time. Wee Changrua gets the same thanks. Luang Vitsanu gets my thanks for his help with the book, and for just being such a good friend in those horrible first weeks of 2005.

Doctors Volker Schoeffl and Gerd Schoeffl need thanks for aiding me in many ways here. Volker needs to be singled out for his help with the chapter on Laos and on sailing trips.

Tom Cecil, Mark Miner, and their posse need thanks for help that they have given us with topo information on the crags. Ditto for Mike Ho and Greg Collum. C-Mac at SuperTopo and Greg Barnes made large contributions of ideas, effort, and time, as did my wonderful editor, DeAnne Musolf Crouch. Jim Gudjonson is thanked for contributing a few photos. Joe and Lisa McKay helped out in Phi Phi and with photography, as well as refreshments. Dick and Beth Balsamo, Jacqui Battaglia, Anne and Michelle Gaultier and the Nongs all need thanks for helping me with a few Thai terms and phrases. Pi Daeng gets full credit for all the meals, and just about everyone listed above thanks her for them as well. Sophie, wherever you are, thanks for rerecording some of this info way back when. Captain Nick Band gets huge thanks for getting us safely around pirates, reefs, sharks, and Burmese gunboats in the Andaman Sea. Josh Morris at Chiang Mai Rock Climbing Adventures deserves kudos for his help with the Chiang Mai chapter. Forest Dramis gets thanks for getting me safely around in my computer.

Hundreds of people helped keep me alive over the years in Thailand: Alex Catlin, Julian Saunders, Jacob Valdez, Nancy Feagin, Scott Morely, and dozens more I cannot picture now but think of often. Elaine Catlin, Tess, and Alg all get thanks for helping me get around in my head. And Michelle Garbert gets very special thanks for contributing in many ways to this project.

Railay Bay and the Phra Nang Peninsula from the Cat Wall

Chapter 1

THAILAND PRACTICALITIES

Paradise! The Phra Nang Peninsula is perhaps the most beautiful playground on Earth. The food is excellent, the water is beautiful, the jungle lush, and the rock steep and full of big holds. I'm not sure you could create a more perfect, not to mention exotic, place to take a climbing trip.

Of course, there are a few other aspects of Thailand that won't escape you. It's hot. Real hot. You can expect to be wearing as little clothing as possible. Many of the crags can be buggy, and those bugs can carry diseases you would just as soon never even hear about, much less fight off. Sand will permeate your gear, wearing it out as fast as possible, and the salt and various chemicals in the air will add to the wear and tear. The gear that stays in Thailand permanently—the bolts—will frighten you...and they should. Everyone will be trying to make a buck off you, and you will grow tired of hearing Bob Marley and "Hotel California" at every bar.

Still, it's paradise, and what you can expect is to have one of the best climbing trips of your life.

When to Go

Thailand is a tropical country, meaning it lies within 23.5 degrees of the equator. This means that Thailand (as well as all the other countries in the tropics) does not have the same kind of seasons we are used to north or south of the tropics. While we have a winter and a summer, Thailand has a dry season and a wet season.

The wet season is made so by the monsoon, a weather pattern that runs more or less around the globe, moving north or south depending on the tilt of the planet. In southern Thailand, the monsoon rains usually begin in June. They can often be nothing more than intense afternoon showers, but as the season progresses—usually starting in late August—long wet periods when rain falls for weeks on end are not uncommon. This begins to ease in October and by mid-November the rains usually end.

Southern Thailand's dry season, a period when long-lasting storms are fairly rare, is generally between December and May. The first few months of this, December through February, are the coolest (unfortunately, they are also the most popular with tourists). The hottest months are April and May, when the sun is passing directly overhead but the cooling rains have not yet begun.

Many people want to know what they can expect on a trip in our "shoulder seasons" (spring and fall). My general answer is that late October and November are like October in Yosemite—you can have the best days of the year, when the temps are cool and the weather is perfect, or you can get caught in storms and get skunked .... It's a roll of the dice. During April and May, you just need to be ready to be hot. Really hot. If you can deal with the summer temps in a place like New River Gorge, West Virginia, then you will feel fine in Thailand in April. If neither of those answers work for you, then you better go in the cooler part of the dry season (December to March) and plan on sharing the beach with a lot of other people.

Northern Thailand is affected in a similar way, but the wet season is shorter and less intense. Also, continental weather patterns that come into play in the dry season can actually bring in cold temperatures. In December and January, you might find yourself seeking the sun at Crazy Horse, near Chiang Mai, while climbing in the sun on the Phra Nang Peninsula is almost unheard of at any time of the year.

Immunizations

Serious infectious diseases are a concern in certain parts of Thailand. At least two months before your trip, start with a visit to a doctor who is well versed in travel medicine. Some medications require an extended period of time in order for repeated cycles to be administered or in order to take effect.

Southeast Asia is home to a lot of the world's infectious diseases, but I have listed below the ones that I understand to be the most common and pertinent to a climbing trip, especially to southern Thailand. The following are not all the possibilities, however, and your doctor could help you choose other immunizations, but these are the ones I believe to be a credible threat in the areas covered in this book and the ones you should at least discuss with your doctor before traveling to Thailand. Keep in mind many tropical-disease doctors would rather treat you for the disease than give you the prophylactic because the immunizations often have a lot of side effects.

Typhoid. It's a serious disease of the stomach and intestine that is fecally–orally transmitted, so it is common in areas where the water quality is bad (i.e., Phra Nang Peninsula and Koh Phi Phi).

Hepatitis A. This liver infection is also commonly transmitted fecally–orally, so you should be immunized.

Rabies. This is one your average doctor will dismiss, but a travel doctor who knows that you will be sticking your fingers into rock pockets in a wild area will know you should have it. Rabies is common and kills over 50,000 people a year.

The bats in Thailand (which often reside in limestone pockets), not to mention the dogs, can carry it. Also, there is now an airborne version of the disease. And think about this: even a friendly dog who gives you a nice lick for feeding him could give you the disease if you happen to have a goby where he licked! Rabies is widely accepted in the medical community as a really bad way to go.

Polio. You probably had a polio booster, but get one again.

Tetanus. Get another booster. No one really knows how long they're good for.

Dengue fever. Other diseases you could encounter include dengue fever, which is spread by the aedes mosquito, is nasty, and in its hemorrhagic form can kill you. However, a lot of people get it and few die. It is common in Thailand and on the rise in the Krabi Province. There is no prophylactic (preventative) medication you can take.

Typhus. Spread by ticks, this is also something you could end up with. Like dengue fever, there is no prophylactic for typhus.

Malaria. Common in rural Thailand, for some reason it does not seem to be much of a problem at Phra Nang or Koh Phi Phi. However, it could be a problem in the other rural areas covered in this book. Malaria is far more prevalent in the rice-growing regions of northern Thailand than it is on the beaches of southern Thailand. Malaria is spread by the anopheles mosquito, which perhaps prefers rice paddies to beaches. Still, it is not completely out of the question. At present, there is no vaccine for malaria.

Japanese encephalitis. If you are trekking up north, you should be concerned about encephalitis, a disease that causes inflammation of the brain and is associated with pigs (common critters up north). Japanese encephalitis is all but unheard of in the south, but it is a reality of life in the small villages of the north. The vaccine is a little pricy, but may be worth the investment.

Visas

A visa is nothing more than a government's attempt to keep track of someone who really doesn't care if the government keeps track of them. In other words, it's a waste of their time. Be that as it may, the Kingdom of Thailand requires you to have one.

There are numerous websites, including *www.thai-info.net* and *www.traveldocs .com*, that tell you what is required for your planned length of stay. You can also go to the website of the Thai embassy in your home country. It will list all the current requirements for visas, depending on your nationality.

Currently, the law states that if you will be in the country for more than a month, you should lay down the US$15 and get the tourist visa. If you plan to be in Thailand for less than a month, you can get away with the transit visa, which is automatically given to you on entry at no charge.

If it appears as if you will go over your visa while in Krabi Province, here is the deal: You can get a one-month extension on a two-month tourist visa by paying 500 baht (the Thai unit of currency) to the immigration office in Krabi town. A one-week extension on the transit visa is also available. The immigration guys will want you to fill out a form and give them two pictures of yourself, as well as copies of the pertinent pages of your passport. It's an easy operation, but you have to do it *before* your entry visa expires. I recommend doing it on a Tuesday, Wednesday, or Thursday. Their offices are closed on weekends and wish to be closed on Monday and Friday.

Reservations for Accommodations

For much of the year, it is fairly easy to get a place to stay on the Phra Nang Peninsula, and Chiang Mai is much the same. However, crowds at Christmas, Chinese New Year, and the Thai *Songkram* holiday, which takes place in mid-April, fill up all the area's accommodations. I have listed those bungalows that take reservations with their phone numbers in the "Getting Situated" section for each of the the major climbing areas. For Railay Beach, you probably will be able to get a reservation via one of the directory websites listed below. My favorite is the first one.

www.railay.com
www.krabidir.com
www.krabiholiday.com
www.krabinet.com
www.krabirailay.com

Phone Calls

The country code for Thailand is 66. Throughout this book, I list the area codes with a "0" in front of them because the "0" is necessary when you are dialing from within the country. If you are dialing from outside the country, you drop the "0" and just go straight from country code to area code. As an example, if you want to call King Climbers:

From the United States or Canada: 011-66-75-637-125 (The "011" reaches an international operator.)

From within Thailand: 075-637-125

Flights to Thailand

Flights to Bangkok are easy to get because it is served by many different airlines. Thai Airways International is often the best deal and has a good reputation for service. Its long-haul flights to Europe and North America have a good record for safety as well. (Safety has not always been the primary concern of Thai's pilots on domestic flights, and it has been costly.) Tickets on Thai Airways also tend to be the easiest to change when you are in Thailand.

However, from the West Coast of the United States, Korean Air and China

Airlines tend to be the absolute cheapest if you are flying no farther than Bangkok.

From Europe, often the cheapest way to get to Thailand is by getting on a chartered flight that works with the various package tour operators. Also, some of the Eastern European airlines offer great deals, as do a couple of the Middle Eastern airlines. *Caveat emptor!*

There are direct flights into Krabi from countries closer to Thailand than either the United States or Europe. These change seasonally, but it has been possible to get directly to Krabi from Singapore, Hong Kong, and Taiwan. It is also possible to fly directly from Europe to Phuket, an airport that is about a three-hour taxi ride (1,500 baht) from Krabi. Before Krabi International Airport opened, this was the most common way of getting to the climbing.

What to Bring

Honestly, you won't need much. You could get away with going to Thailand with two pairs of shorts, two tee shirts, nicer clothes for the plane, a headlamp, sandals, and your climbing gear. My girlfriend once went for three weeks with nothing more than a carry-on pack!

Always carry a photocopy of your passport in a safe place, separate from your actual passport. This speeds up the process of getting a new passport if you should lose it.

Climbing equipment. Obviously you'll need at least one 60m rope (two for getting off the big stuff), fifteen quickdraws, and your personal gear. Keep in mind that the environment is extremely hard on your gear and could substantially weaken it. Old hands to the place bring gear that they use only in Thailand. (When you return home, make sure you thoroughly clean all the gear because the salt will continue to work its voodoo for as long as it's left on the aluminum.) Bigger, more comfortable climbing shoes, preferably slipper-types, tend to be best since your feet swell when you wear flip-flops all the time. No trad gear is needed, though tri-cams can be useful in pockets if you want to back up the bolts and threads. You will want some extra webbing for anchors and threads. Thin webbing works well for threading through pockets, but old rope lasts the longest.

An old rope that you have no use for back home is quite useful in Thailand. If you feel like being a Good Samaritan, you could bring over old rope and re-rig a few anchors with it. We locals like to see it threaded through 2.5-centimeter (1-inch) tubular webbing, which truly makes it bombproof against the ultraviolet (UV) rays. Replacing threaded bits of rock is both a necessity and a community service, and one of your old ropes that you have no use for will go a long way in helping us climbers in Thailand. One of those nasty little hooks commonly used in ice climbing to make abalakovs is very useful for this. Old carabiners are always needed for replacement work as we use them

on most of the anchors. You will only make friends by replacing threads on
the routes you do.

Clothing. You won't need much. Shorts and tank tops or tee shirts are the
norm. You might want light cotton pants at night, not because it's cool, but
because they help keep the bugs off. I personally prefer this to covering my
body in bug dope, but the latter is the more comfortable method. Bring Teva-
type sandals for your feet, as well as a pair of flip-flop sandals. You need both
because soft feet tend to open up when continuously rubbed in the same place
by the sandal straps. By having both kinds, you can alter the contact points.
Oh, and don't forget your swimsuit.

First-aid kit. A personal medical kit is useful. While there are pharmacies that
can get you what you need for rashes, gut problems, etc., it's often easier and
more comfortable to have the stuff available at your bungalow or in your pack
right when you need it. Sunscreen is an absolute must and can also be purchased
in Thailand. Many people like to have rehydration salt mixes to put in their
water bottles. There are a few different types of these available in Thailand, but
their contents seem a bit dubious. Gatorade, however, can be purchased at most
of the shops. If you have a mix you really like, bring it. You will use it.

Flashlight. A headlamp or flashlight is a must. Not only might you need
it when coming off the crag (the sun goes down around 6 P.M., year-round, in
the tropics), but the paths are not lit and you need to see what, or who, you
are putting your foot on top of (see "Wildlife" in Chapter 3, The Kingdom of
Thailand). Depending on the quality of bungalow you are renting, you might
need that light at night there, too.

Miscellaneous. As for toiletries, all the shampoos, soaps, and such can be
bought in the local markets. If you come in one of the shoulder seasons or
during the rainy season, a compact umbrella is often useful.

CULTURE AND CONDUCT IN BRIEF

The dominant religion of Thailand, that of over 95 percent of the population,
is Buddhism. That religion's "live in the moment" philosophy, as well as the
concept that "life is suffering," has had a huge influence on Thai society. For
instance, if the Thais had a national phrase, it would be *mai pen rai*. Roughly
translating to "never mind" or "it doesn't matter," *mai pen rai* is more commonly
used like *c'est la vie* in French: "such is life." *Mai pen rai* is employed to dismiss
the various inconveniences and pains of daily life, no matter how significant,
when dismissing them is all that can be done.

Another term that comes up commonly in Thailand is *sanuk. Sanuk* means
"fun," but *sanuk* is as much an approach to life as it is a noun. The people of
Thailand are generally happy, carefree, and not prone to much that doesn't
have some *sanuk* to it. For instance, you can see *sanuk* with your waiters and
bartenders each evening. Though each of them will have already put in about

a ten-hour day and have probably worked for a month straight, they will be cracking jokes and generally trying to find some fun in their work. In the West, we might dismiss this as not taking the serious approach that work requires, but to the Thais this is just finding *sanuk* in what would otherwise be suffering.

While most of the country is Buddhist, most of the climbs in this book are in areas on the southern coast that are dominated by Islam. Throughout Thailand, a respectful and conservative approach to members of the opposite sex is the standard (this despite the infamous sex industry), but in the south

LIVING IN THE HERE AND NOW

New-age thinking in the West promotes the concept of living for the moment, as if it's something that should be done by all people. That's what we do on vacation. We play, trying not to think about the mortgage, the fact that the house needs a new coat of paint, or the kid's college fund not being quite as big as we might want it. However, living for a better future, as we are prone to do, has some advantages over seizing the day. If you are trying to get everything you can out of "today," it means that the repercussions of your actions are not given their proper due. If you are used to living in the here and now, it's a bit of a stretch, almost like a deeper philosophical thought, to accept the repercussions of those actions. This is perhaps why the environment in Thailand is suffering so badly. When I first came to Railay Beach, the coral was alive. Boat noise wasn't a problem because there simply weren't that many boats, so no laws about mufflers had been created. No one thought of the sewage being put back into the ground because we couldn't see how popular the place would become.

However, times change, and not thinking about the future is coming back to haunt Thailand. The beach is now crowded with tourists for much of the year, noisy boats run back and forth, and all the bungalow operations on the lower peninsula have water quality problems. In the search for a greater profit today, these problems are not being addressed to ensure that life will be better tomorrow. Speaking with friends of mine who are Thai or have lived in Thailand for many years, I don't get a sense this will change without an outside influence. The here-and-now attitude is why it is this way, and the future is too abstract to take from the profits of today. Don't feel bad about complaining that the boats are too loud to let you sleep or that the water in the shower is dirty. Just as we go to Thailand for a vacation so we can live in the here and now, your complaint just might be what reminds Thailand that there is more than just the here and now.

this is even more true. Although Europe has brought over the practice of top-less sunbathing, the locals do find this quite offensive. As a matter of fact, although walking into a bar in a bikini is now completely accepted on the Phra Nang Peninsula, it wasn't long ago that you might be turned away. It should be added that a few of the Muslim restaurants on the peninsula do not have alcohol on the menu.

The people of Thailand love their king, and any sort of negative comments about him, whether they be in jest or not, are considered very disrespectful.

On a different level, touching someone's head is considered offensive be-cause it is the highest point of the body. Similarly, pointing with your feet (the lowest point of the body) or even propping them up on a chair so that they are inadvertently pointing at someone is also considered offensive behavior.

Perhaps the biggest social offense you could commit inadvertently is causing someone to lose face. Proving your point in an argument, if it means pointing out that a Thai person is wrong, is a common way of making someone lose face. This can make an argument over a bill very difficult. Staying calm and smiling throughout the discussion usually helps to smooth over pointing out any mistakes. The most common way we Westerners make someone lose face is by losing our tempers or raising our voices in an argument. Raising your voice is considered to be a loss of self-control to Thais, and that in turn makes everyone in the discussion lose face. You can be sure that if you lose your tem-per in an argument with a Thai, you will not get what you want. Instead, you will have offended everyone involved and will probably find the discussion is simply ended.

A FEW TIDBITS OF LANGUAGE

There are four major dialects of Thai, all hailing from the various corners of the country. However, the most commonly accepted form of the language is that of central Thailand. In Thai, there are five different tones, meaning that not only how you spell a word but whether your tone rises or falls at the beginning, end, or middle of the word all convey the word's meaning. As an example, the word *khao*—as I spell it here in Roman script and ignore the tones—could mean *rice*, *mountain*, or the number *nine*. You can see how letting your voice rise as you lose your temper might change "Don't you lie to me" into "Your cat smells like my umbrella."

The Thai alphabet, which is made up of forty-four consonants and forty-eight vowels, recognizes these tones. The Roman alphabet does not recognize the Thai alphabet's tones, and thus it is problematic for me to write how to pronounce these words. Nevertheless, in the chart provided here, I spell out a few Thai phrases and words as they sound to me and then describe the tone, if it is one I think I can convey in a written description. Try to think of all of the *i*s and *e*s in their hard sounds, like the *e* in the pronoun "he" and the *i* in the pronoun "I." If there are a couple letters in a row, it means you make that sound a bit longer than normal.

However, in my experience, you will have to let your new Thai friends give you the exact pronunciation. Don't worry; they are used to it. I assure you, many of them will tell you "Don't say whatever Sam says to say...he's hopeless." Though I may try, I must admit they are right. I have all that much more respect for them for figuring out *our* crazy language.

One thing to keep in mind is that there are a couple of gender–specific words that should be used regularly in conversation. It is polite to say the word *kop* (male) or *kaa* (female) at the end of most phrases. This is a bit like saying "sir" or "ma'am" at the end of a statement in English, except that rather than using the gender of the person you are speaking to, you use your own gender. Men always say *kop*, and women always say *kaa* ...unless you have a need to show you are of a different persuasion genderwise than it might otherwise appear, in which case you are on your own!

If you really want to learn the Thai language, I suggest the Rosetta Stone computer language course. There you can hear the proper pronunciation. Or just hang around with the Thais when you are over there. They love to help.

English Phrases	Thai	Tonal Inflection
Hello/Goodbye.	*Sawadee kop/kaa.*	rising on the *a*s
See you later.	*Pope con mi.*	falling on *mi*
How are you?	*Sabi de mi?*	rising on *mi*
I am fine.	*Sabi de, kop/kaa.*	
Yes/Correct.	*Chai.*	rising on the *i*
No.	*Mi.*	rising on the *i*
I/me (male)	*Pohm*	falling on the *o*
I/me (female)	*Dee–chan*	falling on the *a*
Do you have...?	*Me* [blank] *mi?*	rising on the *i*
I like...	*Pohm/Dee–chan chawp...*	rising on the *a* in *chawp*
I don't like...	*Pohm/Dee–chan mi chawp...*	rising on the *a* in *chawp*
I understand.	*Pohm/Dee–chan kow ji.*	rising on the *ow* in *kow*
I don't understand.	*Pohm/Dee–chan mi kow ji.*	rising on the *ow* in *kow*
to come	*maa*	
to go	*by*	
I'm going climbing.	*Pohm/Dee–chan by bing khao.*	
I'm going swimming.	*Pohm/Dee-chan by why nam.*	

English Words	Thai	Tonal Inflection
banana	*gloo-aye*	
beach	*haad*	
beef	*noowa*	
bottled water	*nam kuat*	
chicken	*gy*	

English Words	Thai	Tonal Inflection
coconut	*maprow*	
cold	*yen*	
fish	*pla*	
hot	*ron*	
mango	*mamuang*	
market	*dalaat*	
mountain	*khao*	falling on the *ao*
papaya	*malakor*	
pineapple	*sap-arot*	
sea	*tha-ley*	
shrimp	*goong*	
spicy	*bet*	

English Numbers	Thai	Tonal Inflection
one	*noong*	falling on the *oo*
two	*song*	
three	*sawm*	falling on the *a*
four	*see*	
five	*haa*	rising on the *aa*
six	*hok*	
seven	*jet*	
eight	*bet*	
nine	*khao*	rising on the *ao*
ten	*sip*	

A FEW IMPORTANT FACTS

The Thai currency is the baht. There are 100 satang to a baht—but this will mean nothing to you because, as a foreigner, you will never buy items that cost less than 1 baht! Since 1998, the exchange rate has been ranging anywhere from 38 to 44 baht per US$1.

Money can be exchanged in any bank or, at an exchange rate you probably won't like much, at your bungalow's restaurant. ATMs can be found, of course, in Bangkok, as well as on the Phra Nang Peninsula at Railay beween Sunrise Resort and Railay Bay Bungalows and in Ao Nang, on Koh Phi Phi, and in Chiang Mai.

There are two costs for everything in Thailand: *farang* cost and Thai cost. If you are standing at a cashier and notice a Thai paying 3 baht for a bottle of water that you just purchased for 10 baht, don't complain too much. You will not get out of this racially based markup.

Tipping is not generally expected in Thailand, and Thais don't tip other Thais. However, a small donation to the working man's cause, perhaps just part of your pocket change, given to waiters and bartenders, will make your trip a bit more comfortable.

Always tell your metered taxi driver to use the meter as soon as you get in the car. At times of intense traffic, it may be impossible to do this and get anywhere...so barter! And then pay the driver a bit more for the effort.

Email and Internet cafes are common, but connections are slow. Far slower is snail mail. If you need something large sent fast, a service in the Thai postal system called EMS is fairly efficient and quick. Federal Express and United Parcel Service are both dependable out of Bangkok, Phuket, and Chiang Mai but to a lesser degree in Krabi.

Thailand is seven hours ahead of London; twelve hours ahead of New York, thirteen hours ahead of Chicago, fourteen hours ahead of Denver, and fifteen hours ahead of Los Angeles.

Electricity is at 220 volts, as in Europe, and the double round prong is the common type. Some receptacles take both the double round plug and the North American type of plug. The electricity on the Phra Nang Peninsula is not stable. Brownouts are common, as are surges.

All of the international embassies are located in Bangkok. The numbers of a few are listed here:

Australia: 02-287-2680

Canada: 02-636-0540

Germany: 02-287-9000

United Kingdom: 02-251-0191 (also 0192-0199)

United States: 02-205-4000

In any country, dogs make better pets than cats.

THINGS TO FEAR...
State-Run Medical Care

There are some excellent *private* hospitals in Thailand. State-run hospitals are another matter. For instance, the Krabi Hospital, a state-run facility that is the closest to the Phra Nang Peninsula, is not one of the excellent hospitals, though the doctors are qualified.

Nightmares about this place are legion, and you will hear plenty of them if you spend any time here. I had a Thai friend who was in a car accident. She was taken there, but there was no doctor on duty. She had internal bleeding, but the nurses couldn't do anything until the doctor returned. They didn't know when that would be. They would not release her until the doctor could sign off on it—or at least that's what they said. Eventually my friend bled to death in the hospital. She was there five hours and the doctor never showed. Another story I recently heard was about the local snake charmer. He was bitten by a king cobra and managed to make it to the hospital. However, there was no antivenin in stock, so he died in the hospital. It seems these sorts of stories are not uncommon.

I have always touted the Krabi Hospital as a place to be avoided at all costs.

In the days following the tsunami, this underfunded establishment did manage to hold its own in the worst of circumstances. However, I have to stick to my guns here and advise you to try and get to a private hospital in Phuket if you are injured. Perhaps, because of the tsunami, the local hospital will be brought up to a higher standard, but until we see that happen, you should try and move on. There is also a very good hospital in Chaing Mai and we make note of it in that chapter.

Infections

At the climbing areas in southern Thailand, the water—both in the sea and in the shower—is not the purest in the world. On top of that, your skin, which will be sweaty and dirty from a day's climbing in the tropics, acts like one big petri dish. Small cuts on your hands and feet often become infected, and large cuts and road-rash-type abrasions can be downright dangerous. You need to keep on top of any possible infection.

For small cuts, use a topical antibiotic that dries out the area (as opposed to the creams and salves we commonly use in the West). A yellow powdered antibiotic available in the local pharmacies is very effective at this (I have no idea what its long-term effects are). If you get a deep cut, go to the nurse at Railay Bay or the doctor in Ao Nang as soon as possible. They can stitch you up and get you on internal antibiotics, if needed, for the ensuing infection.

Violence

Southern Thailand is not always the "Land of Smiles." By and large, physical confrontations are very rare; however, they are not unheard of. Arguments over bills can happen anywhere, and there have been a number of rapes in the last few years. Regarding rape, the usual rules apply: Don't walk around in dark places alone, and so forth. For what it's worth, half the rapes I have heard of in the last fifteen years were committed by tourists.

Generally, most of the confrontations I have seen in Thailand have been in the south. More often than not, they are started by foreigners raising their voices and making a scene. Thai culture places a lot of value on controlling your temper, and the loss of it and creation of a scene in front of, for example, a restaurant full of people creates a loss of face for the locals. That's bad, and it will only get worse for you. That little 95-pound guy you are arguing with has probably had more hours in a kickboxing ring than you have had on the rock walls. He can kick your ass inside out, so calm down.

If you have a problem with a local and you are sure you are right, take it up with the Tourist Police. The Tourist Police in Thailand have a good reputation for looking out for travelers. They have offices in all the major tourist areas and have a hotline where complaints can be registered. Dial 1155 from any public phone, and you will soon be talking to a local who speaks English and will be helpful...if you are in the "right."

Also, be aware, as I explain in the next chapter, that putting up climbs in areas that are controlled by birds' nest gatherers can be extremely bad for your health. Confrontations with these people, who are usually armed, should be avoided at all costs.

Drugs

Despite what you might have been led to believe, the possession of marijuana, psilocybin mushrooms, Ecstasy, and virtually any other controlled substance in your home country is also illegal in Thailand. Conviction for drug violations by foreigners are not that common, but when they happen they are horrid. You do not want to spend a single night in a Thai prison. If you are going to do drugs—and they will be available—you should be aware that a low-key attitude about it is as important in Thailand as it is in Utah.

Another thing to keep in mind is that many of the drugs you will find here are not as "clean" as you might like. The stimulants that are imported from Burma, such as *yaa baa* (which translates to "crazy drug"), are of varying levels of potency and contain chemicals you may not want in your system. I have known a number of people who have lost it on this drug in particular, and some of them have never fully recovered. Also, I am told that the Ecstasy found in Thailand is often very low quality and dangerous.

For what it's worth, trafficking these drugs into Thailand can get you life in prison or the death penalty. The authorities are very serious about it, and your home embassy is not going to be very helpful with getting a convicted drug dealer out of jail and back home.

Monkeys

Monkeys—and by monkeys, I mean crab-eating macaques—are sweet, lovable, and cuddly little creatures that want nothing more than to entertain you and dole out a little affection. This is true—if your idea of entertainment is having your stuff stolen, if you consider affection to be getting pissed on or having feces thrown at you, and you consider al Qaeda to be "sweet, lovable, and cuddly." Nope, monkeys are evil little humans, and everyone who has lived with them—from Rudyard Kipling to Richard Pryor—has made note of it. You should too.

No doubt you will see the macaques on your trip. You will probably get really close, and they will probably do nothing. However, you should be aware that these little animals are very strong. They can carry some hideous diseases, including rabies, and are quite dirty by human standards. Worse, they are smart; they know that attacking en masse is how to win an Asian war.

You would be well advised to just give them a bit of space. If the macaques are nearby, do not let yourself be intimidated—they prey on that. Never try to appease them with food as this just tells them you are a sucker who is loaded. Instead, puff out your chest, move your stuff, and generally act as if you won't take any crap off them...literally. For better or worse, depending on the situation, baring your teeth with a smile is considered a threat by them. If they are persistent, you might throw something at them and yell a bit. The macaques rarely attack a person, but they will go after your stuff and might keep you away from that stuff once they have control of it. It's best to just avoid them.

Snakes and Bugs

Snakebites kill hundreds of people every year in Thailand. Most of these people are farmers in rice paddies and on rubber plantations, but not always. In the rainy season of 2003, a person was killed on Tonsai Road by a snake. He died within 30 minutes of the bite, so the attacker was most likely a king cobra. Others have been bit on the Phra Nang Peninsula and lived by getting to the hospital as fast as humanly possible. There are nearly 100 species of poisonous snakes in Thailand, and their bites can be catastrophic even if you don't die. The cytotoxic poison of a bamboo viper, for instance, can cause such extreme necrosis of tissue that you lose the bitten appendage. Having a finger removed could be viewed as getting off easy.

All of us who have spent time putting up routes in the Kingdom of Thailand have had our run-ins with snakes. I have almost sat on a Russell's viper while putting my harness on, and my neighbors had a cobra in their bathroom. Climbs from 1,2,3 to Vinland have names that reflect a run-in with a snake. The Cat and the Cobra is a name given to a route after the first ascensionist was pinned down by a reared king cobra.

Of course, he didn't get bitten, nor did I when I stepped over a black cobra in my basement. As a matter of fact, most snakes don't want to bite (the one exception to this may be nesting king cobras, which are apparently territorial). To a snake, a bite will bring on retaliation, during which the snake will most likely die. Also, using that venom on you will cost the snake its only tool for catching some food that day. So it's quite easy to avoid being bitten by simply not bothering the snakes.

The best way to do this is to always look where you are putting your hands and feet. At night, carry a flashlight and use it, even on the lit trails, because snakes' camouflage is quite effective in dim light. Your bungalow itself might make for a nice hunting ground, so make sure you turn on the lights or use a flashlight when you go to the bathroom. Rifling through a backpack or duffle bag that has been left open is potentially dangerous because they make great places for snakes to sleep off the day. The fact is a snakebite is very, very unlikely if you just look before you step.

More likely than getting bit by a snake is getting stung by a centipede or scorpion. The toxins these animals put out are just as nasty as that of many deadly snakes; they just dose it in smaller amounts. Thatched bungalow roofs make excellent centipede habitat, as do other cool, dark places, such as climbing shoes. Shake out your shoes before you put them on, shake your pants before you slide them on, and never go wading through leaves and brush. Just look before you grab, rub, or touch, and you will be fine.

Birds' Nest Harvesters

If you go to one of the climbing areas that is already well established, then this warning will mean nothing to you. However, if you come to Thailand to put up new routes in remote settings, or if you plan on doing the live-aboard climbing thing, you need to be aware of this potential danger.

The delicacy *bird's nest soup* is made from the saliva-nests (think dried bird snot) of a couple species of Asian swift. These birds live in the cliffs of southern Thailand, and their nests can fetch up to US$1,500 per kilogram. Harvesting the nests has been refined over the centuries so that the maximum number of nests can be taken from a rookery without driving off the birds. This means that the men doing the harvesting do not want anyone else getting on the walls and disturbing the birds, not to mention stealing a nest.

Most of the crags of southern Thailand are owned by the Thai government, but the government leases those towers to various businessmen who have small armies of men protecting and collecting the nests. Those men have the right to shoot anyone who tries to get on their walls. The most coveted towers are booby trapped with anti-personnel mines and are under constant watch. Do not think you can sneak onto a tower and not get caught, and do not think that as a foreigner this does not apply to you. You must have permission. Without it, you very well might be killed.

Chapter 2

CLIMBING IN THAILAND

*Every route in Thailand has an expiration date...
we just don't know what that date is!*

Tom Cecil, UIAGM guide and longtime route developer in Thailand

BOLTS: READ THIS BEFORE YOU CLIMB

As this book is being produced just to pay for the replacement of bad bolts in Thailand, this section on our problems with fixed protection is rather long. You might be tempted to skip by it and move directly to the route info... *Don't!* This information is about life and death when climbing, so you should be as well versed as possible on the problem.

This is the ugly side of our little paradise. We have the best rock for rock climbing in the world, but our crags literally consume the best stainless steel and aluminium the climbing industry uses. Virtually every steel bolt manufactured in the last fifteen years has been tried in the rock of southern Thailand, and all of them have failed miserably.

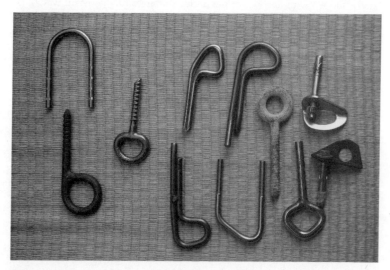

Bolts of Siam

The simple fact is that steel just does not work. It appears that a combination of chemicals is working on the bolts. First, the salt from the sea has its corrosive properties. As I understand it, the ocean, especially in the tropics, gives off a very destructive chlorine gas. It's not given out in amounts that will hurt you or me, but over time it will break down steel. Also, there are the corrosive acids, created by the breakdown of vegetation, that pass through the rock in rainwater. All these chemical processes are sped up by heat, and the heat generated on the walls of southern Thailand when they're exposed to sunlight is intense. The end result of chlorine, salt, acidic water, and intense sunlight means your fixed protection is not very "fixed."

European, American, and Australian manufacturers were equally represented in the dubious distinction of their gear failing on Thai rock. Most of the failures occurred just under the bolt hanger and perhaps a half centimeter (¼ inch) inside the rock. Wet hangers were cracking and breaking as well. A bolt may look absolutely perfect on the outside and be black with corrosion on the inside, so there is no way to simply look at a bolt and decide whether it's good or bad.

We first noticed this problem at Low Tide Wall in 1993. Dean Saydom and I went about replacing the bolts on Strider and Narsilion, only to have them look just as bad the following year. By 1995, bolts were popping out of walls all over the peninsula.

A few of us got together to discuss the problem and its long-term effects on climbing in Thailand. We decided that although new routes were important, the long-term viability of the Phra Nang Peninsula as a climbing area depended more on replacing bolts than anything else. One death at that time could have gotten it all closed down, and people were flocking to dozens of established classic climbs, only to discover that they were not climbable with any degree of safety. With that in mind, we focused on rebolting rather than putting up new routes.

We also decided, based on the fact that most of the bolts were failing under the hanger, that the problem was primarily coming from inside the rock. It seemed that a glue-in bolt would be protected from this and would thus handle the problem, so by 1996 we were replacing standard bolts with glue-ins.

Then two more problems arose. One was that the glue we were sold by one of the manufacturers did not, despite their claims, seal out the water. The other was that we had been wrong about the main culprit. The failures were occurring under the hangers because that is where most of the force is exerted and, thus, where the microcracks in the steel let in the chlorine gas and other chemicals. On top of that, we were replacing the bad bolts with the best thing the industry had, which were good stainless-steel glue-in bolts, but they were not good enough. They were steel and thus inadequate.

We tried every bolt on the market, plus a few that were not on the market but were made by folks in Switzerland and Australia specifically to fix our problem.

None of it worked. By 2000 we had had almost seventy bolt failures, and I can tell you that when it happens to you, it is very scary. Your whole approach to sport climbing changes.

We knew that glue-ins were safer than standard bolts because they were somewhat protected and because of their inherently stronger design, but the breakdown process still occurred. The Union Internationale des Associations d'Alpinisme (UIAA, the internationally recognized authority in setting standards for climbing equipment) got involved and studied the problem, eventually finding what we already knew from visiting climbers who were metallurgists: chlorine gas, acid, and salt in tropical heat were breaking down the steel. Steel, the metallurgists said, just wouldn't work. (Okay, one kind of steel would work, but it costs $33 per foot for unbent ⅜-inch (9.5-millimeter) rod and you need a contract with Boeing, Raytheon, or some company like that to get it.)

Ushba began making bolts out of titanium, specifically for this sort of environment, in the late '90s. It appears so far that their titanium glue-in bolts are holding up. Of course, something could be breaking down and we cannot see it yet. However, if there is a problem, it is manifesting itself differently than it did with all the other bolts. Titanium is incredibly tough and resistant to corrosion. We can only hope. So far, so good. We continue to replace bolts.

Unfortunately, Ushba has not been able to get the bolts for us in the past few years, but we have found another source for titanium bolts. These bolts, which are designed as "staples" (using two holes) are an even higher grade of the metal and are thus thinner in diameter. They are an 8mm rod bent into a U that protrudes from the wall and are usually held in place by a red glue (Hilti RE 500). Our website at *www.thailandclimbingguide.com* and the American Safe Climbing Association website (*www.safeclimbing.org*) will know what venues are taken in the rebolting process; check the Web for discussions of this point.

The Future of Rebolting

The current trend is to do everything with titanium glue-in bolts. Generally, considering breaks we get by buying in bulk, each replaced titanium bolt costs us around $10 (installed). Replacing the average route costs around $100 and takes half a day. Replacing a big route, such as *Lord of the Thais*, runs around $650 and takes three days.

About one-third of the money for this effort has come from donations from visiting climbers, and the other two-thirds has come from the folks doing the retrobolting. I have kept a running tally. A large amount of hardware was donated by Sepi in Switzerland and Christian in Austria, but other than that it has almost all come from those of us hailing from the New World. It seems most Europeans have the misconception that the retrobolting will be done by the government. It won't.

As I stated in the dedication to this book, all of my earnings on this book

Daniel rebolting Cockroach Beach *on Melting Wall*

will be donated to the rebolting cause. So this book is set up to generate money for the rebolting of Thailand. Of course, that is not going to be enough. Rumors of a billionaire paying for it all or of parties where thousands of dollars are raised are greatly exaggerated. So donations via the American Safe Climbing Association are very much appreciated. If you want to help by donating to the effort, talk to someone who you know is doing the work—ask your fellow climbers. A smiling face and a claim of doing this hard work could be nothing more than a scam to get money from you. *Caveat emptor.*

A number of people have put in long hours at great personal risk to replace the fixed protection and to hopefully make this climbing area relatively safe. Shamick Byszewski has done the lion's share of the work in the last few years, and for this he deserves kudos and a big glass of Black Cat when you see him (you will).

Practicalities of the Bolt Problem

Climbing is inherently dangerous, climbing in Thailand even more so. It is important that you keep this in mind before you climb in Thailand. The practicalities of the bolt problem mean that the following hierarchy of bolt preferability generally holds true:

1. Any fixed protection in Thailand should be considered suspect.
2. Though titanium glue-ins have been in use for only a few years and thus have not had a long-term test, they appear to be the best protection available. These are identified as a half-loop of gray metal looking like a sideways U poking out of the wall (see A in the photo). Sometimes these titanium bolts are not countersunk, but instead are a large loop of gray metal jutting from the wall. These are probably just as safe as the countersunk version. A new "staple" version of this bolt is now in use as well. It also appears to be a U of 8-mm (⁵⁄₁₆ inch) titanium protruding from the rock with, usually, some red glue sealing it in place.
3. A good thread (rope placed inside webbing) in solid rock (not tufa or stalactite) is probably the next safest piece of protection. (Keep in mind that thread materials exposed to UV rays and repetitive falls wear out.)
4. The next most trustworthy is actually the Petzl glue-in bolt (see B in the photo). These are breaking down in the elements, but the process seems to be slower on them than it is on many of the other steel glue-ins.
5. After that, all bets are off. Steel staples, the stainless-steel half-loops that are glued in via two holes, as well as the DMM, Lucky, and Fixe glue-in bolts, are all showing breakdown and will eventually fail. Standard expansion bolts, put in prior to the glue-in era, are so bad that they almost need not be mentioned (see D in the photo). Don't trust them.

The rebolting process is extremely expensive, so often there are slight alterations to a climb when the fixed pro is replaced. An example of this might be tying a thread (which is replaceable), when one is available, rather than placing a bolt. You will note that I use the terms "retrobolt" and "rebolt" in this book, but they are not interchangeable. A "rebolt" indicates replacement of exactly what the first ascensionist did; a "retrobolt" indicates replacement of the route, hopefully taking advantage of a few of the natural thread placements that are so often available. This may upset the first ascensionist in some cases; if so, he or she is more than welcome to replace the new thread with a titanium bolt.

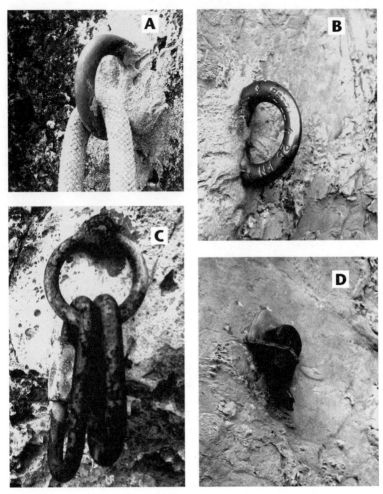

Here are four example of your bolt choices. From top left to bottom right they are in the preferred order for you to clip. A. A good Titanium glue-in. B. A questionable glue-in made of stainless steel. C. A ring bolt of non-stainless steel (as are the malions). D. A machine bolt with the remains of a stainless steel hanger.

Please Don't Make Matters Worse

Over the last five or six years, a trend has emerged that really needs to be re-versed. Climbers who want to put up routes arrive in Thailand knowing all of the above information. Realizing how expensive it is to put up routes with the acceptable materials listed above, they go for a cheaper option. This is often rationalized with "They don't even know for sure if it works," followed by "Well, then they can just fix it with the titanium bolts when they are sure."

That doesn't fly, folks. This problem is now out in the open, written up in all guidebooks and a point of discussion in chat rooms on the Internet. We may not know for sure that titanium works, but we certainly know that the other options do *not* work and that titanium appears to work. By putting up routes with the cheaper materials, you are only putting people in danger and forcing others to do work you should do for yourself. We don't get paid for it; we have to pay for it.

So future editions of this guidebook will recognize first ascent efforts only in that light. If a route is put up using subpar materials, we will say so and let the climbing community tell the ascensionists what they think. Don't make this job bigger than it already is. Also, a little peer pressure on your fellow climbers might help us with this problem.

ACCESS ISSUES AND LOCAL ETHICS (A BIT OF PREACHING)
The One Rule of Climbing
In the not so distant past, the Phra Nang Peninsula was a little-heard-of corner of a developing country where you could do anything you liked. That has changed, and we climbers have found ourselves in the middle of some access issues. The powers that be can shut climbing down here at the drop of a hat, and they might if we don't follow the most important ethic of all. Every climber has his or her own belief system about chipping, bolting, hanging, and what is correct and incorrect, and it is all good for discussions at the bar. Let's keep them there and accept that there is only one true ethic.

This is not a take-it-or-leave-it ethic. This is the one that all climbers must follow or suffer the worst of consequences. Not only must all climbers follow it, they must also enforce it, using whatever means at their disposal. This ethic is:

Do not do anything that will threaten climber access.

That means, if chiseling out a hold is going to make enough people mad to the degree that it becomes an issue, then don't do it. If there are certain areas where the powers that be do not want us to climb, then don't climb there. Your death might get us shut down, so soloing can be frowned on. Try not to do anything invasive such as drilling, in front of nonclimbers. It might compel them to write nasty letters to the Thai government.

As an example, in winter of 2000 a couple of visiting climbers established some routes on some of the unique bits of rock in the area. This area was established in a cave, and caves are quite significant in the local beliefs. Some of the prettiest formations were used as climbing holds, and bolts and slings were hung from naturally occurring works of art. When the area was opened to climbers other than those on the first-ascent group, there was an outcry, and within days action was taken. The bolts were removed, the slings cut away, and the anchors taken out. The trail was covered over and all the topos were destroyed. It was wiped clean. Those visiting climbers spent three weeks preparing routes that no one wanted. If they had looked at the uniqueness of the place they were climbing in and thought of the one ethic, they would have saved themselves a lot of work.

The common climber attitude of "I'll do what I want and I don't care what anyone thinks" doesn't work here. Our actions will have repercussions, and those repercussions could get this place closed to climbing. I assure you, you are not being told this just so I can fill space in this book. This is for longevity of climbing in Thailand, and we must think of it always.

If that's not good enough, then read on. Remember that the local climbing community in Thailand does not have the means to travel to other climbing areas. This is their home crag, and their only crag, and getting it closed down will end their ability to go climbing.

Also, you are an ambassador for our sport to a nation that is just beginning to see the value of it. Remember that, and you will make us look good. Forget it, and you will be violating an ethic that is more sacred than "no chipping in Yosemite" and "no bolting on Gritstone."

Do not do anything that will threaten climber access.

Don't Break Stalactites

Treat each phallic-shaped tube of stone like it's yours...or your boyfriend's! Stalactites and stalagmites are so abundant in Ratburi limestone that, like bars in a jail, they actually prevent climbs from being established. This does not mean that you should knock them off to make room for a climb. They are a revered symbol of fertility. On the Phra Nang Peninsula in particular, where the Princess is supposed to help people with fertility, they should be treated with respect. Breaking them not only brings on the wrath of the park service but also might bring on a bad brush with the Princess.

Don't Use Caves as Outhouses

At the crowded cliffs of Thailand, it is often difficult to get a bit of privacy. Well, the best way to get that privacy is *not* to go into a cave to poo or pee. Whatever you leave there is likely to stay for a very long time. What is better is going out into the woods and doing your business there; even better, walk to the nearest restaurant and use their facilities. This isn't France, so don't do it on the edge of the trail. Burn your paper and it will all be gone in a few weeks. Leave it in the cave, and it will be there for your next visit and the one after that as well.

Don't Scatter Bottles and Butts

It seems that one of the chemicals added to cigarettes makes many a smoker believe that the butt is not trash. Just like a water bottle lid and a candy wrapper,

*The results of the big Earthday! 1994 crag cleanup. From left to right in the photo are
Bao, Dean, an unknown boatman, Egk, Sam Lightner Jr., Luang, an unknown local
climber, and Joanie. (Somporn Suebhait (King))*

that little butt is garbage. Putting it into a pocket in the rock or just dropping it
into the sand is not proper disposal. Please: They came in a pack, so pack them
out. By the way, I realize that some of the worst offenders of this are locals.
Let's try to set an example.

ACCIDENT RESPONSE

Getting hurt in Thailand is a bad thing, and the particulars of all accidents vary
greatly. You have to figure out what to do based on the particulars of the accident you have or encounter. I won't tell you "Do this" or "Do that" because
the situation has to be assessed and then the decisions made based on those
parameters.

First off, I think everyone should carry a credit card in their pocket when
they are climbing. Good medical care in Thailand has to be paid for, usually up
front, and if you get hurt you are going to wish you had the means to do so.

If a person at the crag gets hurt and you are there, your climbing day is over,
as it is for most everyone else at the crag. Everyone has to look out for one
another here. One person must be in charge. Decide immediately. That person
then sends people off to do various jobs. There needs to be (1) a "runner" to
call the appropriate locals and possibly arrange the transportation, (2) a person
to clear or widen the trail, (3) a person to help calm the injured person, and (4)
a person to deal with necessary medical treatment.

Now comes the hard part, which I can't help you with: you need to assess the
severity of the injury and the level of shock. If the person is, in your opinion,
okay to take a road trip for excellent care, then the victim can go to the nearest

large hospital. If the person is seriously wounded and showing signs of shock, attempt to get the victim stabilized in the nearest hospital of any size. A possible option here is to call the Air Asia Ambulance, a new service (see page 93) that has not been used yet for climbing rescues. If it proves to be as efficient as it claims to be (and was during the tsunami evacuation), then it will be the best choice. It will also be the most expensive choice.

Once the victim is on his or her way, make sure loved ones and other partners who might not be there are made aware of the situation. You might have to go to the victim's lodgings to find contacts and such in the climber's personal belongings.

Finally, remember that none of this is free. Be ready to drop cash at a moment's notice, and be ready to bring the hurt person's passport and wallet to the hospital to pay for all this. Large hospitals require a credit card or a very large pile of baht prior to admittance. Boat owners, taxis, and the like are all going to need to be paid. As I said earlier, it's best to have that credit card in your back pocket so you don't have to wait, in pain or unconscious, while someone tries to find it for you.

Let's face it; your best option is to avoid getting hurt.

REST DAYS

The climbing in Thailand is so physical, requiring so much core strength and body tension, that rest days are a must. You will be exhausted after just a few days of it, and if you choose to push through the pain, you will end up either nursing some very inflamed elbows or coming down with some sort of tropical illness.

The first rule for rest days is what *not* to do. Don't let yourself hang out near the crag on your rest day. This is a potentially dangerous temptation that may cause you to develop or regress into Tonsaiman. Tonsaiman is the creature that lives at the base of Tidal Wave. He sits there on a chair, yelling out beta to each of the routes, telling everyone within earshot how things used to be (last month), and occasionally getting up to twirl (you'll see). Sometime in early afternoon he hits the local herb and then starts working out all kinds of bizarre rumors, such as the big resort is putting a tunnel through his favorite crag or there is no reason to give money for rebolting because some millionaire with a 165-foot yacht comes every year to do it for us. *Don't* let this happen to you. Try a few other things instead. I've suggested some rest day activities for each of the climbing areas described in this book.

HOW TO USE THIS BOOK

The routes in Thailand are climbed by people from all over the world. Because of this, most units of measurement are in the metric system. Estimated costs are given in the Thai currency, the baht.

Another result of Thailand being a destination for people from all over the world is that a number of different ideas on ethics, techniques, and even safety equipment have been used here. Because there is no large local climbing community to enforce a standard, climbs often change in character. A route might have been set in a particular line and then actually might get climbed by future ascensionists slightly off that line, thus changing the grade. Future ascensionists might add a thread or, if no one is watching, a bolt. The route then changes in character again.

The retrobolting process also often changes everything, including the length of the route. The point here is that you should know that the route information changes. What this book offers is the best route information at the time I did the ascent. It very well might have changed since then, and you should use your own skills as a climber to decide if the route is correct for you.

After a general description of the crag—its location and a little something about it—the following notations are given:

Sun exposure: This tells you the amount of sun you will be getting at a crag. The route description tells what times of day are best for avoiding the extra heat.

Wall angle and difficulty: The various wall angles indicate not only how steep the wall tends to be but also the difficulty of the climbing at that crag.

Hazards: This tells you what to be leery of at the crag. Almost all of these tidbits contain some mention of how bad the bolts are...that's just standard here.

Approach: This tells you how to reach the climbing area.

A general description of the crag—its location and a little something about it—follows and written route information is then given, in the following format:

Route Number and Name, followed by grade, length, protection, and a
   star rating
F.A. (first ascent)
Rebolting information, if any
Location of the climb and a little something about it.

The routes are numbered consecutively *only* for each crag. The route numbers correspond to the photo or topo drawing for that crag (see "A Note on the Photos and Topos," below).

The route name was usually given by the first ascensionist.

The recommendation scale consists of one to five stars. A single star means the route is pretty bad, while five stars means you should do anything you can to climb the route. There are some routes included that have *no* stars; these climbs are seriously not recommended. This information is only my opinion. Of course, it's the correct opinion!

The grade is based on what appears to be the first system employed in Thailand—the French—with the Yosemite Decimal System rating given in parentheses. Remember that this is paradise, and in paradise the grades tend to reflect a happier world than you might otherwise live in. What this means is you will likely find the grade to be a bit soft compared to equivalent routes in France or Red River Gorge. So let's call this the Thai Scale, not the French Scale. As for the YDS, well, it's just soft...like Red Rocks! That said, if you are vertically challenged, you might find the grade to be extra hard. Thai climbing tends to be big pulls on big holds. It can be reachy. For a comparison of the different rating systems, see the UIAA chart at the back of the book.

The route length is an approximation, in meters. This information, due to rebolting efforts and to the whims of visiting climbers, can change. You should not take this information as an absolute but, instead, as the best information at the time of this writing. Make sure you tie a knot in the end of your rope to prevent your partner from taking a plunge if the anchor is slightly beyond your rope's length.

The protection indicates what you need to climb the route. For most of these routes, that means a number of quickdraws. I list the number of quickdraws, rather than the number of bolts you will be clipping, because the number of bolts changes with the rebolting process. Also, the nature of Thailand's rock leaves lots of room for threads, and visiting climbers often add threads to an existing route. For this reason, the number of quickdraws I estimate you'll need is a bit high...one or two more than necessary when I did the route. However, this is an estimation. This information can change, and you should be aware that such a change affects whether it is safe or not. We cannot keep this current on a week-to-week basis.

First ascensionists, when known, are listed, with the approximate date of the ascent, as is any current rebolting information. Putting together all this information in a climbing area that attracts people from five different continents is, at best, difficult. The information is often hearsay and sketchy, so if you find your name is not given for your route, I apologize.

The climbs in this book have been established over a period of fifteen years by people from all over the world. Often they did not leave a written record of their work, so establishing who did what was done with some speculation. Last names, in particular, are often not known. We tried to get the names of the first ascensionists correct, but if we are wrong, we apologize. Please let the author know of any errors or omissions and it will be changed in future editions.

A Note on the Photos and Topos

The route information is shown in two different formats: photograph with a route overlay or a drawn climber's topo. My goal when putting this book together was to do all of them as photos, but some crags just don't allow that option. Perhaps the jungle encroaches too close to the wall, or perhaps it's in a cave and the back wall is too close. When this is this case, we drew the pictures for the topos. You're going to curse them, because I am no artist. My goal was to keep them very simple, and they're intended for you to use in conjuction with the written text to find the route. They are not perfect, but I think keeping them simple has made finding the climbs easier than creating a really complex drawing.

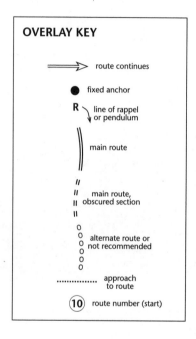

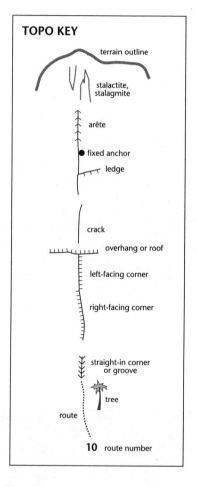

Chapter 3

THE KINGDOM OF THAILAND

THAILAND'S HISTORY...40,000 YEARS IN 4,000 WORDS

Putting a definitive date on the first human habitation of Thailand has eluded science. The facts seem to tell us that people began living in caves in northeast Thailand (and perhaps western Laos) around 10,000 BC, although these people may not have been the very first human inhabitants. Some anthropologists believe human habitation of Southeast Asia began as far back as 40,000 years ago. If the first humans in the area lived in forest dwellings and not in caves, then their existence has long been wiped clean by the environment itself.

What we do know is that the world's first farmers, and perhaps the first real metal workers, were the early inhabitants of Thailand. Rice was being grown in the region as far back as 4000 BC, a time when the people of China, who are often credited as the first rice farmers, were still living on wild millet. Bronze was being worked into various tools around 3000 BC, putting the Thais in the Bronze Age at least 200 years ahead of the traditionally accepted "first" bronze workers in the Middle East.

In the eighth century AD, in what is the modern Szechuan Province of China, a tribe of people known as the Tais were being displaced by the Chinese. This tribe wandered south in the valleys of the Mekong, Salween, and Red Rivers. The tribe that went down the westernmost river, the Salween, became the Shan of northern Burma, while the tribe that went down the easternmost river, the Red, became the Laotians. The tribe that came down the Mekong and settled in the fertile valleys of modern Thailand have kept their name, though the modern spelling is changed slightly. The original inhabitants of this area, living here prior to the first Tai migration, seemingly were assimilated into the Thai tribe.

Dvaravati and Srivijaya: AD 600–1000

The Thai went about creating regional political groupings known as *meuang,* a word that is still used today when describing the municipalities in the Kingdom of Thailand. These *meuang* traded in a network spanning from modern Chiang Mai to Yala in the south. Commonly referred to as the Dvaravati period and spanning the seventh to the twelfth centuries, this collection of *meuang* had its center in what is now northwest Thailand, where the Mon tribe was centered

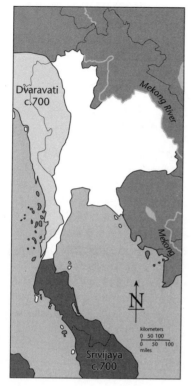

Figure 1.

(see Figure 1). The Mons had been Mahayana Buddhist missionaries who first brought Buddhism to the region during India's Ashoka period (second century BC). They apparently liked what they found and settled down, then went about cultivating the first examples of art and architecture, as well as coined currency, to come from Thailand.

The southernmost *meuang* of the region were more closely aligned to the Srivijaya Empire. Srivijaya was centered on what is now the island of Sumatra, and its main form of commerce was through trade on what could be called an oceanic Silk Road. Ships trading through Srivijaya could link people in China, Vietnam, and northern Thailand with people in India. India in turn was linked to Persia, the Middle East, and Rome. During times when travel on the traditional Silk Road was interrupted by war—something as common then to the steppes of central Asia as it is now—this trade route was very useful. Large, slow-moving boats, precursors to the Chinese junk, carried goods on either side of the Malay Peninsula. At the Isthmus of Kra, the narrowest part of Malay Peninsula, about 100 miles north of what's now Krabi Province, goods were transferred by land and then put on another ship on the other side. At that time, Pha Nga Bay and the area around Phi Phi and Phra Nang were in all likelihood flush with goods from China, India, and perhaps even as far away as Rome.

Angkor and the Khmers: AD 600–1100

The territory that comprises modern Thailand was controlled at different times by different countries; this period also saw the rise of perhaps the most well-known of these ancient empires, the Khmers. The Khmer Empire developed as an agricultural society in what is now central Cambodia.

Khmer conquests of the region began in the seventh century, and within a few hundred years they controlled most of what is now modern Thailand. The Khmers built Angkor (see Figure 2), a city that was home to perhaps a million people in the eleventh century, just north of Tonle Sap (it was another 800 years before the Europeans had a city of such stature).

The Khmer referred to the people of Thailand as the "Shyam," perhaps a reference to the Sanskrit word *shyama* for "golden." (The discovery of this term by an English trader in the late 1500s led to the foreign-used name "Siam.") Although the Khmers never took over the southernmost bits of the Malay Peninsula, instead leaving everything south of Nakhon Si Thammarat on the Isthmus of Kra to Srivijaya, they did tie the northern and central parts of the region into one state and thus set the stage for the first true Thai country.

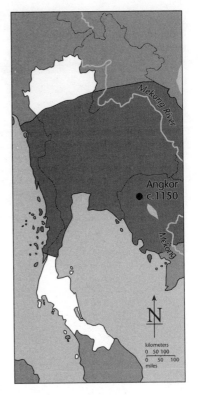

Figure 2.

Sukothai and Lan Na: AD 1200–1300

Most Thais consider Sukhothai to be the first Thai nation. Perhaps due to corruption, or maybe because of an epidemic of malaria, Angkor fell into rapid decline in the early thirteenth century. Thai leaders of *meuang* in the central Mekong Valley began to take advantage of the weakened condition of Angkor, and in 1238 a Thai prince named Indraditaya overran the Khmer soldiers at their outpost in Sukhothai (see Figure 3) and declared himself the sovereign of the city.

Sukhothai, a name that translates to "rising happiness" or "dawn of happiness," expanded quickly. By the end of the thirteenth century, it controlled much of what today is northern Laos, eastern Burma, and Thailand. About this time, the Srivijaya Empire collapsed, and with that, Sukhothai's influence in the south of the Malay Peninsula expanded. Within 100 years, the kings of Sukhothai reigned over an empire that stretched from China to Singapore. Sukhothai's crest of power was short-lived, but its influence on the future of Thailand cannot be overstated. During this period, the Thai writing system was created, art and architecture took on a distinct Thai flavor, and Theravada Buddhism was adopted from the Sinhalese on Sri Lanka and became the state religion.

Interestingly, another kingdom, Lan Na, came to exist in the far north of

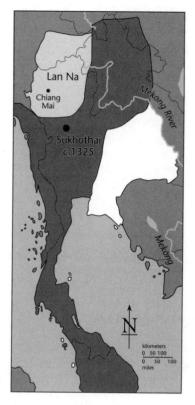

Figure 3.

Thailand at the same time Sukhothai rose in power. Centered around Chiang Mai, which was the kingdom's capital for most of its 300-year existence, Lan Na was smaller and had far less military power than Sukhothai. Lan Na served as a buffer zone between Sukhothai and the Mongols of China. This buffer was put to good use in the late 1200s when King Mengrai of Lan Na successfully repelled a Mongol invasion.

Both kingdoms were bases on which the future Thailand was built, but Lan Na outlived Sukhothai. This first truly "Thai" kingdom was not able to maintain its powerful position much beyond King Ramkhamhaeng's death in 1299.

Ayutthaya: AD 1300–1800

In 1350, a Thai general named U Thong took control of Suphan Buri and, soon, all of the areas around it, including Sukhothai. A cholera outbreak in 1351 forced U Thong to move his capital to Ayutthaya (see Figure 4), a defendable position surrounded by rivers. U Thong immediately went about expanding his control, forcing the various *meuang* within Sukhothai's borders to submit through military force. U Thong changed his name to Ramathibodi and asserted his power as an absolute monarch whose power, like that of his predecessors in Angkor (and unlike those of Sukhothai), was divine.

In 1431 Ayutthaya's army sacked Angkor and completely closed the books on that city's era of power. It soon fell into complete neglect and was overrun by the jungle (only regaining some stature in the world hundreds of years later as a tourist attraction). Meanwhile, Lan Na was attacked and battles continued with that kingdom for almost a century. Within 100 years of the fall of Sukhothai, Ayutthaya was in control of an empire that extended from the modern Thai-Malay border to China and included parts of modern Burma and all of Laos and Cambodia.

As a capital city, Ayutthaya had an enviable location. It was in the delta of the Chao Praya River and had an excellent seaport. Canal systems ran through the city, creating a Venice-like transportation (and waste disposal) scheme, and the fields around it had complex irrigation systems that kept the region well fed.

The sixteenth century was a pivotal time for much of Southeast Asia, even if the people of the region could not quite see it yet. In 1498, Vasco da Gama sailed around the Cape of Good Hope and into the Indian Ocean. He traded with the city of Calicut, on the Malabar Coast of India, and made a large profit. The profit enticed more exploring traders, and by 1511 the Portuguese were moving onto the Malay Peninsula. An embassy was set up in Ayutthaya, and the royal family was given complete control of all matters of trade.

Despite a constant state of war, trade bloomed and the city grew in wealth. None of this prosperity was lost on the powerful Burmese, who sacked Ayutthaya in the late sixteenth century. The city was retaken fifteen years later by King Naresuen, but war with the Burmese continued until even bigger powers moved in. The Portuguese were soon followed by the Dutch, British, and French, all of whom were vying for exclusive trade rights for their nations and, eventually, colonies.

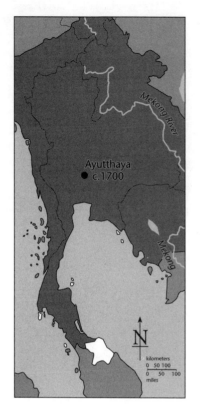

Figure 4.

An interesting side story to the court of Ayutthaya came about in this time. King Narai (next in line after King Naresuen) befriended Constantine Phaulkon, a Greek trader, in the 1670s. Phaulkon, whose clear understanding of the European world was helpful to the Thai king, was awarded the equivalent of a cabinet position in 1675. Though many Thais were suspicious of Phaulkon, he actually served Ayutthaya well, blocking the British, Portuguese, and Dutch from each gaining too much control of the lucrative trade with Ayutthaya. As the European powers toiled with one another and with the Thais to gain control of the trade, Phaulkon managed to play them off against one another (a continuing theme in Thai history). Eventually, he allowed some French troops to be garrisoned in the capital, and some of the more xenophobic ruling elite moved against him. A well-founded anxiety about the intentions of the French, whom the locals called the *farangset*, was fanned by royals who vied for Narai's throne. In 1688 Phra Phetracha, the general in charge of the royal regiment of elephants, overthrew the king and had Phaulkon beheaded. The French, who had overtaken the Portuguese in trade under Phaulkon, were sent packing. Phra Phetracha immediately cut off relations with the Europeans; the legacy of this separation would continue for 150 years.

War with Burma was the constant theme of the seventeenth and eighteenth centuries. The Burmese slowly gained the upper hand and in 1765 laid siege to Ayutthaya. It fell in 1767, and almost everything of any cultural significance was either burned or hauled off to Burma. To the Thais, this was Pearl Harbor, 9/11, and the Civil War all rolled into one big catastrophe. The Burmese were Buddhists, but they even burned Buddhist manuscripts and tore down temples. Thousands of Thais were enslaved, and the capital was left in smoldering ruins. The Burmese invasion might have destroyed any chance for the emergence of the modern Thailand we know today if it hadn't been for a wacky military tactician named Phraya Taksin. Taksin was a half-Thai, half-Chinese general who managed to reorganize the army and force out the Burmese. He reestablished the capital at an even more defendable position, a small fishing village on the Chao Praya River delta called Thon Buri.

Without question, the Thai people needed Taksin's military brilliance to repel the Burmese, but Taksin quickly proved a bit too quirky to rule the kingdom. Shortly after Taksin named himself king in 1769, he began to tell everyone he was the reincarnation of the Buddha. This didn't sit well with the ruling elite, and Taksin was removed from power. The former general was executed in the traditional royal manner: he was sewn into a velvet sack and beaten to death so that not a drop of his blood would be spilled on the earth.

Bangkok and the Colonial Era: AD 1800–1900

One of Taksin's aides, General Chao Praya Chakri, managed to take a leading role in the kingdom's affairs and was made king in 1782. He went about restoring symbols of Thai culture, badly damaged during the Burmese wars, and built a new capital across the river from Thon Buri on Rattanakosin Island. This capital soon took on Thon Buri's popular name of Bangkok, and though Chakri's name was changed to Rama Thibodi when he took the throne, his original surname is the name of the current dynasty. Chakri is now commonly called Rama I (1782–1809). His kingdom, then called Siam, saw Rama I's efforts to solidify the borders and restore the Siamese/Thai culture to what it had been.

His great-grandson, Mongkut, really led Siam into the modern age. Mongkut, or Rama IV (1851–1868), had spent the twenty-seven years of his brother's reign in a monastery. He was a devout Buddhist, but he had thoroughly studied the ways of the West. Mongkut left the monastery fluent in Sanskrit and Pali but also English and Latin. He studied Western science, especially astronomy, and remained current on the political events of Europe and North America. When he took office as Rama IV at the age of forty-seven, he immediately went about establishing full relations with the West.

Treaties allowing trade were signed first with the British in 1855, then with the United States in 1856, and with most of the powers of modern Europe by 1868. He set up a new system of currency to help accommodate all this trade and installed foreign advisers in his cabinet to help him in his negotiations with the various governments of Europe and North America. Rama IV instituted an education system along modern European lines rather than that of traditional Buddhist teachings, and he was the first king since the Sukhothai era to let his face be seen by the common people. It is Rama IV who was portrayed by Yul Brynner in *The King and I*, and although the movie (and the other films about the same subject) greatly overdramatizes Anna Leon Owens' position in the Thai court, Mongkut did offer elephants to Abe Lincoln for use in the Civil War. I believe Lincoln declined the offer.

Rama IV died suddenly of malaria in 1868, but his son, Chulalongkorn, or Rama V (1868–1910), added greatly to his father's modernization. Rama V was tutored by Western teachers (one of whom was, for about five years, Anna Leon Owens), and he went about developing a Western-style legal system and a modern rail system for the country. Rama V made slavery illegal and was the king who abolished the requirement that all subjects should prostrate themselves before the monarch. For these reasons, he is still very popular with the Thais, and his likeness is often hung in restaurants and businesses. But it was his political moves with the colonial powers that he should best be remembered for.

Rama V ruled at a time when European powers were chopping up the world in their grand design. Vietnam was taken apart, piece by piece, by the French. The French went on to add Cambodia and Laos, and their designs on Thailand were no secret. However, their chief competitors, the British, were rapidly approaching the Siamese borders from the south and west. The British had colonized India and, with it, modern Bangladesh and Burma. They also controlled the Straits of Malacca and Malaysia.

It's not uncommon to hear young Thais extol the uniqueness of their country, how it was the only one in this part of the world not to be colonized, as if it were because of military superiority. However, the lack of colonization has far more to do with Rama V's brilliance in playing the colonial powers off on one another than it does with Thailand's elephant cavalry. Rama V convinced both the British and French, through years of separate negotiations with their ambassadors, that each would be better off with a Siamese buffer zone between them. Some concessions had to be made, most notably to the French, who annexed the Siamese territory of Luang Prabang (in modern-day Laos) and Siem Reap (in modern-day Cambodia), but by and large this system worked and did keep Thailand completely independent through the colonial period.

The Modern Age: World War II

The Chakri Dynasty had its biggest test just before the outbreak of WWII. Through a bloodless coup in 1932 by a group of Thai students who had been living in Paris, Rama VII was forced to accept a change in the way Siam was to be governed (he was playing golf in Hua Hin when he was notified of the coup...I'm not sure what he shot that day). Because the king was a popular figure with the people, a constitutional monarchy was adopted in 1933, leaving the king with limited powers and handing the majority of control over the country's direction to a governing council. This proved too much for Rama VII, and in 1935 he abdicated the throne and moved to England. He named no successor, so the cabinet that had been ruling the country, led by a French-educated general named Pibul Songgram, named Ananda Mahidol, Rama VII's ten-year-old nephew, as the new king.

In 1939 Pibul had the country's name changed from Siam to Thailand. He continued to rule Thailand as the Japanese swept through Southeast Asia. Pibul cozied up to the Japanese, and in an interesting story he instructed his American ambassador, Seni Pramoj (who later became the Thai prime minister), to hand a declaration of war to U.S. Secretary of State Cordell Hull. When Seni Pramoj met with Hull, Pramoj stated he had something that he was to give to the secretary but that he really didn't want to hand it to him. Hull, recognizing the declaration for what it was, told him, "Then don't give it to me." This action would later be cited as proof that the Thai people never really wanted to declare war on the United States, and in 1945 Secretary of State James Byrnes accepted that the declaration was null and void. (We did the same thing for the French!)

Even so, a state of war between the Japanese garrisoned in Thailand and the United States and Britain did exist from 1942 to 1945. This really amounted to no change in Thai policy other than allowing the Japanese to occupy and use Thailand as they saw fit (Pibul was left in "power"). It wasn't much different from how the Swedes or the French treated the Germans during the same period. Few large-scale battles took place in Thailand during the war, but many POWs were interned in the country, including those who built the infamous Death Railway and the bridge over the River Kwai.

At the end of the war, General Pibul was forced to step down as head of the cabinet by the Thais who had led a Japanese resistance force. A pro-American stance was adopted that has not really changed since. In 1945 Ananda Mahidol, Rama VIII, returned from Switzerland. Under very mysterious circumstances that to this day are kept unclear, Ananda was shot and killed in his bedroom in 1946. Although the death was labeled a gun accident, it appears that he may have been murdered by one of his orderlies. His brother, Bhumibol Adulyadej, was the next in line, as Rama IX. A few years later, Ananda's attendants were arrested and executed, perhaps to repay the karmic debt (they failed to protect the king and therefore they had to die) or perhaps to keep them quiet. No one really knows.

To say the least, the death of Ananda is an ugly slice of Thailand's history. Hushed conversations about the subject are common, but everyone in Thailand is officially forbidden to discuss the event since much of the dialogue circulates around the concept of regicidal plot. As a matter of fact, by virtue of my just bringing it up, I think this book can be taken from you as you enter the country, so don't mention it to any customs officials.

During the Cold War, Thailand's military leaders took an anticommunist stance and began to support, as well as promote, many of the plans of the French and United States in Southeast Asia. Through the mid decades of the twentieth century, military leader after military leader came to rule the country despite its declaration of being a democratic nation. The one common theme through this period of revolving military leaders was Thailand's pro-Western/anticommunist stance.

The Vietnam Era

The actions of the United States and France in the First and Second Indochina Wars (Vietnam War) are common knowledge to us in the West, but Thailand played a significant role in the wars as well. Fearing a communist takeover—a very real possibility in all of Southeast Asia—the Thais went about fighting the war alongside the Americans, Australians, indigenous people of Indochina, and other countries from the region. With the Mekong working effectively as a "Bamboo Curtain," the U.S. military built airbases all over the country, the largest and most active of them being in Udon Thani in the northeast. Much of the war in Laos and Vietnam was run from Thailand, and the country went through a veritable boom in its economy with the influx of U.S. funding and U.S. soldiers spending their "leave" in Bangkok.

Then in the latter '70s, when the U.S. military involvement in the war had ceased, the alliances were turned inside out. As the Vietnamese took control of Cambodia (and, effectively, Laos), their former allies against the Americans—the Khmer Rouge—were forced out of power and into the jungle on the Thai-Cambodia border. The Arab proverb "My enemy's enemy is my friend" expresses how war makes for strange bedfellows, and the Thai support (with U.S. and Chinese acknowledgement) of the Khmer Rouge was no exception. Pol Pot's murderous army effectively created a buffer zone along the border, separating Vietnamese-controlled Cambodia from Thailand.

Current Events

With the Cold War fizzling out in the late 1980s, Thailand entered a new era. The military loosened its grip on the government, including allowing elections in 1988. In 1991 the military staged another coup, the tenth since 1945 (for those keeping count), but placed another civilian, Anand Panyarachun, in control of the country as prime minister. His administration passed a new constitution, but in 1992 there was another election that was overruled by the former military rulers.

All this time, King Bhumibol Adulyadej, although very limited in power as the monarch, had been growing in stature among the common Thai people. King Bhumibol publicly reprimanded the military. His status as a man who cared for his people had elevated him to such a lofty place that without having governmental power, he nonetheless could sway the government. A civilian government was reestablished, and in September 1992 Chuan Leekpai, a businessman from Trang (just south of Krabi) was elected as prime minister.

In an election, Leekpai was replaced by Chavalit Yongchaiyudh, a former general and logging tycoon. Chavalit was voted out of office amid numerous accusations of corruption and the 1997 economic collapse, to be followed again by Chuan Leekpai. In 2001 billionaire businessman Thaksin Shinawatra defeated Chuan.

Many feel that Thailand is headed into troubled waters. The king, who is aging, has been a strong force in holding the country together and the military at bay. Who his successor will be remains a bit of a mystery, with his daughter being the popular choice but his son being the more likely pick. The crown prince has a reputation for being a thug and not much of a man of the people (I shall not go any further than that, or this book *will* be taken from you by customs!). Also, an Islamic movement in the south, funded in part by the Jemaah Islamiyah and al Qaeda, continues to create problems for the government. This could negatively impact the tourist industry, which would create strife and thus strengthen the movement. What does the future hold? We shall see.

GEOLOGY AT A GLANCE
The landscape of southern Thailand is dramatic, and it is considered by geologists to be the most perfect example of karst topography in the world. These karsts, the spires and buttes that give us climbing and give a whole host of wildlife a unique habitat, run from Guilin, China, to the Mulu region of Borneo.

Karsts are made up of limestone, a sedimentary rock that is composed of dead organic material. It began to form around 360 million years ago when a mountain range (that has long since disappeared) began to erode onto a tectonic plate called the Sunda Shelf. The erosion deposits, which contained everything from broken bits of stone to fern leaves and the remains of proto-dinosaurs, settled off what was then the south coast of prehistoric Asia (see Figure 5).

A warm, shallow sea that was a perfect habitat for marine life then bound the coast. A huge reef, perhaps the biggest reef in the world's history (far bigger than Australia's Great Barrier Reef) grew up off this coast and added to the organic material being deposited from the land. Over time, the bits of coral, plankton, and dead fish hardened together. The sediments from the land continued to bury this reef, eventually creating a sedimentary rock now known as the Ratburi Limestone Formation (see Figure 6).

Then about 30 million years ago, an event that took place thousands of miles away had a huge impact, literally, on all of Asia. When the subcontinent

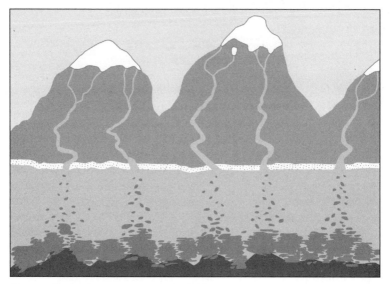

Figure 5. Erosion deposits on the Sunda Shelf.

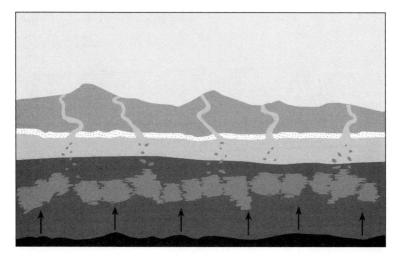

Figure 6. Sediments create the Ratburi Limestone Formation.

of India rammed into southern Asia, it not only drove up a huge mountain range, it also twisted the Malay Peninsula around in a clockwise motion and lifted the Sunda Shelf. Because all this organic limestone had been laid on top of the shelf, it lifted the limestone as well.

At the same time that the sedimentary rock began to push toward the surface of the ocean, the ocean levels began to drop because of the various ice ages. From

Figure 7. Sedimentary rock rises while ocean level drops.

Figure 8. The Ratburi limestone is exposed over millennia.

time to time, the Ratburi Formation poked out of the sea, while at other times, it dipped back into the sea, depending on global temperatures (see Figure 7).

As the sediments that had been laid down over the millennia rose and ocean levels fell, the weaker bits of sediment eroded away. What was left behind was the hardest of the sediments, that being the Ratburi Limestone, made up mostly of the original reef components (see Figure 8).

Thai karsts are limestone, but they are exposed to a number of elements that give them unique shapes compared to other limestone. First are those fluctuating

Figure 9. Acidic rainwater erodes Thai karsts into wild shapes and caverns.

sea levels, which have recently eroded away the karsts from beneath, often leaving big overhanging walls. Changing tides have also eroded weaknesses within the karsts, leaving canyons and huge caves. The karsts have actually been eroded so much from underneath that they are often hollow. The caves in the Ratburi karsts are some of the deepest in the world, and the Sarawak Chamber in Gunung Mulu National Park on Borneo is thought to be the largest underground chamber in the world. It is large enough to hold forty Boeing 747s end to end.

Limestone is inherently porous, so rainwater passes through it as much as it runs off it. (Indeed these rocks act as giant aquifers for southern Thailand.) In the tropics, where there is lots of rain and sunshine, a huge amount of organic matter grows on top of the limestone. As this organic matter dies and breaks down, which is an acidic process, it mixes with the rainwater that passes through the stone (see Figure 9). The acidic rainwater helps to break down the limestone, allowing it to erode into wild, almost melted shapes.

The stalactites, stalagmites, and various flowstone formations that make this rock so unique are created by a very complex turn of natural history. An ancient reef gave us stone, then fluctuating sea levels eroded it into overhanging walls, and, finally, acidic runoff created holds...and it only took about 360 million years.

WILDLIFE

Karst topography gives rise to very diverse wildlife, and the karsts of Southeast Asia are some of the most varied ecosystems in the world. In one square mile, shallow reefs (where diversity is aided by deep drops into cooler water) run onto tidal pools and then beaches. A mangrove might exist behind this, then a huge wall running up a 3000-foot peak. All of these different levels of the biosphere contain different species ekeing out an existence.

I won't go through Mother Nature's entire smorgasbord, but you probably are interested in a few of the larger critters you are likely to see. Keep in mind that the Phra Nang Peninsula is a wildlife sanctuary...not a very well-protected one, but still a sanctuary. Over the years, I have come to realize that tourists can have one of the biggest impacts on protecting the environment. As long as we show an interest in visiting the wild, diverse places where these animals live, the areas will be kept protected. Let the national park, or even the owner of your bungalow, know that you like coming to Thailand as much to see the gibbons and reefs as to participate in the climbing. Also, set an example and be kind to the critters. It's the only way these areas will stay protected.

Gibbons

The Laem Phra Nang has been declared a gibbon sanctuary, which I think means we humans will allow the gibbons to live here if they wish. So far, a few of them wish. They are quite gangly, off-white apes who live in small family groupings. However, you will be very lucky to see one because they are shy. However, the calls of white-handed gibbons, which sound something like a soprano humpback whale, can be heard most any morning between 8:00 and 10:00. If you get to see one, you are very lucky.

Crab-Eating Macaques

Evil. Yeah, I'm supposed to say how wonderful the wildlife is. I can do that for virtually anything else. I can even tell you why leeches (no, we don't have leeches) are worth meeting up with, but I have a hard time saying the same for the local macaques (as I explained in the "Things to Fear" section of Chapter 1). Crab-eating macaques, or long-tailed macaques as they are sometimes called, weigh up to 40 pounds (18 kilos), are excellent swimmers, and are quite common on the Phra Nang Peninsula. There are a number of large and aggressive troops of them, including a group that guards the trail from Railay East to Phra Nang Beach, another that frequents the Railay Beach Club and the Tonsai bungalows, and a third that haunts the Fire Wall, Melting Wall, and Cat Wall.

The real problem with these animals is their similarity to us. They are greedy and ill-tempered, and they will not hesitate to steal from you and even bite if you protest. Since they can transmit a number of diseases, including rabies, this is a very bad thing. Be careful with the macaques.

Dusky Languars

Another species of primate, dusky languars, are fairly shy. They are larger than the macaques, though much more pleasant and far less common. You can distinguish them from macaques by their larger size, their darker color, and the gray and white hair on top of their heads that points skyward like the 'do that Don King sports.

Palm Civets

Palm civets are related to the mongoose, though they look a bit more like a North American raccoon. Civets are great climbers. If you have any olfactory sense at all, you will find their scat on various ledges across the Phra Nang Peninsula. Their Thai name, *musong*, was given to one of our routes because it had obviously been climbed numerous times by a civet.

Snakes

The most common snakes you'll see are the so-called coconut snakes. These live off bugs in the coconut trees and are quite harmless. They are very thin, green, and anywhere from one to four feet (30 centimeters to more than 1 meter) long. Don't pick them up because it is possible to mistake them for one of the green vipers, which are anything but harmless. There are a dozen different species of green viper, all of which could cost you a hand or more if they bite. Cobras are one of the most common snakes in southern Thailand. Phra Nang is home to four different species of cobra, including the king cobra and a type of spitting cobra. In general, these guys avoid contact with people and are rarely awake and moving in areas of human habitation during the day. If you spend a lot of time near the water, you might see a yellow-lipped sea snake. These can be up to five feet (1.5 meters) long and have black- and silver-colored bands. If you see one in the water, take a good look and then swim the other way. Ounce for ounce, this snake has the most deadly venom in the world!

Most people don't see the snakes; they are there, but they really don't want you to notice them. Unfortunately, some of our snakes try to be stealthy until you get right on top of them, when they do what snakes do to defend themselves. See "Things to Fear" in Chapter 1 for advice on avoiding snakes.

Water Monitors

These big lizards are impressive to see. They are usually a dull brown color with yellow eyes and can be up to 2 meters in length. Though they are not poisonous, they should be given a wide berth. Their bite, like that of their cousin the Komodo dragon, almost always carries a nasty infection.

We grow 'em big in Thailand! This is about the only way to safely display a big centipede... in a bottle of liquor.

Scorpions, Wasps, and Centipedes

Okay, these creatures don't seem that exotic when you list them in a book. However, we grow all of them pretty big in Thailand, and when you see them, they will have your full attention. The scorpions and centipedes are quite poisonous, and a bad sting can kill a weak or small person. At the very least, their sting will make you wish you were dead. The wasps are common to the cliffs and can be dangerous because their nests can get quite large. While doing first ascents, some climbers have been stung by dozens of them at once. This will ruin your whole day. If you see a wasp nest on a climb, it's best just to climb something else.

Red Ants

Known locally as *mot daeng*, these little

devils are right down there on my *kee* list with macaques. You will see plenty of them. When one bites, it releases a pheromone that tells all the others in the area to bite whatever they are standing on. If that's you, you will be amazed at how many parts of your body you can swat in one second. *Mot daeng* inspire great leaps and unbelievable feats of speed.

Golden Orb Spider

This spider is so large that it has been called the bird-eating spider. It constructs a web that will all but stop you, and it has an appearance that absolutely *will* stop you. I'm told none of the spiders in Thailand are deadly, but the black and yellow lines on this critter and its sheer size make me wonder. They are pretty common. Look for them in their webs in the jungle along the trails.

Animals That Are Sadly Rare

If you are lucky, you will get to see one of the rarer animals in Thailand's deteriorating biosphere. Malaysian sun bears, which are small but aggressive, have been seen on the Phra Nang Peninsula. Great hornbills, one of the largest birds in the region and certainly the most interesting, have also been spotted at Phra Nang. Sea otters, pangolins (a scaly anteater), and pythons have also made an appearance, though I have never had the pleasure. There have also been lorises, jungle cats, and giant fruit bats on the peninsula. At one time, the water around the area was no doubt the home of the dugong, or sea cow, although now their territory has been forced south. Fortunately for those of us who like to hang out on the beach, the huge saltwater crocodile is also gone...but it would have been nice to see one before they were wiped out.

Chapter 4

BANGKOK

The "City of Angels," as Bangkok has been dubbed, is the capital of modern Thailand and the center of all things governmental and financial. It is home to more than 9 million people, making it one of the largest metropolitan areas in the world, and to look at it up close is to see that the city is the epitome of the term "concrete jungle." Dingy white, block-shaped, two- and three-level concrete buildings that provide shops on the lower floor and housing on the uppers have all but replaced the traditional teak houses. Six-lane boulevards are so clogged with traffic that taxi drivers in the know stay strictly to the *sois* ("small alleys"), and the air pollution from all these cars is estimated to cost the city US$2 billion a year because of respiratory illnesses. Urban planning seems nonexistent (or perhaps no one is following the plan) as high-rise banks cast permanent shadows across residential neighborhoods while 40-by-100-foot neon signs make the night glow.

Your initial impressions of Bangkok will no doubt be tinted by these modern

THERE IS A LOT IN A NAME!

The name Bangkok is actually a combination of two words, *bang* and *makok*, that translate to "village of olive groves." This nickname, which is now internationally recognized, was given to the city when the very first bricks of the capital were being laid in an ancient olive grove. Bangkok's common name in Thai is Krung Thep, which means "City of Angels" and is also a condensed version of the slightly more austere royal name for the city. The correct transliteration of the full royal name is *Krung Thep mahanankon amonratanakosin mahintara ayutthaya mahadilok popnopparat ratchathani burirom udomratchaniwwet mahasathn amonpiman avatansathit sakkathattiya wisanukamprasit*. This translates to, roughly, "City of Angels, Great City of Immortals, Magnificent City of the Nine Gems, City of the King, City of the Royal Palace, City of the Gods Incarnate, Erected by Visvikaran at Indra's request." When contacting your travel agent, please simply use "Bangkok."

realities of a developing economy. However, the modernization of Bangkok has not wiped out all of its charm, and there is a lot to see in, and learn, from the city. Spending a few days here acclimatizing, getting your tickets south to the climbing areas, and seeing the sights is well worth your time.

This book is not the ultimate guide to Bangkok—that would be another book in itself, and many exist that you will no doubt come across when planning your trip. This book gives you enough information to find a place to stay and to see some of the city's best sights. If you need more information, see the References at the back of this book, or go to a bookstore in Bangkok (easily found at most historical landmarks, on Khao San Road, or in large hotels) and pick the one you like.

ENTERING THE LAND OF SMILES

When you deplane at Don Muang Airport, you will be herded toward a row of a couple dozen immigration agents in taupe-colored booths. You get your passport stamped and receive a visa (see Chapter 1), and then you take an escalator down to the baggage claim level. You get your bags and go through one of the doors marked with a green customs sign for "nothing to declare"...unless you are doing business and need to declare something.

After you exit this customs area, you will be in a large room with barriers at either end that are holding back folks waiting for friends and relatives. It is at this point that your first *tout* encounter will happen. That is, someone in a suit will step up and ask you where you are going and whether you need a limousine or a room. My recommendation is to politely brush them off by saying you already have whatever they want to give you.

At this point, it's a good idea to go over to one of the bank kiosks and exchange some money. You will get a slightly better rate in town, but not much better, so get what you need for a day or two. ATMs, which work in both English and Thai, are available just outside the retaining fences.

If you are going straight to the domestic terminal for a flight to another part of Thailand, a 500-meter walkway connects the international and domestic terminals. You find it by turning left when exiting the customs area, then walking until you get to the end of the international terminal...there should be a sign here directing you to the walkway. Also, there is a free minibus running between the two terminals every 15 minutes all day.

If you are planning to get a cheaper hotel near the airport just for the night and have not chosen it ahead of time, you can go to one of the kiosks in the arrival hall and discuss it with the booking agent there. One of the touts will no doubt help you get over to the kiosk.

If you know where you are going to stay in Bangkok, proceed out the doors to the taxi stand. You will pay a fixed rate, which changes, to various areas of the city. Expect to pay 200 to 300 baht, plus an airport charge of 50 baht. Also, tell the driver to take the expressway and pay the extra 40 baht this will cost. It saves a lot of time—hours in bad traffic!

ACCOMMODATIONS

Bangkok is a very large city, so it has a number of accommodation options. As you will no doubt be commuting all over the city to see the sights, there's no reason to be centralized in one place. Instead, here I point out a few choices, from least to most expensive, that I like. Rates, given in baht, are estimates only, so confirm the rate before you make your reservation or check into the hotel.

Inexpensive

For inexpensive, or downright cheap, you will want to be near the infamous Khao San Road in the Banglamphu District of the city. Khao San, located close to the Grand Palace, is the place to get tickets to elsewhere in Thailand (or the world, for that matter). It is the hangout for young, wandering travelers of Asia, and therein lies both its best attributes and its worst. As a tourist, everything you need for your trip is nearby: Money can be exchanged at an excellent rate, travel agencies line the street offering deals to anywhere, and the food is cheap.

However, it's a real scene, absolutely jammed with tourists at all hours of the day and night, listening to techno as they discuss the bar scene at the place they just came from and what the bar scene might be like at the place where they are headed. Also, perhaps because so many people are coming in from so many different places across the globe, there is the distinct possibility that your cheapest places to stay will be the home of many a bedbug. If you have ever had bedbugs, you know what a nasty reality this is, so be wary.

The Khao San Palace
www.khaosanroad.com
02-282-8876
This place is down an alley near the middle of the street. Like everything else on Khao San Road, a huge sign out on the main road gives you some idea of its location. The place itself is okay but, for better or worse, it sees a lot of traffic. Rooms vary from 400 to 800 baht, depending on what you want.

Sawasdee House
02-281-8138
If you want something a bit quieter than what is offered on Khao San Road proper, go to the end of Khao San Road, cross Chakraphong Road at the police station, and then pass through Wat Chana Songkram (don't pet the dogs in here). On the other side you will find a few places to stay that I think are a bit quieter and cleaner. This one was my favorite of the bunch. It offers rooms from 200 to 700 baht per night.

Riverview Guest House

02-234-5429

This is another option for people traveling on a tight budget, but it is not near Khao San Road. Instead, Riverview is in the "*farang* quarter," near the Oriental Hotel and behind the River City Shopping Center. It's in an odd neighborhood of machine shops and motor repair places, but the tall building overlooks the Chao Praya River. The rooms are clean and range from 400 to 800 baht.

Moderate

I list only one place in the moderate price range, and it is not in the Khao San Road area. However, it has its pluses.

The Swiss Lodge

www.swisslodge.com

02-233-5345

This moderately expensive, quaint little hotel is in one of the liveliest parts of Bangkok: the Silom Road area. The cost is listed as 3,800–4,400 baht, but a substantially discounted rate as low as 2,280–2,640 baht is often found at the website. Return customers usually get a lower rate as well. This part of the city is famed for the two streets that make up Pat Pong, the red-light district, but girlie bars are only part of what makes it popular with tourists—and they are certainly something that can (and should) be avoided. This is also a good area for restaurants and shopping, and the night market is excellent. The Skytrain, a brand-new elevated train that connects various parts of the city (see "Getting Around the City," later in this chapter), can be caught just a few hundred meters out the door of the hotel. The hotel concierge can tell you all about the various goings-on.

Expensive

In the expensive price range, Bangkok is a city with no peers. At one point in the 1990s, five of the ten most highly rated (I believe by *Conde Nast Traveler*) hotels in the world were in Bangkok. My two favorites are the Sukhothai, a boutique hotel with amazing restaurants just off Sathon Road, and the Oriental, the perennial world champion in this category, located on the banks of the Chao Praya. Once you stay at either of these places, you will feel neglected everywhere else. As soon as you check in, the staff knows your name. They keep records on what you prefer for breakfast and the type of newspaper you read, and I have even had the concierge ask me, "How is the climbing in Krabi this season?" No, it's not spooky, it's cool! If you are ever going to splurge on a hotel, this is the trip to do it. Travel agents are able to get good deals at these places from time to time, so if you feel like really splurging (5,700–13,200 baht per night)—do it in Bangkok. You can also look for deals on the web.

Oriental
www.mandarin-oriental.com/bangkok
02-659-9000

Sukhothai
www.sukhothai.com
1-800-223-6800 (from U.S. and Canada), 02-284-4980

Airport Area Hotels

If you are planning on just overnighting in Bangkok and then going on to Krabi the next morning, it is best to stay out near the airport and avoid the 30-minute commute in and out of town. A number of hotel options are out here, and new ones are popping up fast. Check the web for the best deals.

Amari Airport Hotel
www.amari.com/airport/
airport@amari.com
66-2-566-1941

This five-star hotel is literally across the road from the airport. An indoor walkway connects the two, making travel as painless as possible. The breakfast buffet is excellent here (something to note even if you are not staying in the hotel but are waiting around the airport for a flight). Unfortunately, rooms at the Amari start at around 6,650–7,700 baht per night. If you fly in on Thai Airlines and have an onward ticket on Thai Air, a substantial discount is available. This has changed a lot over the years and always seems different... it has been as low as 760–880 baht, but I believe 50 percent of the regular room rate is the standard discount now. You have to ask for it when you make your reservation and not when you check in.

Asia Airport Hotel
www.asiahotel.co.th/asia_airport.htm
airport@asiahotel.co.th
66-2-992-6999

This is a good alternative to the Amari. The rooms are clean and run from 1,200–3,500 baht. If you book ahead and notify them of your arrival time, they will send a van to pick you up. They will also run you to the airport the next morning.

Quality Suites Airport Hotel
www.asiatravel.com
1-800-780-5733 (from U.S. and Canada), 66-2-677-2240

The Quality Suites Airport Hotel is about 5 km from the airport and has a shuttle (you have to book ahead of time to get picked up). It is a good, clean, cheaper alternative to the Amari. They advertise a 1,862–2,156 baht rate on the web, though this is certainly subject to change. I have heard anything from 1,700 to 4,000 baht.

GETTING AROUND THE CITY

There are three options for traveling around within Bangkok.

Metered Taxis

The first, and most commonly used by travelers, is the metered taxi. These rove the streets looking for fares, just as they do in most other cities of the world. They are quite inexpensive, but metered taxis often don't go far from the driver's home area during rush hour. If traffic is intense and you are trying to cross the city, most drivers might tell you they are not taking fares. If this is the case, you will have to hop in a tuk-tuk.

Tuk-Tuks

A tuk-tuk is a large, motorized tricycle. They have a top speed of about a million miles an hour and can get to that velocity in roughly three seconds. To say the least, tuk-tuk rides are a rush. However, there are some drawbacks.

First, you will be exposed to Bangkok's air and thus be coated with smog particulates. Second, tuk-tuks do not have meters and thus a ride in one will require some negotiation of price. The price for your travel should be a bit cheaper than in a metered taxi, but it all depends on your bartering skills. Finally, tuk-tuks do not come with airbags, seat belts, roll bars, or even doors. A wreck in a tuk-tuk is likely to leave a mark, so pick your driver wisely.

Skytrain

The third means of getting around in the city is fairly limited but very civilized. The Skytrain is comfortable, has nice views, and connects many of the areas most commonly frequented by tourists. A map by Nancy Chandler (see the next section) shows the Skytrain routes.

SEEING THE SIGHTS

There are a lot of choices on books about Bangkok, but for the purposes of visiting the city, there really is only one map. Your first order of business should be to buy Nancy Chandler's Map of Bangkok. Not any map of Bangkok...Nancy Chandler's Map of Bangkok (originally published in 1974, now in its twenty-second edition). It's available in most shops in Bangkok that sell tourist information; it costs around 200 baht and is worth every satang. Or it can be ordered prior to your trip for about US$10 from this website: *www.nancychandler.net*.

This map is an indispensable tool for getting you around the City of Angels.

The usual tourist sights are listed on it, but so are unique shops, public transportation particulars, and historical tidbits. It is amazing that so much is put onto one piece of paper. Once you have that map, here are a few things to look for.

Sam Paeng

A trip to Thailand is not complete without an afternoon in Sam Paeng, the Chinatown of Bangkok. This is the commercial heart of Thailand, and it is perhaps the most exotic part of one of the world's most exotic cities. Everywhere you go, there are scenes you want to capture, so take your camera, but keep in mind it's going to be impossible to truly describe this place to your friends back home. No macroscopic lens could capture the mixture that is Sam Paeng: the sounds of the tuk-tuks and Chinese music; the smells of ginger, incense, and dried squid; the absent stares of the people as they pass by you, noticing your existence for nothing more than to keep from stepping into you as they go about their daily commercial activities. Everything from rhino horns to signed Harvard diplomas are available in Sam Paeng, and most of it at a fairly good price, especially if you are Chinese and speak one of the dialects of Teochiu Chinese.

It's an amazing place, and I'd like to tell you how to get around, but I can't. Sam Paeng is a maze of "walk-only" streets teeming with food stalls, knockoff Rolex salesmen, and Chinese temples. The best way to see the area is to take a cab or a tuk-tuk to one of the temples marked on Nancy Chandler's map. Then take a left turn, then a right, then a left, so that you are hopelessly lost. Later in the day, you'll pop out at some big, impassable street or at the Chao Praya River, and then you will be able to find your way home. Take your camera and a few baht, and keep a good hold on them. Lots of *farangs* have lost their cameras here, only to find them for sale in the "Thieves Market," one of the more colorful parts of Sam Paeng that can easily be found with Nancy's map.

Chatachuk Market

More commonly referred to as the Weekend Market, Chatachuk is home to over 15,000 vendors of everything imaginable. It is generally a Saturday and Sunday event, though a few of the shops sell stuff on weekdays. It generally runs from 8 A.M. to 8 P.M., though things really don't start kicking until around 10 A.M. and cool down around 6 P.M. A full day will give you time to buy any conceivable item for friends and family members back home. All of the taxi drivers know the name "Chatachuk," and again, Nancy Chandler's map does a good job of showing what sections of the market specialize in what items.

The Snake Farm

The Snake Farm is the common term for the Queen Saovabha Memorial Institute and Red Cross Center. There is another "Snake Farm," but you want the one near the corner of Rama IV and Surawang. This is the place where they milk the various snakes for venom so they can make antivenin. The snakes are brought out and shown to tourists at 11 A.M. and 2:30 P.M. every day. There is also a video explaining the antivenin process. Some of the more exotic critters, such as the king cobra and a few of the Siamese cobras, are also brought out and put on display so you can see how they behave around people…. You get to be really close to them and can even pet the banded kraits. I once saw the master of ceremonies kiss a cobra, though he was bitten and had to be rushed off. Various vipers live in terrariums around the park, so you can see them in a seminatural state and see just how well they blend in with their environment. It's really cool, and I have found it a great place to take a date. Seriously! All my ex-girlfriends loved this place.

The Grand Palace, Wat Phra Kaeo, and Wat Pho

The Grand Palace and Wat Phra Kaeo with its Emerald Buddha, plus Wat Pho with its reclining Buddha (across the street from the palace), is basically a three-for-one stop. No expense was spared here.

A demon guard at the Grand Palace. (Jim Gudjonson)

The architecture and decor of the palace, where themes range from Thailand's Hindu past to more modern European lines, are awe-inspiring. The interior of the palace is more or less a museum, with artifacts from all eras of the past on display.

Wat Phra Kaeo, a temple within the walls of the Grand Palace, is an amazing place created solely for the purpose of housing the Emerald Buddha. This statue is so sacred in Thai culture that only the king is allowed to change its robes. The Emerald Buddha itself is perhaps a bit overshadowed by the ornate frescoes and architecture of its home. One of the national symbols, the temple is highly revered, but the Buddha itself, which is generally accepted to be made of jade or jasper and not emerald, is held very far away from the viewing area and is a bit lost in all the gold that surrounds it. Its traveling history, having been hauled off by the Laotians and Burmese at various times, is more interesting than the Buddha itself and can be read about as you move through the *wat* (temple).

Perhaps more impressive, at least in sheer size, is the 150-foot (45-meter) reclining Buddha, stretched out in Wat Pho, which is across the street from the palace. This huge Buddha is covered in gold leaf and has mother-of-pearl inlays for eyes and in its feet.

ARRANGING TRAVEL WITHIN THAILAND

Almost all travel inside Thailand takes you through Bangkok. If you booked your domestic travel ticket online or with a travel agent before departing for Thailand, then the information in this section is not necessary. However, if you are on a "roam as you will" trip or are looking for the absolute cheapest way to get around, this section can serve as a guideline.

The best place to find a travel agent in Thailand is on Khao San Road. Travel agencies make up roughly a third of the businesses on that famed street, so you won't have a problem finding one. My personal favorite is Olavi Tours, but there are lots of choices. They generally charge a very small percentage over what the airline or bus company charges them for the tickets.

As a special note, if you are going to Laos (or any other Southeast Asian destination), you will also want to do your shopping on Khao San. These agents often advertise that they can get you a visa as well as the tickets you need. In my experience, this has been a good way to go rather than waiting in line yourself at the embassy of the country you will be visiting. You will have to give the agency your passport for an evening, plus some money, but so far this has not been a problem for me.... Of course, I can't be sure that a photocopy of my passport wasn't sold to the Mossad or Hezbollah!

Planes

Flying in the developing world does tend to put many of us Westerners on edge, and flying in Thailand is no exception. Although these airlines do not suffer the accident rates you find in Africa or South America, the pilots do tend to have a bit of bravado that wouldn't go over well with the Federal Aviation Administration, and no one worth noting is paying close attention to the service records of the planes. A number of accidents have happened since I have lived in Thailand, including one in which the pilot tried to force his way down because he felt he was losing face with the pilot of another aircraft. However, thousands of people fly every day in Thailand, and they rarely have a complaint. Also, your only other option requires getting on a bus at some point, and that is far more dangerous than flying.

Trains

In second class, you get a sleeper berth (ask for the lower berth, not the upper one: the upper one is further from the tracks and thus rocks harder from side to side). Snoozing away the ride is comfortable if you don't mind being rocked to sleep. There are just a few hang-ups with the trains. The first is that they fill up fast and are therefore hard to book. Another downside to the train is that you get the berth they sell you. Stories of people having bedbugs in their berths are getting fairly common, and if you happen to get a berth with these loathsome creatures, you will probably have to stay in it for the ride.

Buses

Private buses leave from Bangkok often right off Khao San Road. This is the means of travel I like least, though it is commonly used. The reasons I don't like them are that they are often kept so air conditioned that you feel slightly hypothermic; they are also less comfortable than the flight that got you to Thailand, and, most important, they are not very safe. Bus drivers seem to treat the road as if they own it, and if not everyone on the road agrees with this approach, there can be problems. Also, they seem to take the road at one speed, that being all-out, and turns be damned. Bus accidents are not uncommon in Thailand, and when they happen, they tend to be grand in scale. One accident in the early '90s was actually a head-on between two buses, killing almost everyone on board both.

When you reach your destination, you will need to rummage through your bags immediately. It is fairly common to hear stories of a person riding in the baggage compartment of the bus to go through all the bags for valuables while the patrons are uncomfortably riding up above. Oh, and it costs about the same as the train and leaves at an inconvenient hour that I cannot recall. I hate the bus.

Chapter 5

THE PHRA NANG PENINSULA IN SOUTHERN THAILAND

You best start believin' in ghost stories...you're in one.

Captain Barbossa

Although the Phra Nang Peninsula is a relatively small landform in Thailand's southern reaches, for climbers it's central: it encompasses about 99 percent of the climbing that's worth doing in the whole country. Most climbers travel from Bangkok to the Phra Nang via the Krabi Province of southern Thailand. *Krabi* is a word that means "sword" in Thai. The province, which covers about 2,900 square kilometers (1,800 square miles) is not much bigger than the state of Rhode Island and is home to just under 400,000 people. Some anthropologists believe Krabi's caves were home to people as long as 35,000 years ago, making it one of the oldest inhabited regions of Southeast Asia. Indeed, without giving up too much and thus threatening access, I will tell you that at times you will be quite close to the humble abodes of the first inhabitants!

The capital, the largest city, and the heart of the province is Krabi town. This modern tourist boomtown has around 30,000 inhabitants and has been a seaport since well before written records of the area were kept. The airport is about 15 kilometers east of the town of Krabi and perhaps 40 kilometers east of the main climbing area on the peninsula.

GETTING TO KRABI PROVINCE
By Plane

Krabi has the closest airport to the Phra Nang Peninsula, and it is served by a number of airlines, each offering at least a couple flights per day. The times change regularly, as do the number of flights, so it's best to check the current rates and schedules when you are ready to book. The flight time from Bangkok is about an hour and 20 minutes. All of the airlines have good service and cost about 2,800 baht per leg of the journey. The earliest flight of the day to Krabi from Bangkok is usually around 8:15 A.M., with the latest arriving sometime around 9 P.M. It's best to book ahead as the flights fill up in the high season. Thai Airways has at least three flights per day during the high season, all on

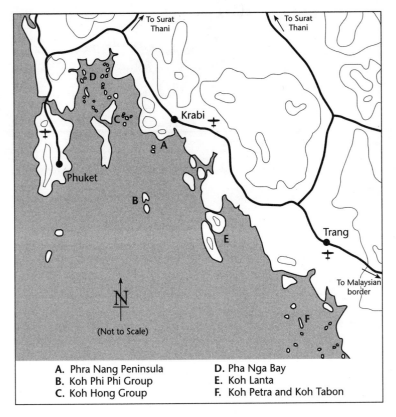

To Surat Thani

To Surat Thani

D

C

Krabi

A

Phuket

B

E

Trang

To Malaysian border

N

(Not to Scale)

F

A. Phra Nang Peninsula
B. Koh Phi Phi Group
C. Koh Hong Group
D. Pha Nga Bay
E. Koh Lanta
F. Koh Petra and Koh Tabon

Boeing 737-400s. Bangkok Airways serves Krabi with ATR turboprops. Air Andaman uses either ATR or Boeing 717s.

By Train

The train is an excellent way to get to the south cheaply. You get to leave late in the day, around 7 P.M., so a day of sightseeing in Bangkok can be had before you get on board. Second class costs around 400 baht for the 12-hour ride. You don't just get to ride a train...you have to take the bus too, because there are no tracks to the town of Krabi. Granted, the bus ride is only for a few hours, and it's a scenic jaunt through southern Thai villages and beautiful karst spires, but they wake you at like 5 A.M. to make the switch at Surat Thani.

By Bus

Private buses get you from Bangkok to the pier in Krabi town in about 14 hours. Buses cost about the same as the train and leave at an inconvenient hour that I cannot recall. If you arrive via a bus, you will probably be dropped off in downtown Krabi.

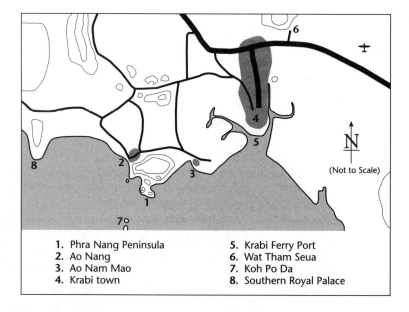

N (Not to Scale)

1. Phra Nang Peninsula
2. Ao Nang
3. Ao Nam Mao
4. Krabi town
5. Krabi Ferry Port
6. Wat Tham Seua
7. Koh Po Da
8. Southern Royal Palace

PHRA NANG

The Phra Nang Peninsula extends off the mainland about 3 kilometers. It is separated from the rest of the world by the Khao Ao Nang Massif, a huge chunk of that Ratburi limestone we climbers love so much. The name Phra Nang translates simply to "Princess Nang" (Nang being a proper name). This peninsula, which contains the majority of Thailand's climbing, is the sanctuary of Princess Nang. The land lies in a Buddhist country, is owned primarily by Muslims, and is visited mostly by Christians, but Phra Nang commands respect from all of us.

The most common version of the Princess's story is that she was shipwrecked on the peninsula hundreds of years ago. At that time, there was no land between the Thaiwand Massif and the Diamond Cave–Tonsai Massif. There were two families of fisherfolk living in the area, one on Koh Phi Phi with a boy named Boon and the other on the peninsula, who were wishing for a girl. The childless family prayed to the sea spirit Phaya Nayk, and he granted them the wish for a baby girl, but only if they agreed that he could marry her when she came of age. The girl was soon born and given the name Nang.

Nang became friends with Boon, and as they grew older, they fell in love. They planned to marry, but at the wedding ceremony Phaya Nayk reappeared and punished everyone for going against their word. He grabbed Nang and made for the sea. A holy man, perhaps the fellow conducting the services, asked the wedding guests to quiet down. When they did not, Phaya Nayk turned everyone into stone. Boon was banished to Kho Phi Phi and the Princess to the peninsula.

A refurbished junk in Phra Nang Bay

Her home was destroyed and her family turned to rocks. The Princess Cave on
Phra Nang Beach became her bedroom, and the inner cave is her bathroom. The
hills across the bay, just above where the King of Thailand's southern residence
sits, are the remains of Phaya Nayk.

One *Farang*'s Interpretation

There are a lot of versions of this story. Like so much of oral history, the variations in these tales are often convoluted and have perhaps changed over time.
But while the legends about the Princess vary in detail, they are fairly consistent
on the major points. It is difficult to say what exactly happened on this peninsula so many years ago, but based on these legends, raw historical facts, and
the words of people who have been possessed by the Princess (yes, *possessed*),
I have come up with my own interpretation of this very important story. It is
only mine and should not be taken as the absolute gospel.

I believe the Princess was a young, ethnically Indian girl who was born in
roughly 1680 on the Julian calendar. The 1680s were a very turbulent time in
what was then known as Siam, with a lot of politics and gamesmanship being
played out by all the major powers in this region (see "Thailand's History" in
Chapter 3). For whatever reason, she was sent to China as a baby, perhaps as part
of some sort of political arrangement between the two nations. A storm came up

when they were near the southern Siamese coast, so the ship headed for refuge and in the process it was dashed on a reef in what is now Phra Nang Bay.

At that time a married couple, who were probably sea gypsies of the Orang Lonta tribe, were living in the large cave on what is now Phra Nang Beach. They had tried to have a child, but for reasons that could not be explained, they could never conceive. Then one night, when the sea god Phaya Nayk had released a great storm around them, a child washed ashore. It was literally a gift from the gods. They had wanted a child and now, here, from the sea, had come a baby girl. They called her Nang, and she grew up with them, learning to fish and live mostly on a boat that her father had built but also in the cave on the now celebrated Phra Nang Beach. As she grew older, she ventured farther and one day met a boy from another fishing village on the island of Phi Phi. The families didn't get along but could see the two were very much in love. They eventually allowed the two to marry.

On the day of the celebration, Nang's mother and father sailed out to greet the wedding party as they approached from Phi Phi. When they did, another storm came up, and within minutes the boats were swamped and sinking. Nang had stayed behind to prepare herself for the wedding, so she was spared, but her family and her fiancé were not so lucky. They were lost in the storm.

So there she was, on a remote beach with no one around and no hope of ever meeting anyone. All she loved had been destroyed by the sea—twice. She vowed to never leave the peninsula and to never marry. She died there of a broken heart and is still there, in spirit.

Consistently in all the legends, Nang is said to be very lonely, and since that time this area has been known to be dangerous for fishermen. The legends say she wants a new man every year to help her deal with the loneliness. Supposedly a fisherman disappeared from the waters around the Phra Nang Peninsula roughly every year before we tourists started showing up.

When the bungalows were new and only a couple of houses had been built in the Railay Beach Club, a holy man was asked to come out and survey the place. It was discovered that sometime in the past, a cemetery had been created on the peninsula, presently on the ground where the Rayavadee Resort lies. The land around it was deemed okay for the use of the living, but the area beyond the two *klongs* (creeks) was for the spirits. (One of those *klongs* flows out past Bobo's, the other near Diamond Cave and Coco's.) Of course, over time people wanted more land. Holy men came out and spoke to the spirits, asking them if the land could be used. The spirits said "Okay," provided they were paid the proper respect, and then moved into the caves and valleys of the Tonsai Massif (Diamond Cave, Dum's Kitchen, etc.). This massif is a hollow maze of stone, and it is accepted by many locals as the land of the spirits.

So much for legends, you say. More than just a couple of superstitious old men believe in this legend, and hundreds of tourists have seen strange events

Just a sampling of the shrines honoring the Princess on the Phra Nang Peninsula

that are obviously tied to the stories. When tourists (*farangs*, or foreigners) started coming in addition to fishermen, tourists began to disappear instead of fishermen. A young boy was lost here a few years ago and a huge search was conducted, but he was never found. Many tourists claimed to have seen the child walking with a woman in a wedding dress on Po Da Island. In another incident, an athletic man drowned off Railay Beach in the middle of the day during high season (i.e., lots of people were around). His girlfriend watched as he was pulled under by something, but there were no marks on him to show this. Possessions have happened at a local restaurant: the possessed, usually someone new to the area, recites a version of this story. Believe it or not, one boy or man has disappeared or died, either on the peninsula or on Koh Po Da, every year for as long as the old folks can remember. At the same time, many a tourist has seen a Thai woman in a wedding dress walking on the beaches at night.

No doubt you will notice that this place is rather romantic, and it is widely known by the Thais that a trip to the Phra Nang Peninsula increases fertility. Shrines exist all over the peninsula in the Princess's honor. Even the most die-hard Muslims give the Princess her due, and the big resort here has had to have ceremonies in her honor because of all the problems they had during their opening season. Tracts of land, which are extremely valuable, are left without buildings to honor some part of the legend.

A number of us climbers even considered the possibility that the problem with our bolts could perhaps be remedied by paying a bit of homage to the Princess. However, we could not find anyone to forge us a titanium phallus, so we gave her a few bolts, some flowers, and a lot of incense instead. Since then, certain walls have been kept sacred and not climbed on, and you won't find too much local support for sinking a bolt into any bright pink, phallic-shaped stalactite. (These are said to help appease her loneliness.)

Of course, you don't have to believe any of this. It could all be a bunch of hocus-pocus mumbo jumbo that only we Thailand "lifers" fall for. But no matter what you think now, these legends and the belief in the princess will affect your life on the peninsula. And if you spend enough time there, you will believe.

A Climbers' History of the Phra Nang Peninsula

A long, long time ago, in the distant past, say 'round 1987, there was no climbing on the Phra Nang Peninsula. It was a remote bivy site for fishermen that the occasional wandering tourist happened to stumble across on a day trip from sleepy Krabi. Mr. Gift, an enterprising man who is well known locally for having the best ideas first, bought some land where the Rayavadee Resort now lies and started a bungalow operation. A few tourists showed up on purpose, and a few more bungalows opened.

Then came Francois Brunier and Dominique Potard, two of the most pleasant and gregarious Frenchmen you could ever hope to meet. They had climbed at Kho Phi Phi in 1988 and returned the following year to explore the rarely seen Phra Nang Peninsula. On their second trip, they put up many of the first routes on Nam Mao Beach (at the area now called 1, 2, 3) and made a plan to begin guiding people to Thailand specifically to climb. Sometime that year, it appears a route went up, via "the journeymen" Kurt Albert and Thierry Renault, in Phra Nang Cave. Volker Schoeffl, Frank Dicker, and a few other climbers including Max the Kiwi, Cyro Glad, Mark Newcomb, and me, showed up a season later, all putting up climbs and living in *Sawan* (Paradise). After having had the best climbing trips of our lives, we left that year knowing that, no matter what, we would return the following season.

That next season arrived none too soon. Many close friends of those who'd come the year before made the trip, and thus a lot more routes were established.

Remarkably, the peninsula had until then gone unmentioned in Lonely Planet's *Thailand* guidebook. The underground traveler scene, those who discover places the way Richard did in *The Beach* and not from Lonely Planet, had found Phra Nang. A couple bungalow operations bumped up to 24-hour power, making it possible for phone calls (via radio phones) to be made from the peninsula. A number of the now-prominent local climbers moved to Railay, formerly working in bars or as boatmen, to get their first taste of the sport.

At that time, roughly 1991, knowledge about the climbing was merely in the heads of the few climbers who had been to Thailand. The names, the ratings, and the proper boatmen to get you to the routes was coveted information, but anyone who had this knowledge was willing to share it. Climbing on the Phra Nang Peninsula was still a shadow of what was done on Koh Phi Phi, both in the number of routes and in international recognition.

Another year arrived, and then another, and with each passing season the number of climbers and established routes grew tenfold. Everyone who came to climb was equipped to put up new climbs, but since there was no local climbing scene and no truly local guidebook, there was only one obvious place to store the info where all the climbers could and would easily find it: the Sunset Bar. The bar was the center of the climbing scene. The route log was kept behind the bar and closely guarded by Murphy and Egk. It was a hodgepodge of climbing info and endorsements, topos, and complaints about the new 200-baht bungalow prices, all on marijuana ash- and beer-stained paper napkins, rotting Lonely Planet guidebook pages, and even Singha labels. As a "guidebook," it was in such disarray that one needed to have already climbed the route to be able to make sense of the information in the log.

After another season or two, there was some discussion of rewriting the log. The problem was that no one wanted to do it. A local climbing scene had sprouted up, but it was far more interested in letting people top-rope Money Maker for 100 baht (and a chance at some "soft rock") than getting involved in the philanthropic cause of rewriting the log book. I was busy climbing in the morning, playing volleyball in the afternoon, and in the evening writing down in the log what I'd done that day. Then Egk met Sophie. Sophie was a tan Swede with eyes as blue as the sea and white-blonde hair that hung like wavy clouds from heaven—and to our benefit, she was a bit bored just watching Egk and I play two-on-two volleyball. With a little coaxing, and an offer of all the rum and cokes she could drink, we managed to get Sophie to rewrite the log. For that we say, *Thank You, Sophie* (7a+), and I reopen the offer of all the rum and cokes she can drink if she ever returns. Of course, only a few days after the log was rewritten, it disappeared, but that's another story.

A number of guidebooks now have been written about the area, and it has been featured in numerous climbing magazine articles, not to mention the *New York Times*, the *Washington Post* and *The Guardian*. With this exposure, we now see thousands of climbers visiting the area every year. An entire industry has been built around the sport, and countries all over Southeast Asia are looking to draw the same crowds to their walls. The Phra Nang Peninsula has grown so much in stature in the climbing world that it is probably the most common climbing area that all climbers, including alpinists, sport climbers, and traditionalists, from dozens of countries, visit.

A Note on New Routes

Not long ago, doing a new route on the Phra Nang Peninsula was as simple as it could get. But times have changed, and without squeezing someone else's routes or climbing on rock that has potentially bad ramifications for access, much of what could be done has been done. That said, a few gems are left to be found. While you are searching, keep this point in mind: Remember that all routes should be established with titanium glue-in bolts and threads.

Off-Limit Areas

Phra Nang Cave has been closed to new routes at the request of the big resort where it's located, for good reason. There is loose rock up there, and it would be tragic to kill a sunbather while you were climbing. Climbing here, even if protection exists, could definitely get the whole area closed down.

The area behind the Railay Beach Club has been kept wild for years, and it continues to be one of the last untouched wild habitats left on the peninsula. It has become the last home for some rare critters, including gibbons, and the walls are the last remaining untouched places for the Asian peregrine falcon to nest. Please let these animals have one area that is people-free.

The walls left of the Diamond Cave North Face—in other words, the walls to either side of the actual Diamond Cave—have been deemed off-limits for climbing by the park service.

The walls behind Phai Phlong Beach will perhaps become off-limits as construction of the resort there is finished.

The walls of various islands in Pha Nga Bay are off-limits due to birds' nest harvesting. The best way to stay current on what is acceptable and not acceptable out here is to talk to a knowledgeable local, like Luang at Hot Rock, about where the nests are being gathered.

A Few Things to Keep in Mind Before You Leave for Phra Nang

If you arrive on the Phra Nang Peninsula near Christmas or Chinese New Year without a reservation, you will probably have to spend a few nights out on the beach. This sounds romantic, but actually it's quite a pain.

There is at least one ATM on the peninsula, but you can't always count on it being loaded with cash. Stores exist on the peninsula, but items are sold at quite an inflated price. You're better off getting supplies in Krabi.

GETTING TO PHRA NANG

Phra Nang is separated from the rest of the world by those large rock walls you have traveled so far to climb. There are no roads onto the peninsula, so all visitors get there by boat. During the dry season, which is winter to us northern-latitude folk, the main gateway to Phra Nang is via the beach town of Ao Nang, west of Krabi (see the map); boats from Ao Nang land at either Tonsai Beach (North Peninsula) or Railay Beach West (Central Peninsula). If you are coming during the rainy season, there are two ways to get to the peninsula: via Krabi itself or Ao Nam Mao, on the peninsula's east side; boats from Krabi or Nam Mao land at East Railay Beach (Central Peninsula).

Getting a boat to and from Ao Nang to the peninsula can be difficult after dark. It's possible, at a higher rate, but you can't count on it.

It is common to arrive on the peninsula at low tide. This is a bit of a pain because it means lugging your stuff through knee-deep water for a ways, or even a couple hundred yards over reef off Tonsai Beach. It's best to have your sandals on before you get to the peninsula.

Via Ao Nang

The easiest way to get to Ao Nang from Krabi airport is to hire a taxi. Taxis to Ao Nang cost about 400 baht and the trip takes about 40 minutes. Keep in mind that most taxis down here don't have a sign on the top of the car that say "taxi." You need to look for a guy who looks like he wants to put you and your stuff in his car. He will probably find you.

Also, if you see other tourists standing around the baggage claim area with backpacks, it's a good guess they're headed your way. Sharing taxis to Ao Nang is common. Keep in mind that, depending on your flight from Bangkok and the way things are scheduled in the year, month, and the particular day you arrive (everything changes regularly down here), there may be a taxi-van that can take a bunch of you to Ao Nang. Watch for these being loaded with backpacks in the parking lot. It's first come, first served and should cost about 100 baht per person.

From Krabi town proper, if you come via the bus, you can use public transportation to reach Ao Nang. *Sawng-thows,* usually small, white pickup trucks with a cover over the back and two benches on either side, run between Krabi and Ao Nang every 15 minutes. You hail them down, pile your stuff on top, and find a place to sit or stand. (I have seen a Nissan *sawng-thow* leave Krabi for Ao Nang with twenty-nine people on board, so don't get in an argument over your personal space!) *Sawng-thows* start the trip from Krabi at a stand about half a block from the jetty. They drive along the waterfront picking up people and then head out of town. The ride is about 45 minutes. Ask around for "*sawng-thow* to Ao Nang" and you will be pointed in the right direction. Just yell when the little white truck goes by and it will stop.

Ao Nang has sprung up from being nothing more than a sandy bend in the road to a beach resort town. You will probably be let out of the taxi or *sawng-thow* on the ninety-degree corner in town. Before you even get out of the vehicle, a boatman will be there asking you if you want to go to Railay Beach.

At this point, you need to specify whether you want to go to Railay Beach or Tonsai Beach, based on where you plan to stay. The boat will probably hit both objectives, but not necessarily. Different boatmen are in different "cartels" and are thus kept from certain destinations, so make sure your boatman is going to your place. Once you get there, you can move from one beach to the other, but moving all your stuff up and down the beach is not always easy, so it's best to know your approximate destination ahead of time. The boat price for getting to the peninsula from Ao Nang is 50 baht per person. Excessive luggage can bring on an extra charge of 50 baht.

Just so you know, there is a trail connecting Railay and Tonsai beaches, and a boat can haul you between them for 20 baht. Keep in mind that if you are planning on staying on East Railay Beach, it is best to go to Railay (East or West) in a boat. Carrying your stuff to, say, View Point Bungalows from Tonsai Beach is an epic you don't want to have when jet-lagged.

A Note for Rainy Season Travelers

The rainy season, which is stormy, pushes swells onto the peninsula's west-facing beaches and thus makes boat travel dangerous. If you are arriving in the rainy season (roughly May to October), you need to go to the town of Ao Nam Mao to get a boat to Phra Nang. This is because from Ao Nam Mao you are in protected waters. Catch a boat from the jetty directly to the peninsula. The cost is 50 baht. If there is a breeze, you might not want to do this, as you will probably arrive with wet stuff.

GETTING SITUATED

The Phra Nang Peninsula is broken into three different sections by various chunks of rock or impassable human barriers (i.e., the big resort at Phra Nang Beach). Each section is labeled on the map here according to its most prominent beach.

The North Peninsula, which is closest to Ao Nang, is accessed via Tonsai Beach. Tonsai Road, formerly Tonsai Trail, starts at the north end of the beach under Cat Wall, makes a big horseshoe into the jungle, and returns to the beach under Tonsai Crag. At the back of Tonsai Road, another road extending to the east eventually degenerates into a trail that goes over the hill and down to Railay East, about a 30-minute hike. Most of the bungalows are along Tonsai Road; bars and restaurants are along the beach. Nights are often filled with reggae and techno, and the beach is not as nice as Railay West or Phra Nang. If you have kids or are not going to be partaking in the party scene the majority of

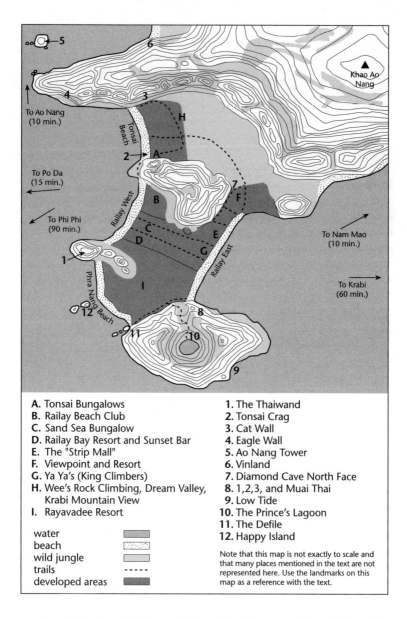

A. Tonsai Bungalows
B. Railay Beach Club
C. Sand Sea Bungalow
D. Railay Bay Resort and Sunset Bar
E. The "Strip Mall"
F. Viewpoint and Resort
G. Ya Ya's (King Climbers)
H. Wee's Rock Climbing, Dream Valley,
   Krabi Mountain View
I. Rayavadee Resort

1. The Thaiwand
2. Tonsai Crag
3. Cat Wall
4. Eagle Wall
5. Ao Nang Tower
6. Vinland
7. Diamond Cave North Face
8. 1,2,3, and Muai Thai
9. Low Tide
10. The Prince's Lagoon
11. The Defile
12. Happy Island

water
beach
wild jungle
trails   - - - - -
developed areas

Note that this map is not exactly to scale and
that many places mentioned in the text are not
represented here. Use the landmarks on this
map as a reference with the text.

evenings, Railay is probably your better choice. If you want to socialize and be in "the climbing scene," this is the place.

The Central Peninsula, which is equidistant to most of the crags, is accessed via either of the Railay beaches. Railay West is the beach you will arrive at from Ao Nang; Railay East is where you arrive from Nam Mao (and possibly Krabi).

Railay Beach was the center of the climbing scene for years, but it has become a little higher end than most climbers want to shell out for. The accommodations here tend to be the better option if you want quiet nights or if you are traveling with kids, because they are in a much nicer location than the places on Tonsai. East Railay Beach can be reached via a 30-minute walk on Tonsai Road, via a trail from West Railay Beach, or by boat from Ao Nam Mao or Krabi.

The Southern Peninsula, which has only one very expensive place to stay, is accessed via the famous Phra Nang Beach or Railay East.

EATS

Almost all of the bungalow operations on the Phra Nang Peninsula have a restaurant. On Tonsai Beach, a couple small restaurants are independent, and Bobo's on Railay West is independent. From time to time, vendors sell really good barbecue chicken and *som tam* (spicy salad) in front of the various convenience stores. The quality of the food is generally pretty good, but it would be hard to single any one place out. Ask your fellow climbers. You will probably find they are frequenting a number of locations because there really isn't too much difference among them.

ACCOMMODATIONS

If you are staying in one of the cheaper places, keep in mind that your best friend is your mosquito net. The bugs are often nonexistent during the day but a complete nuisance at night. A fan can help to keep them off, but nothing works like a good net. Make sure there are not a lot of holes in your net *before* you rent a room.

By the way, my recommendation is against air conditioning because it keeps you from acclimatizing to the heat at night and thus makes your climbing days much more uncomfortable. It's also a good way to catch a cold. A fan is a good alternative.

Also, the cheaper places tend to be constructed of natural materials that make a good home for critters. Make sure you tuck your net in at night to keep out such nasties as centipedes and snakes. Personally, I prefer a netted bungalow to a non-netted one, regardless of how nice the place is. No matter how hard you try, a few bugs are going to get in. You just sleep better with the net.

Most of the bungalow operations have restaurants and travel agencies, and most are within easy walking distance of the crags. Prices drop in the low season, and if the place looks empty you can often get a good deal. Most of them offer phone service from the "lobby," with 80 baht per minute the standard rate for calls to the United States and 100 baht the standard rate for calls to Europe. Internet service is usually available for around 3 baht per minute. Don't bother bringing your own laptop; they won't let you plug in. Most of these places only have power during the night.

Remember: all the information below is subject to change at any time ... and probably has since I wrote it!

North Peninsula: Tonsai Beach

At the north end of the beach and Tonsai Road is Viking Village (under Cat Wall); at the south end of the beach and Tonsai Road is Tonsai Bungalows (under Tonsai Crag). Most of the places to stay are along Tonsai Road in between these two. The cheapest places to stay are found at the very back of Tonsai Road or on the trail going over to Railay East.

The bungalows on Tonsai are cheaper because there is a glut of them on the market. All the bungalows on Tonsai Beach are in the less expensive category, although each establishment tries to have its own low-, medium-, and high-end rooms. These have varying levels of comfort, from nothing more than a mosquito net, mattress, and shared toilet to tile, air conditioning, and hot running water. Here are a few of your dozen or so choices on Tonsai Beach.

Banyan Tree Beach Resort
75-621-684
As far as I know, we don't have any banyan trees in Phra Nang. Then again, considering the high level of service of the Banyan Tree in Phuket, it's a good name to go by. Power runs from 6 P.M. to 6 A.M., and the least expensive units are 350 baht per night.

Countryside Resort and Tiew Khaow Bungalows
A couple hundred meters up the small road at the back of Tonsai Road are a few less-expensive places to stay. It is common to find bungalows for as little as 200 baht per night, and Tiew Khaow, just under the generator wall, has units for as little as 100 baht per night.

Dream Valley Resort
www.krabidir.com/dreamvalresort/index.htm
75-622-583
Dream Valley, a very popular place with climbers, offers all the amenities and has bungalows from 150 baht to 1,200 baht per night. Their power is on from 5 P.M. to 8 A.M. They will do your laundry for 35 baht per kilo (but don't give them an all-white shirt that you really need to stay all-white!).

Krabi Mountain View Resort
www.KrabiMountainView.com
75-622-610
The KMVR has an office, a restaurant, and a really big generator at the very north end of Tonsai Beach. However, you have to walk a few hundred meters

up Tonsai Road to find the bungalow operation. It's a clean place with nice rooms from 600 to 1,000 baht per night. You can barter them down if you will be there a while. That rate is a bit steep, so I have no doubt they will be adding some "less-expensive" bungalows soon to compete with the neighbors.

Tonsai Bungalows
75-622-588
This is the original place on this beach. It is also the closest bungalow operation to the Tonsai Crag. It has units varying from 300 baht for a bamboo bungalow to 2,500 baht for a fancy new one made of concrete and tile. It's not as quiet as the places farther from the beach and bars.

Central Peninsula: Railay Beach

The prices on Railay West are higher than on Tonsai. There is very little that is under 1,000 baht per night during high season; however, if you are staying a while, you will be able to negotiate a price. The bungalow operations down on the actual beach are now catering more to European package tours than they are to climbers, but that has its perks too. All of these establishments, with the exception of the Railay Beach Club, have restaurants with good food. Railay Bay Resort, Railay Village, and Sand Sea Bungalow are the closest to the beach. The Railay Beach Club at the north end of Railay West has the longest stretch of beachfront property. Many of these places will send a car for you to the airport and then have a boat waiting for you at Ao Nang.

The best deals can be found at the north end of Railay East. You get there from Railay West by walking a trail east through Railay Village or Railay Bay Resort.

Diamond Cave Resort
www.thai-tour.com
2-622-589
Diamond Cave and Viewpoint Resort, two of the places at the north end of Railay East, are good choices if you are looking for a lower rate and are not afraid of a little hike to get to the best beaches. Both offer rooms with fans and air conditioning from 800 to 2,000 baht, depending on the amenities you want.

Railay Bay Resort and Spa
www.railaybay-resort.com
railayresort@hotmail.com
75-622-570
Home to the infamous Sunset Bar, this was *the* climber hangout for a long time. The climber ghetto was recently torn down to make room for a pool and spa, both of which seem to be well liked. Rooms range from 2,000 baht to 7,600 baht per night.

Railei Beach Club
www.raileibeachclub.com
reservations@raileibeachclub.com
75-622-582 or 6-685-9359

The Club is a collection of private homes on the north end of Railay Beach and was the first establishment on Railay West. It is commonly referred to by the locals as *lanka daeng*, a term that means "red roof" but also implies a slang idiom for an insane asylum. Many of the private homes can be rented through a central office. There is a sign about 100 meters from the north end of the beach showing you where the office is. These are nice homes, but power is on only from 6 P.M. to 6 A.M. and there is no air conditioning. Prices range from 3,500 to 8,000 baht per night, depending on how many rooms you need. There is a daily cleaning service, and international calls can be made from the office.

Sand Sea Resort
www.krabisandsea.com
sandsearesort@hotmail.com
2-622-170

One of the first bungalow operations on the peninsula, this place has served as a home away from home for many a climber. Once a US$2-a-night place, it's now more likely to charge about thirty-five times that. Prices range from 1,450 to 3,450 baht per night. With that comes a pool, breakfast, and a supreme location.

Sunrise Tropical Resort
www.sunrisetropical.com
info@sunrisetropical.com
75-622-599

Newly renovated, Sunrise is on Railay East. Though it's not on the best beach, you're only 200 meters from Railay West, and this is the closest affordable place to Phra Nang Beach. All of the usual conveniences are available; prices range from 2,500 to 4,000 baht per night.

South Peninsula: Phra Nang Beach

All of the land behind Phra Nang Beach is currently owned by the Rayavadee Resort. Finding a room with them is easy because they are listed on many a discount website . . . you might try *www.krabi-hotels-guide.com/rayavadee-premier/* first. This deluxe place has everything. However, they are not used to climbers. I know one climber who stayed here and was kept out of the resort by the ever-vigilant security guards because she "did not look like" she should be staying there. Take your key with you when you go to the crag.

CLIMBING SHOPS

Hot Rock
hotrock@aonang.com
75-621-771
Railay West, Central Peninsula
Luang, the owner of this shop, was one of the first climbing guides in Thailand, along with Tex, Somporn Suebhait (King), and Dean Saydom. He has a very nice shop behind the coffee shop in Bobo's on Railay Beach West. Equipment is available, and the clothing he stocks (which his wife often designs) seems to set the trend for what is cool *next* year. Luang also operates a speedboat that can take up to six people out to Phi Phi as a day trip.

King Climbers
www.railay.com
75-637-125
Railay East, Central Peninsula
King Climbers, in Ya Ya Bungalows in East Railay Beach, has done a lot to support climbing in Thailand. Among other things, they worked very hard in the mid-'90s to allow climbers to access the walls. They have also strived to get a certification program put in place for the local guides, and they have acquired backboards and rescue equipment in the event of emergencies on the peninsula (out of their own pockets). For these reasons, we should support them.

King's shop has gear and shoes for rent or purchase. Somporn Suebhait (King) has climbed in Australia (his wife, Robin, is Australian), and he understands climbers. He is well-versed in what is going on with the climbing scene and has a guidebook with the very latest in climbing info.

Wee's Climbing School
www.geocities.com/wee_rocks
Tonsai Beach, North Peninsula
Wee Changrua is a true rock climber. While most of the Thai climbers see themselves as "climbers" because they guide at 1, 2, 3, Wee understands what it is to be a "climber." He wakes up thinking about it and goes to bed with pain in his elbows from the day's games. He is in touch with the scene at a base level, so he understands why you have come all the way to Thailand to climb. (Wee himself has climbed all over Europe.) He has a shop near Dream Valley Resort on Tonsai Beach, where you can get chalk, shoes, and other gear, as well as his current guidebook.

Cliffsman
www.thaiclimb.com
Railay East, Central Peninsula

If you haven't seen their stickers on cars at your local crag, you will see them somewhere on the Phra Nang Peninsula. Cliffsman is located at the end of Railay East in the big Viewpoint Resort building. They stock gear to replace yours and are up on some of the latest crags.

GUIDE SERVICES

It seems hard to believe, but just a dozen years ago King, Dean Saydom, Luang, and Tex were just learning to climb and were making more girlfriends than money by offering top ropes on *Money Maker* (6a) in Phra Nang Cave. The boys would boulder around the base of the route until a tourist came over to the route, then they'd let the person top-rope for something like 80 baht. This eventually evolved into taking people higher up the Phra Nang Wall and rappelling back to the beach. When we voluntarily closed Phra Nang Cave to climbing, one of the guys came to me and asked how they would be able to continue to guide. I told them that I didn't believe guiding, in the long run, would work in Thailand. The climbing was too hard, the people who came to climb were generally already experts at the sport, and there just wouldn't be enough slices of pie to go around.

I was very wrong.

Guided climbing and instruction have blossomed into a large industry at Railay Beach, and the venues chosen for it actually work pretty well. The well-featured rock is, at its lowest grades, very good for teaching the basics of climbing, and the easy access draws many tourists to try it. Climbing here has become so popular that Lonely Planet's *Guide to Thailand's Islands and Beaches* has listed it first in its "Highlights of Krabi Province."

Most of the guiding schools are *run* by very competent people, but some of their newer employees are lacking knowledge of climbing. The good guides will tell you that what they teach is sport climbing—specifically, how to go sport climbing in Thailand. Like so many industries in Thailand, guiding is unregulated and thus unencumbered by frivolous lawsuits. This means that the guides are capable of teaching you some things that you might not be able to do in the states.

For instance, the school I worked for in Jackson, Wyoming, is not allowed to teach lead climbing, where you actually lead the route. Leading is necessary, however, if you want to be able to climb on your own, and the Thai schools will teach you how to do it. I have seen the better instructors even explain such technical safety points as the proper placing of quickdraws so they will not unclip or cross-load and how to prusik back up a stuck line. These are things I, and most experienced climbers, learned through trial and error, with the errors often being nearly fatal.

The flip side of the freedom to teach this information is that inexperienced people, sometimes with as little as a couple months of climbing under their belts, can become guides. People in Thailand often seek out the tourist sector for jobs, and the good money made as a climbing guide has produced numerous "guides" who simply showed up, bought the equipment, then hung up a sign that offers instructed climbing. They very well may not know as much as you do. Also, even if they are experienced, they may not be able to convey the information to you clearly if their English isn't polished.

Finally, I should point out that I have never been guided by any of these schools listed below, so I cannot endorse any of them. I know them, and some of them I consider to be good friends, so I can say that I know they have good information in their heads. However, the ability to climb, and the ability to teach, are two very different things.

Again, make sure you get the right guide by selecting them based on your own common sense. Choosing to be guided by anyone is strictly your decision. Remember, sometimes a little information is a lot more dangerous than none at all. If you are going to choose a guide in Thailand, here are a few things you should think about.

First, I wouldn't just jump into it. Learning how to climb properly and safely is as important as learning how to correctly fly a plane. I would recommend any beginner or novice to go over to the Muai Thai area and 1, 2, 3 area and watch how the various guides go about instructing. You don't need to stand there for so long that you actually get a free lesson (this would be rude), but you can at least see how each guide goes about his or her craft. If the guide spends most of his or her time yelling, "Left foot up, now right foot, no—*higher,*" as some of them are apt to do, you would probably be better off with someone who teaches you the basic principles rather than force-feeds the movements to you.

Another thing to watch for is the guide's ability to speak English. The international language is taught in all Thai public schools, but climbing instruction is so important that you need to be able to clearly understand everything he or she says.

Also, read through this book and remember a few of the things I warn against. One of the biggest warnings is to *never,* ever, top-rope or lower off one bolt or one carabiner *anywhere,* but especially in Thailand. If you see a guide doing this, or any of the other little things I warn against in this book, you can be sure he or she isn't qualified to take you out.

Hot Rock
www.hotrock@aonang.com
75-621-771
Located in Bobo's on Railay West, Central Peninsula.

King Climbers
www.railay.com

75-637-125
Located in Ya Ya Bungalows on East Railay, Central Peninsula.

Krabi Rock Climbing
Located in the Ya Ya Bungalows on East Railay, Central Peninsula. This establishment is managed by a female guide named Pueng. If you are more comfortable learning from a woman, Pueng knows her business. She has been at it for a long time.

Tex's Rock Climbing
Located on Railay East, Central Peninsula, near the big generator. Tex does a lot of work with kids.

Wee's Climbing School
www.geocities.com/wee_rocks
Located on Tonsai Beach near Dream Valley, North Peninsula, and also at the north end of Railay East, Central Peninsula.

MEDICAL EMERGENCIES
Illness
For much of what might ail you, like having a bad shrimp with last night's dinner or an unidentifiable rash after thrashing about in the jungle, a visit to the nurses' clinic at Railay Bay Resort in Railay West, Central Peninsula, will be enough. They have all the creams, antidiarrhetics, and ointments you might need.

If you are pretty sick and really think a doctor is called for, a medical clinic in Ao Nang is operated by a doctor who speaks fluent English. Dr. Somboom's clinic is open from 7:00 A.M. to 8:30 A.M. and then again from 5:00 P.M. to 8:30 P.M. These hours may change, so it's best to make an appointment. The medical clinic in Ao Nang is brand-new, so there is no word yet on how often the doctor is in. The clinic can be reached at 75-695-303. It is located up the road from the ninety-degree corner, on the left side, about 200 meters past McDonald's.

If you are extremely sick, I recommend you stop at the Ao Nang clinic and then request to be forwarded to either Bangkok Phuket Hospital or Phuket International Hospital, both of which are in Phuket. The Krabi Hospital is not the place to go, but it does have a fully equipped ambulance that can transfer patients to Bangkok Phuket Hospital in Phuket when they are stable.

Climbing Accidents
If a person at the crag gets hurt, a runner has to go to one, or a few, of the places listed below and explain the situation. The people at these places probably will get right after it, but if you sense that they are not on it, you might go to the

nearest bungalow and call the places listed below if that seems faster. Go to a bungalow operator, explain the situation, and either (1) make sure a van taxi is sent to the ninety-degree corner in Ao Nang if the person is going straight to Bangkok Phuket Hospital or Phuket International Hospital or (2) take the Krabi Hospital ambulance, also on the ninety-degree corner, if the victim needs to go straight to Krabi.

Another choice is to get the injured person to Phuket via a speedboat. This will mean some bouncing around, but it will cut about an hour and a half off the transit time. If you do this, make sure that an ambulance is waiting at the boat dock in Phuket...this must be arranged before you get there! The bungalow operators will know which speedboat is available at the time, but a good choice is Luang at Hot Rock.

SONIA'S FLOP

I had just clipped the anchors of *Freedom Safari* and was looking back at my friend Elaine when I saw Sonia take to the sky. Well, the sky didn't take to her, and gravity took hold and slammed the poor girl down like something in the World Wrestling Federation. "I need a hospital now," she yelled, so coherently that I didn't quite believe she was serious. Then I saw her tibia, and her fibula, and a lot of flesh around them, all collecting dirt, leaves, guano, and whatever else was at the base of the wall. I agreed, she needed a hospital. "Sam, what do we do?" Mark yelled from the ground. I sent him to the bungalows to line up a boat and a taxi, either to Krabi or Phuket, depending on the patient's wishes and likelihood of surviving the trip.

I then lowered down and we began the rescue operation. We made a stretcher out of a rope bag and two bamboo poles. We packed her leg up with towels, shirts, and webbing. One guy began slicing out a much larger trail. This wider trail later became Tonsai Road. We had Sonia into a boat in less than 90 minutes, which was pretty fast, considering that the last rescue, led by the local "rescue team," took something like five hours from less than 100 feet from the beach.

Sonia was coherent and wanted the fastest route to Phuket, which was a speedboat. Sadly, after 20 minutes of looking, no one could come up with a speedboat driver, so she had to opt for the taxi. By her own choice, which wisely meant avoiding Krabi Hospital, she went to Bangkok Phuket Hospital. This was a committing choice because the chance of shock setting in on the long, bumpy taxi ride to Phuket was a real possibility. However, she made it and was well cared for. She's had multiple surgeries now but is faring well and plans to come back to Railay. I'm still wondering where my rope bag is.

There is a new service that can, theoretically, airlift an injured climber off the peninsula (or off Koh Phi Phi): Air Asia Ambulance. At the time of this writing, this service had not been put into action yet in a climbing rescue, but if it turns out to be what it is billed as, this will be the most efficient (and most expensive) way to get to a good hospital (this service was in full use during the post-tsunami rescue). Make sure you have your credit card ready when you make the call. The phone number is 01-932-8309.

Without getting angry, make sure the locals understand the urgency of the situation. But remember: If accidents keep coming at the current rate (early 2005 showed a rate of one per week), it will get very expensive for people to keep dropping their jobs to help.

If you go to Krabi Hospital, get the victim stabilized and then transfer the person to Bangkok Phuket Hospital or Phuket International Hospital. These hospitals have been very good in the past. Be sure you are assertive on this point if the person can be transferred. The doctors in Phuket International are well trained and very dedicated.

Hot Rock
75-621-771
Located in Bobo's on Railay West, Central Peninsula. Luang's mobile phone is (06) 120-7913...try to get him or his wife. He has a speedboat and can take a person directly to Phuket.

King Climbers
75-637-125
Located in Ya Ya Bungalows on Railay East, Central Peninsula. Somporn Suebhait (King)'s mobile phone is (01) 797-8923...try to get him or his wife, Robin. If a rescue involving spinal injuries or requiring multipitch descent is required, King is your best option because he has the most experience with it and has the required equipment. If King is called in from Ao Nang, he will have to drop what he was doing and thus lose a day of work to help you out. He won't ask for it, but it would be nice if you offered a little financial support.

Tonsai Bungalows' Climbing Shop
75-622-588
The climbing shop at Tonsai Bungalow is good to contact first if the accident is on Tonsai, North Peninsula.

Wee's Climbing School
Located on Tonsai Beach near Dream Valley, North Peninsula, and also at the north end of Railay East, Central Peninsula. If Wee Changrua is climbing nearby, let him know what has happened.

REST DAYS

The fact is, most of us need to rest on our rest days. A journey to the market in Krabi to stock up on supplies is good, and it can be augmented with a trip to Thai Farmers Bank. There isn't much worth seeing at the bank, but it does boast Krabi's most powerful air conditioning! Lubricate your 'biners, go hiking, chase girls or boys, lie on the beach, and dream about new routes on Koh Po Da and Chicken Island. Or try one of these adventures.

Wat Tham Seua

This is a *wat* (temple) near Krabi. Supposedly, a few centuries ago the *wats* at Nakhom Si Thammarat were being built for all the people of southern Thailand. People from all over made a trek to Nakhom Si Thammarat to help in the construction. A large number of these people from the southwestern coast passed through Krabi, staying in the caves that are now Wat Tham Seua for shelter. So many people went to Nakhom to help out that the temple was completed early, and the people returned the way they had come, having not gotten to help out with the construction. When they passed back through the caves outside Krabi, they met up with many people, all of whom were disappointed to hear that the temple at Nakhom was completed. Rather than cry over the spilled milk, they simply decided to construct a *wat* where they were. Wat Tham Seua is what they created.

At this *wat*, there are lots of Buddha statues in small caves, and each of those caves has been home to monks seeking enlightenment. The jungle has been kept in pristine condition here, and a nice walk through it is quite spectacular. If you want to get a good view of Krabi, go early or late and hike up the endless steps to the karst summit above the *wat*. Don't go at midday unless you are really good with the combination of exercise and heat.

Krabi Thai Cookery School

A useful way to spend a rest day is to learn to cook Thai food. With its hands-on approach, the Krabi Thai Cookery School is one of the better places in Thailand to learn this. Khun Ya, the head chef, will show you how to make your favorite dishes. You will receive a cookbook and, if you don't burn everything in the place, a diploma saying that you graduated. The school sends a car to pick you up in Ao Nang. Reservations are required. You can reach them at (075) 695-133 or via *www.thaicookeryschool.net*. Your bungalow can set up the class for you, but it's much better for the school if you make your reservations yourself. The cost is roughly 1,000 baht.

Sightseeing by Boat

Luang at Hot Rock on Railay West, Central Peninsula, is now taking people on tours of Koh Phi Phi, Pha Nga Bay, and all points between in a speedboat.

The price is 7,000 baht per day, but that's pretty cheap when you consider all you will get to see. He has snorkeling gear on board and can take as many as six people. It's a fun way to see a lot of wild limestone islands, and it's a really good option if you are not going to have enough time to visit Koh Phi Phi or the other islands for an extended period.

Snorkeling at Koh See and Yah Wa Sam

Get a few people together and hire a boatman to take you out to do some snorkeling. Baang Ee, one of the Ao Nam Mao boatmen, is a good guy who knows these places well. Make sure your boatman uses the moorings and doesn't just toss out his anchor, or the first table coral you're likely to see will have an anchor line through it. Take plenty of water and sunscreen. If you don't own snorkeling gear, you can get it at the bookshop next to Railay Village in Railay West, Central Peninsula. Most of the dive shops do not rent their gear to snorkelers.

Diving

We are lucky to have an excellent and safe dive operator on Railay Beach. Safety is the key with diving, and Phra Nang Divers, located in Ao Nang and with a second on Tonsai Beach, takes safety very seriously. They are a certified PADI dive center, which means they have been accredited by the Professional Association of Diving Instructors. For 9,000 baht they offer a four-day open-water course in which you can become certified to dive in most open-water situations. If that's too much time, they offer what I call the "hold your hand" dive, where they take you through the basics in the morning and then let you dive in the afternoon, while "holding your hand," for 3,500 baht. If you already are a diver, they have day trips to Koh Phi Phi and Shark Point for 2,400 baht and local diving for 1,500 baht. This includes two tanks, other equipment, and meals and beverages. If you really want to go for it and take a few days off from the one true sport, then go on their three-day live-aboard trip for 16,000 baht. This is all the diving you can manage at Hin Daeng and Hin Muang, Thailand's two world-class dive sites.

Sea Kayaking

Okay, this isn't very restful. As a matter of fact, this activity will pretty much ruin you for climbing the next day, but there is a lot to see and it's a lot more peaceful than seeing it from a longtail boat. If you want to see something really cool, go out with John Gray Sea Canoe. Find them in Ao Nang or at *www. johngray-seacanoe.com/*. These guys will take you through cave systems and mangroves in Pha Nga Bay that will blow your mind. Finally, if you just want to kayak around the local beaches, there are sea kayaks for rent at many of the bungalow operations.

Chapter 6

CENTRAL PENINSULA CLIMBS

Most people arrive on the Phra Nang Peninsula in the shadow of either the Thaiwand or Tonsai Buttress, and for this reason I start with the central peninsula climbs. Most advanced climbers spend at least a few mornings at Tonsai and Dum's Kitchen, and your trip will not be complete without a day on the Thaiwand.

To some this might be a confusing way to start because it's not linear, from north to south, or vice-versa. However, the two most popular crags are at the center; many a climber has come and found the center of the place was so good, he didn't need to go any further.

THAIWAND: SINGLE-PITCH ROUTES

Sun exposure: This wall is shady most of the day in the dry season, with some glancing sunlight in early morning and late afternoon. However, it catches direct sun during May, June, July, and August.

Wall angle and difficulty: The Thaiwand is generally slightly overhanging, though very steep sections and slabby sections can be found. Routes run the gamut, from easy to very difficult.

Hazards: Many of the routes here are more than 30 meters in length, so you need to be able to rappel. If you venture onto the bigger routes, you need to know how to descend, as well as how to climb, an overhanging wall. Just tossing the rope and rapping might leave you in space, so learn how to back-clip a rappel before you climb here. Also, keep in mind that some approaches, particularly those at the far right of the crag (routes 14–18) and the lower pitches of *Candlestick* (the first of the multipitch routes, below), are exposed and potentially dangerous. One more thing…reflected sunlight at this crag can burn you despite the fact the crag is shady. For the most part, the wall is composed of solid rock, and the bolts here are farther from the sea than those on most of these cliffs. Still, the Thaiwand inspires more than its fair share of accidents, and the bolts seem to break down just as fast here as they do anywhere. The high proportion of lower-grade routes along its base are a draw to many less-experienced climbers, and their lack of knowledge has led to some nasty falls. Anyone climbing on the Thaiwand should be very experienced, and any climber

CENTRAL WALLS

Tiger Wall

1,2,3

Wee's Present

Thaiwand

Happy Island

Escher World
(behind the Thaiwand)

Po Da
(15 minutes)

trail

Tyrolean Wall

Dum's Kitchen

Tonsai

* Diamond Cave North Face
and the Generator Wall
cannot be pictured here. They
are left of the frame.

with a lot of experience should not feel bad about pointing out mistakes he or she sees being made by others.

Approach: At the south end of Railay Beach, tucked under a scraggly bit of bamboo, is a trail that runs straight up and into the jungle. This trail breaks apart and re-forms, working up and then hard right for a few hundred meters. Eventually it turns straight up the hill and comes out at the base of the middle of the wall. Routes 1–13 are left of the approach; routes 14–18 must be approached by climbing a rickety ladder onto a ledge that runs west from where the trail ends.

The Thaiwand is the face that launched a thousand ships. Older Thai locals refer to this spire as Khao Luk Choee, a name that means "bat man's headstone." As with the Escher World (on the Phra Nang Beach/South Peninsula side of this tower), the name refers to a guano collector, not a superhero. The man's occupation gives us the translation "bat man," while the distinct shape of the spire from the bay provided the word "headstone." Greg Collum and I knew nothing of these names, nor did any of the Thai climbers, when we first started calling it the Thaiwand. Our name was in reverence to the Eigerwand, which, like this spire, absolutely dominates the sky above a beautiful place.

A number of legends are associated with the Thaiwand, including one that says that one of the caves is the final resting place of an ancient king with a gold-filled coffin. I've checked, and he's not there. Still, there are plenty of treasures on this mountain.

Climbers have been drawn to it by its sheer size since very early in Railay Beach's climbing history. Being over 200 meters from water to summit, this spire's overpowering size and angle kept climbers at bay for some time. Nowadays, people hear of it from friends and see pictures in magazines and can't help but be drawn to the wall. The Thaiwand is best known for its multipitch routes, but there are some great short routes to do along the wall's base, too.

If you are climbing a route that is the starting pitch for one of the longer climbs and a party approaches that plans to go high on the wall, you might consider letting them go ahead. Try to keep your rope and gear close to the wall when belaying so others can pass by you on the trail.

If last night's dinner is not sitting too well, walk back down the trail a way and then into the jungle to relieve yourself. This spire is very overhanging and its base gets a minimal amount of rainfall in the wet season. For this reason, there is a limit to how fast organic matter can be broken down here. What you leave behind might be there a long time.

I should point out that all of the rock on the Thaiwand is featured enough to be climbed, but that does not mean it needs to be. This wall, like Tonsai (and 1, 2, 3 on the South Peninsula side of this tower) is pretty much full, and any routes crowded into the middle of the wall will simply detract from each climb's overall beauty and unique position. Also, the national park service has requested we halt drilling up here except for replacement work. Please adhere to this request.

All climbers should be very careful when climbing here, keeping in mind that many of the routes, even the single-pitch routes, are longer than half a rope length and thus require a rappel. Near the base of the *Lord of the Thais* rappel, fixed lines lead straight down to the lower cliff and then into the water. This has become the main trail of access, but originally it was set up to allow an injured person to be lowered straight into a boat. Time will tell if this system works or if the cleared trail simply becomes a rain gully from the wall's base.

1. PRIMAL SCREAM   6a+ (5.10b), 15 meters, 8 quickdraws★★★
F.A. Greg Collum, February 1992

This climb is on the left side of the wall just before the old trail cuts off into the jungle. Lots of threads.

2. SOLUTION 41   6b+ (5.10d), 18 meters, 6 quickdraws★★★
F.A. Gordon Brysland and Terry Schmidt, April 1994

A bit sharp. Find this one just right of *Primal Scream* with which it shares an anchor.

3. SPICY SPECK DREAMS   7c (5.12d), 20 meters, 7 quickdraws★★★
F.A. Valentin Mak, February 1994

This tweaky climb is about 3 meters left of *Orange Juice*.

4. ORANGE JUICE   7b+ (5.12c), 20 meters, 7 quickdraws★★★★★
F.A. Greg Collum and Jay Hanvik, February 1992
Retrobolted: January 1997

This climb goes up an orange- and yellow-streaked wall. The start is amid the roots of a large tree. An all-time classic. Don't fall before the first bolt.

5. LIVE AND LET THAI   7a (5.11d), 25 meters, 10 quickdraws★★★★
F.A. Will Hair, January 1994
Retrobolted: March 2000

This climb goes up the face and then the arête right of *Orange Juice*. The first ascensionist envisioned us staying out on the face and doing a 7c, but no one went for it. A great route as it stands.

6. EQUATORIAL   6c (5.11b), 35 meters, 12 quickdraws★★★★★
F.A. Greg Collum and Trevor Massiah, February 1994
Retrobolted: February 1998

Running up the clean face and then the blunt, gray arête right of *Live and*

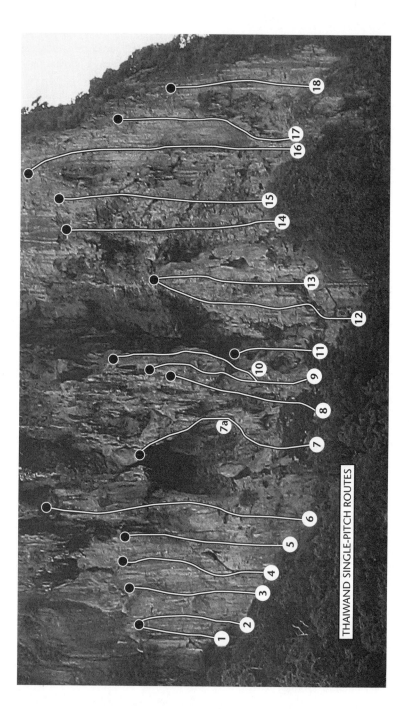

THAIWAND SINGLE-PITCH ROUTES

Let Thai is this great climb. The anchor is in a cool cave. A 60-meter rope will not reach the ground from the anchor. This is an excellent climb, but you will push your 60-meter rope to its end to get down, so watch the end.

7. ORGAN GRINDER   6c (5.11b), 25 meters, 12 quickdraws★★★
F.A. Greg Collum and Trevor Massiah, February 1994

This climb goes up a brown bit of rock beneath the giant cave, then traverses the cave's lip from the right side. Long slings should be used below the roof to alleviate rope drag. Also, there is an anchor in the cave to break it up or to just do the bottom third, which is rated an easy 5. It had not been retrobolted at the time of this writing, so the bolts are very bad.

8. MONKEY LOVE   6b (5.10c), 25 meters, 8 quickdraws★★★★
F.A. Greg Collum and Larissa Collum, February 1994

This climbs the face right of the cave on lots of threads.

9. OUT OF THE STICKS   7a+ (5.12a), 30 meters, 10 quickdraws★★★★
F.A. Sam Lightner Jr., Gerd Schoeffl, and Volker Schoeffl, January 1994
Retrobolted: January 1997

This route shares a start with *Caveman* and then goes straight up through some powerful moves, traverses out a roof, and goes up an arête. Pumpy.

10. CAVEMAN   7a (5.11d), 32 meters, 12 quickdraws ★★★★
F.A. Greg Collum and Larissa Collum, February 1992
Retrobolted: February 1998

This climbs up the slab with *Out of the Sticks*, then goes right (above the small cave at ground level), goes farther back into the big cave, and goes up a rounded arête and face. A standard rope will not reach. This route can be cleaned via the top anchor and a second anchor in the mouth of the cave, but you cannot safely lower all the way to the ground on a 60-meter rope.

11. CAVE ROUTE   5 (5.8), 15 meters, 5 quickdraws★★★
F.A. Sam Lightner Jr., January 1993

This climbs into the cave in the cleft to the right of *Caveman*. Bad bolts!

12. LORD OF THE THAIS   6a+ (5.10b) pitch 1, 25 meters, 10 quickdraws★★★★★
F.A. Sam Lightner Jr., Greg Collum, and Larissa Collum, February 1992

Starting below the largest cave, this climbs up to the ledge about 4.5 meters off the ground, then traverses out right and up a clean face to a ledge. It's polite to let people pass if you are only doing the first pitch (see full *Lord of the Thais* description in Multipitch Routes, below).

13. MALA MUJER   6b (5.10c), 25 meters, 10 quickdraws★★★★★
F.A. Pep Masip, January 1995
Retrobolted: March 2000

This route goes straight up from the approach ladder to the *Lord of the Thais* anchor.

14. "ETCETERA, ETCETERA, ETCETERA"   6b+ (5.11a), 25 meters,
10 quickdraws★★★★
F.A. Sam Lightner Jr. and Jacob Valdez, March 1993

The start to this is found on the ledge that is accessed via the approach ladder. Go up and right on the ledge to its high point. The route goes out the juggy overhang. This climb is often done as the first pitch of *The King and I*. A short traverse past *The Sluggard Prince* anchors puts you on the top of the first pitch of *The King and I*. Use a long sling on the anchor of this route if you are doing this, or you will have a lot of rope drag.

15. THE SLUGGARD PRINCE   6b (5.10d), 25 meters, 10 quickdraws★★★★
F.A. Gordon Brysland and Olle Whelin, April 1994

This climbs the face right of *"Etcetera, Etcetera, Etcetera."* It's done mostly on threads, and some of them are not real big!

16. THE KING AND I   7a (5.11d) pitch 1, 25 meters, 13 quickdraws
★★★★★
F.A. Sam Lightner Jr. and Jacob Valdez, March 1993

Just beyond the high point of the ledge, a series of long tufas and stalactites comes down almost to the bottom of the wall. This route climbs up the face on the right side of this formation and then has an anchor at a stance on top of it.

17. FIT TO BE THAI'D   6a+ (5.10b), 25 meters, 10 quickdraws★★★★★
F.A. Sam Lightner Jr. and Greg Collum, January 1992

An anchor in a cleft at the end of the approach ledge allows you to belay this climb. It traverses out right and then up a series of dagger holds and stalactites. This route was the first on the wall and can be continued to the summit on natural gear. However, even if you are capable, I highly advise against it...lots of dagger rock, ants, and sun exposure.

18. TAMING THE EAST   7a+ (5.12a), 20 meters, 8 quickdraws★★★
F.A. Sam Lightner Jr., Gerd Schoeffl, and Volker Schoeffl, January 1994
Retrobolted: February 2000

To reach the base of this, you need to traverse across the slabs at the start of route 17 to a comfortable ledge at the edge of the wall. The anchor is above in dagger rock.

THAIWAND: MULTIPITCH ROUTES

Sun exposure: Even though the Thaiwand will probably be in the shade when you climb it, the reflected sunlight, both off the water and from the clouds, can give you a nasty burn. Make sure you put on that sunscreen!

Wall angle and difficulty: The Thaiwand is generally slightly overhanging, though very steep sections and slabby sections can be found. Routes run the gamut, from easy to very difficult.

Hazards: Don't be high on the Thaiwand during a thunderstorm...people have been hit by lightning here. For more on that, go talk to Luang at Hot Rock!

Approach: See the Single-Pitch approach info for the Thaiwand.

To me, the best aspect of Thai climbing is that we have the opportunity to do multipitch sport routes. Quality climbs of this type are all but unheard of in the United States, and although they exist in Europe, the options are in a limited number of areas and are often very sporty! In Thailand we have a fair number of bigger sport climbs, and the Thaiwand is one of the best venues for them.

You probably understand this, but I should still say that this sort of climbing is not just a farther-off-the-deck version of what you do at the sport crag. These big climbs have peculiarities to them that you need to understand, and if you don't have a lot of multipitch experience, this is not the place to get it. Thailand's walls can be very unforgiving, and a number of accidents have resulted from climbers getting in over their heads.

I make a couple of exceptions in my pitch-by-pitch information here. One is route 2, *Inaka*. With full pitches of dagger rock, bad bolts, loose stone up high, and lots of black munge in the overhangs, this is a terrible climb. For posterity it would seem that I should have gone back and redone it in the winter of 2004, but I couldn't bring myself to undergo the torture. My advice on this route is simply *don't do it.*

For similar reasons, I need to say the same thing about the upper reaches of *Fit to Be Thai'd.* This climb was the first on the wall, but it is very sharp, requires some creative use of natural gear, and has a fair bit of loose rock on it. The crux pitch is very difficult to protect, and rappelling or being rescued off the climb is a nearly impossible option because the dagger rock will cut up the rope and whoever or whatever is being lowered.

Besides the locking 'biners and belay/rappel devices you need for a multipitch climb, there are a few things you should have with you for an ascent of one of these routes. They all require two ropes to get down. Extra slings to run through threads, and perhaps a knife to cut away the old ones, are also useful. Water pours from your body during this kind of activity in the tropics, so bring at least one bottle (and please don't leave it up there or throw it off!).

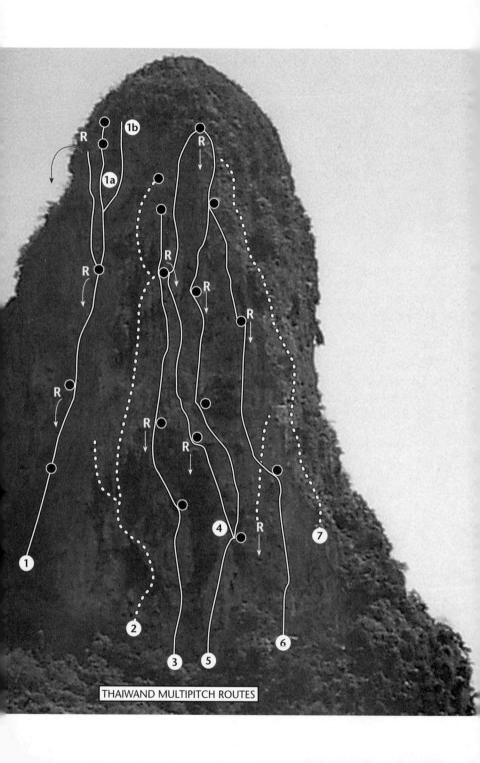

THAIWAND MULTIPITCH ROUTES

1. CANDLESTICK

6c (5.11b), 80+ meters, 15 quickdraws, extra threads★★★★

F.A. Drew Spalding and Jay Foley, January 2000

Candlestick is the farthest left of all the climbs on the wall. The climb gets sun early in the morning even in the dry season. This route, or compilation of routes, carries a fairly easy grade by Thaiwand standards, but the grade is a bit deceiving. You can get to the top of the wall, but the climbing is not all safe. The lower pitches, which I will call 4th class here, can be belayed. They have fixed ropes that can aid you, and there are threads. However, the rock is very sharp and ledgy, so your belayer will probably not stop you before you hit something. Also, the main rappel off, which is about 31 meters (reaches with stretch), leaves you on a small ledge that must be traversed. This is very exposed and a slip will most likely be fatal (read how to avoid it below). All that said, the climbing over here is fun. Just be prepared for a tropical "alpine" experience.

You reach it by following the trail up and through the jungle at the far left side of the wall. When it turns nearly vertical, put on your stuff and start climbing. The 4th class goes on for 50 meters or so.

Pitch 1: This starts as 4th class climbing, following fixed lines and a cut in the vertical jungle. Eventually you work right to a large ledge where the first pitch of 5th class can begin.

Pitch 2: 6a (5.10d), 30 meters, 15 quickdraws. Climb up and right on rambling ground. A ledge fall, if your belayer is not on top of it, is possible here. Two-thirds of the way up, you can trend left to the cave anchor for The Red Line finish. The better option is to continue on to the right anchor, where you can belay both of the other routes, which go higher, and even the upper portions of The Red Line if you wish.

Pitch 3: 6b+ or 6c (5.11a or 5.11b), 35 meters, 15 quickdraws. From the small cave, a direct finish goes up and left, then back right to the "glowing tunnel." This is an excellent bit of climbing known as the *Crystal Flame*, 6b+ (labeled 1a on the photo). The upper third of this climb can be avoided, thus allowing you to easily lower back to the belay off an anchor at the mouth of the glowing tunnel. I recommend you keep going. It's just too cool a finish to be missed. You can rappel from the top using two ropes to get back to the cave or use one rope and set up a hanging station at the mouth of the tunnel.

From the cave you can also do the original finish, which is 6c (labeled 1b on the photo). This is a traversing line that goes out right of the cave and up the steepest bit of the headwall on jugs. Fun climbing. Getting back to the cave is a pain. It's easiest to just get lowered and pull yourself back, climbing occasionally and back-clipping yourself where appropriate. Rappelling it would be difficult. Let your second follow it to clean, then "fief" back down your side of the line to get back to the cave. This pitch was rebolted with titanium in 2002.

Descent: As I said, you can reach back to the top of the 4th class with one rope and some climbing, but it's not safe. The safer option is to go with two lines. Tie the trailing line to the station at the start of pitch 2, then rappel from the small cave on two ropes. You can use the line that was tied to the anchor to pull yourself that way and thus avoid climbing across the exposed ledge unroped.

2. INAKA   7b (5.12b), 124 meters, 15 quickdraws, extra threads

F.A. Kaori Tsuji and Koji Okumura, February 1996

This route is a mess. Don't do it. There is a lot of loose rock and sharpies that can cut a rope. Be aware there are people below you.

Pitch 1: 5+ (5.9), 15 meters, 6 quickdraws. This is the first pitch of *Organ Grinder* and the original start to *Continental Drifter*. Belay from the cave.

Pitch 2: 7a (5.11d), 16 meters, 8 quickdraws. Proceed up to the right of the cave.

Pitch 3: 7b (5.12b), 15 meters, 10 quickdraws. Continue on through mungee rock on more difficult ground. Don't fall!

Pitch 4: 7a (5.11d), 50 meters, 14 quickdraws. Razors and gravel to the *Continental Drifter* anchor.

Pitch 5: 6b+ (5.10d), 28 meters, 9 quickdraws. Proceed through the flowstone and stalactites up and left of the belay, then over dagger rock to an anchor. There are some threads on this pitch.

Descent: Get down by rapping off the top pitch to the *Continental Drifter* anchor, then from there down that route.

3. CONTINENTAL DRIFTER   7c+ (5.13a), 110 meters, 14 quickdraws★★★★

F.A. Sam Lightner Jr., Volker Schoeffl, and Gerd Schoeffl, January 1994

This route is good, but not as good as *Lord of the Thais* or *The King and I*. It is in dire need of retrobolting. Check with the locals on status. All belays are on ledges, though a couple are pretty small.

Pitch 1: 7a+ (5.12a), 38 meters, 14 quickdraws. The original first and second pitches are to go up the first pitch of *Organ Grinder*, 5, then do the second, 6b+, by going through overhangs up and right of the cave to the anchor below the big bulge. The better option is to do the first pitch of *Out of the Sticks*, 7a+, then move on past a few bolts to the anchor.

Pitch 2: 7a+ (5.12a), 18 meters, 8 quickdraws. Up and left through the bulge, climbing on the hidden arête and some very strange features.

Pitch 3: 7a (5.11d), 37 meters, 13 quickdraws. Pretty much straight up, veering a bit left, then up past a beautiful fin and over the bulge. A very good pitch. Be careful with the fin.

Pitch 4: 7c+ (5.13a), 17 meters, 7 quickdraws. Treat this like a sport-climbing pitch in the sky by lowering back to the lower anchor when done. This is a great bit of climbing...powerful and technical. Sadly, the bolts are in sorry shape and it is totally bolt-dependent for pro.

Descent: Get down by lowering off the last pitch, then rappelling the route. Two 60-meter ropes will reach the ground from the top of pitch 2. These bolts are currently very bad.

4. CIRCUS OZ   7a (5.11d), 123 meters, 14 quickdraws★★★★
F.A. M. Matheson, G. Tempest, Richard Smith, and "El Gordo," date unknown

This route is, in my opinion, a contrivance of *Lord of the Thais*...and *Continental Drifter*. My detractors say that I just want to own the Thaiwand...not true. I feel that too many routes in one place take away from each route's beauty. Decide for yourself. *Circus Oz* is popular and gets you as far off the deck as you will get in this area. Its third pitch is quite fun if you have the means. A fall on the last bit of the last pitch could be very dangerous, even deadly, because there is some sharp rock and you are falling into a dihedral.

Pitch 1: 6a+ (5.10b), 25 meters, 10 quickdraws. This was originally the first pitch of *Lord of the Thais*.

Pitch 2: 6b+ (5.11a), 25 meters, 10 quickdraws. Force yourself left of the obvious line of bolts, then go up more to the inside of the giant "keyhole" cave until you reach the last *Lord of the Thais* rappel anchor.

Pitch 3: 7a (5.11d), 45 meters, 14 quickdraws. Move left and up. Going straight up will put you on *Lord of the Thais*, so stay to the left, moving through the bulge and up to an anchor just up and right of the anchor of *Continental Drifter*. Most people end up on the *Continental Drifter* anchor, then end up with a slightly exposed traverse and more rope drag for the last pitch.

Pitch 4: 6b+ (5.10d), 28 meters, 8 quickdraws. Move up and into an open book–dihedral, then traverse out and right to the top anchor of *Lord of the Thais*. Falling into the dihedral from the traverse is a bad option.

Descent: To rappel, go down the *Lord of the Thais* rappels 40, 40, and 50 meters. Some back-clipping is helpful.

5. LORD OF THE THAIS   7b (5.12b), 125 meters, 14 quickdraws★★★★★
F.A. Sam Lightner Jr., Greg Collum, and Larissa Collum, February 1992

I challenge you to find a better route in the world. This climb was the first big sport route on the wall. Only the crux bolts were replaced in March 1997, and they are starting to show their age. The anchors were replaced in January 2000.

Pitch 1: 6a+ (5.10b), 25 meters, 10 quickdraws. From the cleft at the base of the "keyhole" cave, basically the end of the approach trail (see the single-pitch routes, above), go up and right past bolts and threads to an anchor shared by numerous pitches.

Pitch 2: 7a (5.11d), 28 meters, 14 quickdraws. Straight up, then right

UNEXPECTED HELP

I had a hangover that could have killed a water buffalo. That was normal. What was not normal was the place I had chosen to sweat out the Mekong Whiskey haze. Greg and I had gotten up early, still buzzing, then spent two hours thrashing through untouched jungle. We had clawed over razor-sharp boulders, past deep dark holes, and through virtually every ant nest in southern Thailand until we reached the rock. We had spent the next eight hours waterless, with no breeze, mostly in the sun, meandering up the spire's northwest arête. We'd gone back and forth, up and down, on six or seven pitches of dagger rock, placing dodgy gear and never contemplating a fall on the mid-6 terrain lest we slice the rope and be grated like Parmesan all the way down to the Andaman Sea. Now we'd crossed over the arête near the summit and were contemplating an unknown number of rappels back down to terra firma. It was 6 P.M.; we had only three ropes, a small drill, and no gear left. In 30 minutes it would be dark, and in our stupor both of us had forgotten headlamps.

All things considered, the hangover was the least of our worries.

Greg did the first rappel, dropping over small bits of orange and white rock mixed with the dreaded dark gray sharp stuff, not saying a word as the rope popped across the daggers. He slipped under a huge overhang and swung out over the darkening jungle, then back in, and clung to the wall. Moments later he began drilling. I fixed the rope and headed down. Twenty minutes later I was on the sharp end, swinging wildly over the dark jungle. I got in an anchor and Greg descended. We had already decided we would assume three full-length ropes would make it to the ground and that if we wanted to put a route up the middle of the face, we would have to leave them behind. Greg committed us to that—or to spending the rest of our lives on the wall—when he came down on the second fixed line. We had only one left.

Greg then admitted that, well, he now had doubts about us reaching the ground. I thought we would but had to concede that getting close was not an option. At that time, the only two climbers capable of mounting a rescue on the entire continent were the two of us, so if we ended up not reaching the ground it would be a long wait. Still, we were committed. I told Greg again I thought we would make it. He agreed that I should go see. In pitch black I descended from the cave, sliding down about 25 feet (7.5 meters) until I reached a ledge. Below there was no sign of the ground, just darkness. I could hear Supertramp playing at Sunset Bar and the crickets and tree frogs singing in the jungle far below. Maybe Greg was right.

"What do ya see?" he said calmly. There were no longtail boats running at that hour and not a hint of wind, so no need to yell.

"Blackness ... I see a black future for us."

"Hmmm."

"Oh, hell," I replied. "I'm going for it." I heard him laughing, but it wasn't a reassuring laugh.

The wall quickly disappeared into darkness, and I was twisting in space. After 20 seconds of descent, I pulled up the end of the rope and tied a knot in it, then dropped it. Twenty seconds later, I was at my knot.

I hung there for half an hour, listening to Supertramp and trying to come up with excuses to lay on the blonde Italian who was now waiting for me at Coco's. Nothing would work, and I'd just have to hang my draws on a new project ... if I ever got out of this. I was perhaps 30 feet (9 meters) above the ground, I guessed by looking at the nearby trees. In the faint starlight I could see the wall, but there was just no way to reach it. I'd stopped swinging far above, and basic Newtonian physics said I wouldn't reach it unless someone came along and gave me a shove. On a high spire, across hundreds of yards of untrampled jungle, in southern Thailand at 8 P.M. on a February night in 1992, that wasn't very likely.

Then it hit. There hadn't been a sparrow's breath of wind for days, but suddenly I was pushed by a gust. I swung a bit, then it hit again. This time I worked the swing like any kid on the playground. Moments later, I was clinging to the wall, and the wind quit blowing. I tied off the rope, climbed down from what is now the second clip on *Lord of the Thais*, then yelled for Greg. We spent the next three hours crawling through the trail-less jungle, using fireflies and an occasional star as the only light.

We spent the next two days recovering, then we began chopping a trail and scaling the ropes. The Thaiwand had been climbed, and *Lord of the Thais* would be redpointed in a couple of weeks. Those ensuing weeks were a lot of fun, but they might not have been if it weren't for that breeze that swung me to the wall. The whole day had been touch and go, and I'm pretty sure that at its end, someone gave us a little help.

through a bulge, left through another bulge, and up a pumpy face to a large alcove-ledge with an anchor. The noncrux bolts on this pitch are a horror. Often people top-rope this pitch off a single bolt just below the anchor ledge...*Don't do that here! Ever!*

Pitch 3: 7a+ (5.12a), 28 meters, 12 quickdraws. You won't find a better pitch in Thailand.

Pitch 4: 7b (5.12b), 27 meters, 14 quickdraws. It ain't over 'til it's over. Up and right through a power bulge, then a pumpy overhang to a small stance belay. "Hanging on near the top feels like you're clinging to the underside of a 747," said Kyle Mills. Retreating back to the belay from the top of this pitch is not an option, so if the weather is bad you should bail before doing the pitch.

Pitch 5: 6b (510d), 12 meters, 4 quickdraws. A little sharp. Over the bulge and up, then left to the top anchor.

Descent: The rappels are 40, 40, and 50 meters. You will need to back-clip at least two bolts to get into the second anchor and one to get into the third anchor. Tying a knot at the end of the rope is always the safe option, but this can be a hassle here because the rope can more easily get tied around a stalactite when it's knotted (this happens regularly during wind).

6. THE KING AND I   7b+ (5.12c), 115 meters, 14 quickdraws★★★★
F.A. Sam Lightner Jr. and Jacob Valdez with Pia, Egk, and Somporn Suebhait (King), April, 1992

This fun climb is most commonly done via an easier variation. By climbing *"Etcetera, Etcetera, Etcetera"* and traversing to the top of the first pitch, you can bypass the original pumpy 7a first pitch. This option is an easier way to get to the great 6a second pitch. To get down from the small cave at the top of pitch 2, you can either do two rappels, reversing using the belay stations, or one rappel

BASE JUMPERS

Some guy showed up in 1999 with the idea he would BASE jump off one of our cliffs. We had an epic day getting a nonclimber to the top of *Humanality* (route 2 on Tonsai), complete with heat strokes and temper tantrums. He got there, then almost passed on the jump. Peer pressure sent him down, and he was safely on the beach in a matter of seconds.

However, he was not the first BASE jumper that I had seen here. A few years before, when I was on the pitch 3 belay of *Lord of the Thais,* I was looking up when I saw a bit of webbing falling. I then realized there was no one above us, so I wondered who could have dropped the webbing. I watched as the webbing slithered through the air, until I finally realized that it was not webbing at all; it was a snake. It went by me, perhaps 30 feet from the overhanging wall, righting itself on the wind with quick slithering motions. The hiss of the air around its body made me instinctively duck because it sounded just like a falling rock. I watched it pass, then sail into the trees. It hit a horizontal branch so hard it wound around it a few times like a spaghetti noodle on the end of a fork. I watched a bit more, not taking in rope and ignoring the pleas of my partner, rationalizing that the Thaiwand is steep enough for her. The snake uncoiled itself and slithered down the tree.

Now that's a real jump. None of this sissy parachute stuff.

with two stretchy 60-meter ropes (it's close). People do this variation to avoid the difficulties of the original first pitch, not to avoid it for its quality.

Pitch 1: 7a (5.11d), 30 meters, 13 quickdraws. From nearly the far end of the base ledge on the Thaiwand, move up through a series of bulges and up a pumpy face right of the stalactite. Belay on top of the stalactite.

Pitch 2: 6a (5.10a), 35 meters, 14 quickdraws. What a fun pitch. Move up and left, then straight up to a small cave below the overhanging headwall. An anchor mysteriously appears midway up this pitch (slightly right of the climbing). Ignore it and go on to the cave.

Pitch 3: 7b+ (5.12c), 38 meters, 14 quickdraws. Go out the left side of the cave following the line of holds and gear. Do not belay off the old bolt just after the obvious dyno. Keep going through the headwall and over some prickly stone to the stance belay on pitch 4 of *Lord of the Thais*.

Pitch 4: 6b (5.10d), 12 meters, 4 quickdraws. Use the last pitch of *Lord of the Thais* to reach the rappel station.

Descent: To get down from the top, use the *Lord of the Thais* rappels.

7. FIT TO BE THAI'D   6b+ (5.11a), 115 meters, quickdraws, slings, stoppers, Friends, steel-toed boots★

F.A. Sam Lightner Jr. and Greg Collum, February, 1992

This climb, the first on the spire, is a heinous undertaking. It is definitely not the easiest way up the Thaiwand! This dangerous route is not fun. Loose rock, sharp holds, and edges that can cut a rope make retreating even more dangerous than climbing. This is probably not what you came to Thailand for. I don't list the pitches here because it is a gear route and you would make them on your own. The first pitch is bolted as *Fit to Be Thai'd*. From that anchor, you traverse around the arête (and into the sun), then up multiple pitches of dagger rock with plenty of red ants. When it gets too hard and too loose to move on, traverse back around the arête and start looking for the *Lord of the Thais* rappel station.

WEE'S PRESENT WALL

Sun exposure: This wall is deep in the jungle and thus is almost always in the shade.

Wall angle and difficulty: Wee's Present is vertical to slightly overhanging, with the one "harder" route taking the steepest line. The climbs are mostly moderate, with one being pretty difficult.

Hazards: The trail can be a nightmare after rain, and there are often a lot of mosquitoes here. As always, be wary about the bolts.

This small wall just above the resort at the south end of Railay Beach has some good climbs.

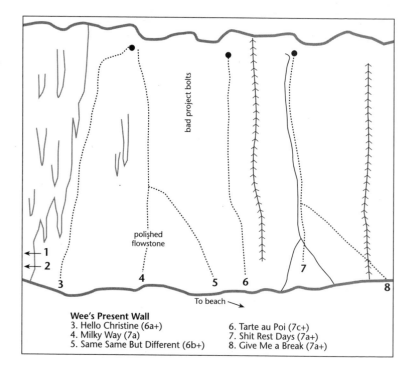

Wee's Present Wall
3. Hello Christine (6a+)
4. Milky Way (7a)
5. Same Same But Different (6b+)
6. Tarte au Poi (7c+)
7. Shit Rest Days (7a+)
8. Give Me a Break (7a+)

About 40 meters left of the main wall (described below) are four climbs that you will probably want to just give a miss. They are on sharp rock and are not very pleasant, so they are not included here on the topo. They are, from left to right, a 7b, a 6b, a 6c, and a 5. These were all established by Wee but are not Phra Nang classics. Ditto for the routes up and right of the wall. To the right of the main Wee's Present Wall are some even less enticing lines…give them a miss! Stick to the routes described below, and you will be getting the worthy stuff.

High on the wall between *Same Same but Different* and *Tarte au Poi* are a few ugly, incomplete bolt placements. These are probably relics of someone attempting to bolt a project with 10 mm bolts in ⅜-inch holes. I've been there…it doesn't really work. However, the mess should have been cleaned up.

Approach: Find Wee's Present Wall by accessing the start of the trail to the Thaiwand, then go up and left when the Thaiwand trail breaks right. It's about 5 minutes from the beach.

1. I DON'T KNOW   6a (5.10a), 15 meters, varying number of
                                              threads, take 6 quickdraws★★

F.A. Wee Changrua, date unknown

The first two routes are just past the stalactite on left side of the clean, white face. They climb fairly sharp rock and tufa stone. These names may be telling a story!

2. A MAN CAN TELL 1,000 LIES   6a (5.10a), 15 meters, same as above★★
F.A. Elke Schmitz, date unknown

3. HELLO CHRISTINE   6a+ (5.10b), 20 meters, 6 quickdraws★★★
F.A. Thomas Arnold, February 1997

This climb starts on the right side of the obvious stalactite flow on the left side of the wall. A bit prickly at the top, this route could be considered slightly run-out for people who are maxed at its grade.

4. MILKY WAY   7a (5.11d), 20 meters, 8 quickdraws★★★★
F.A. Thomas Arnold, February 1997

This route shares an anchor with *Hello Christine* and *Same Same But Different*. It starts in front of the big tree just right of *Hello Christine*. The belayer needs to be focused for the start.

5. SAME SAME BUT DIFFERENT   6b+ (5.11a), 20 meters, 8 quickdraws★★★
F.A. Mark Urbezat and Thomas Arnold, February 1997

This starts just right of *Milky Way* and traverses into it, then shares an anchor with it and route 3. Sort of a powerful move (or two) for the grade, but hard to rate it any harder!? The belayer needs to be on the ball because the crux is the first few moves off the ground. After that, it is quite a bit easier.

6. TARTE AU POI   7c+ (5.13a), 27 meters, 8 quickdraws★★★★
F.A. Hubert and Wee Changrua, August 1997

This route goes up the blunt arête in the middle of the wall. It is a bit sporty in spots, therefore you should have confidence in yourself so that you don't test the bolts to their max. A standard 60-meter rope is required for lowering from the anchor.

7. SHIT REST DAYS   7a+ (5.12a), 25 meters, 7 quickdraws★★
F.A. Thomas Arnold, February 1997

Beginning a few feet right of *Tarte*, this climb ascends, in its upper reaches, a broken crack. By and large, good crack climbs in limestone are rare. This one is not rare.

8. GIVE ME A BREAK   7a+ (5.12a), 25 meters, 8 quickdraws★
F.A. Thomas Arnold, November 1997

Completely forgettable, this "route" traverses into *Shit Rest Days* to give a boring climb a bad start. About 50 meters beyond this section (climber's left), near a large cave, are four more routes (see overview above).

TONSAI

Sun exposure: During the dry season, this area starts getting sun in late morning, though the more overhanging routes create their own shade for a while longer.

Wall angle and difficulty: Very steep. This is one of the steepest climbing venues around. There are exceptions, but this is mostly a moderate to expert area.

Hazards: Seaside climbing means questionable bolts. Also, people regularly drop things off *Humanality* (route 2), and stalactites have broken above climbers.

Approach: Access is as easy as it gets because the majority of the routes start off the beach, and when you need a break, a bar and restaurant are within 50 meters of most of the climbs. Routes 6–9 are accessed via a 5-meter "ladder." To access routes 10–13, climb the ladder, then traverse up and right to a broad ledge.

Dominique Potard's 1991guidebook made reference to this part of the Phra Nang Peninsula as a place to "explore." Just ten years later, it had become the center of the climbing scene. This is the place for more advanced climbers. There are a lot of very steep, gymnastic routes on high-quality stone in this area. Routes 14–23 are the roof routes. Routes 24–39 are on Central Tonsai.

1. TARZAN   5+ (5.9), 10 meters, you must place a few threads★★★

F.A. Sam Lightner Jr., Volker Schoeffl, and Gerd Shoeffl, December 1993

You want something unique…this is a tree climb! Starting behind the bar and up the old *klong* (stream) is this ficus tree. It actually overhangs! This is the common start to *Humanality*. Clip the slings, but don't fall.

2. HUMANALITY   6b+ (5.10d), 87 meters, 9 quickdraws★★★★★

F.A. Greg Collum and Trevor Massiah, January 1995
Retrobolted: February 1998

This is an excellent climb. I could go so far as to say it is the most appreciated contribution to Thai climbing that Greg and Trevor have made, and that is a huge statement (look for their names elsewhere in this guide). You will have to get up early to avoid having a party ahead of you. Pitches can be combined if you bring a few long slings to hang on the anchors. This is an all-time classic. If you don't like it, you should go home! Two rappels with 60-meter ropes will reach the ground. Make sure you tie a knot in the end of that rope.

Pitch 1: 6a+ (5.10b), 20 meters, 8 quickdraws. Find the start to this via *Tarzan.* Traverse right on the ledge and go up and out the bulge, then right to an anchor.

Pitch 2: 6b (5.10c), 22 meters, 9 quickdraws. Keep going up to a nice ledge.

Pitch 3: 6b+ (5.10d), 25 meters, 9 quickdraws. Keep your mind open to all sorts of possibilities. Good belay ledges.

Pitch 4: 6b (5.10c), 22 meters, 7 quickdraws. Continue on to a small stance at the base of the overhanging headwall. A variation pitch has been added here, though it isn't recommended and is not shown on the overlay.

Descent: Rappel to an anchor right of the top of pitch 2.

3. EVICTION   7c+ (5.13a), 30 meters, 14 quickdraws★★★
F.A. Alex Catlin, March 1994

This route starts on the ledge above *Tarzan*, going out the roof and up the huecoed face. One rope will reach the anchor but not the ground. It has not been rebolted.

MR. STINKLE'S BAD LUCK

Humanality was an instant classic. Greg didn't even get the last bolt tightened up before a line had formed at the base of the wall. One fellow, who we will call Mr. Stinkle, had a bit of bad curry the night before, but he felt the grumbling in his stomach was probably dismissible. (A word of advice: Heed that grumbling when you hear it.) Mr. Stinkle was about to burst when he reached the alcove at the base of the last pitch. Rather than explode, he dropped his drawers and let it run … and run it did. The line at the base of the route got very short in almost no time.

The ledge, of course, was a nasty mess, and Mr. Stinkle was to blame for it. Everywhere he went for the next week, he was harangued with, "Dude, are you going to shit here?" He knew it had to be cleaned up, but his rope had been damaged in a longtail propeller the day after the chocolate rain incident on *Humanality.*

Finally, he went back up to clean up the mess, using someone else's rope and a big bottle of bleach. Somehow, his bad fortune was still running: he spilled half the bleach on the rope. Climbing ropes and bleach are not a good combo. Mr. Stinkle managed to clean the route and get down, but he then had to buy someone a new rope—in southern Thailand at a time when there was no such thing as a new rope. I quit following his bad luck at that point.

4. BIRD'S NEST DROOP   7c+ (5.13a), 20 meters, 8 quickdraws★★★
F.A. Greg Collum, February 1994

Also starting off the ledge to the right of *Eviction*. The start of *Humanality* is right here as well. As far as I know, this one has not been rebolted.

5. HUMAN FRAILTY   6b (5.10c), 87 meters, plenty of gear and guts are needed★★
F.A. Greg Collum and Trevor Massiah, January 1995

Greg Collum has been in on the first ascent of more Phra Nang classics than anyone else. However, this was not one of them. The climbing is okay, but the lack of gear and the fact that it feels a bit like a squeeze of *Humanality*'s brilliance makes it worth the miss.

The Ladder Routes

6. COWABUNGALOW   6B (5.10c), 25 meters, 8 quickdraws★★★
F.A. Will Hair, February 1994
Retrobolted: December 1999

Start this one at the base of the 5-meter ladder. Hit the ledge and take a hard left. Go up the stalactites and tufa rock. Long slings help at the start. This route can be a link to the second pitch of *Humanality*, though the other start is better.

7. SWEATING MEKONG   6c+ (5.11c), 20 meters, 8 quickdraws★★★
F.A. Will Hair, March 1994
Retrobolted: March 1999

Up the ladder and 3 meters right of *Cowabungalow*...just on the other side of the bulge from *Vikings in Heat.*

8. VIKINGS IN HEAT   6c+ (5.11c), 20 meters, 8 quickdraws★★★★
F.A. Max Dufford and Greg Collum, December 1992
Retrobolted: December 2004

This route goes pretty much straight up from the ladder.

9. HIN RONG HAI   6c (5.11b), 20 meters, 7 quickdraws★★★★
F.A. Max Dufford and Divinder Singh, December 1992
Retrobolted: December 1996

Go up the ladder, then right for a couple meters, then up the perfect rock to a powerful bulge. When Max put in the first bolts, water spewed out of the holes, hence the name, which means "Crying Rock." Like many of the routes at Tonsai, the retrobolting effort initially repaired this one with a type of glue that did not seal out the water (we were misinformed by the manufacturer). It has since been repaired, as have most of the routes on this buttress.

Ladder-to-Ledge Routes

10. SILKAT   7a (5.11d), 11 meters, 5 quickdraws★★★
F.A. Shamick Byszewski, April 1997

This climb starts about 11 meters right of route 9 on a wide, flat ledge. Look for a belay bolt that will help to keep the belayer on the ledge. Goes up a corner to a roof.

11. TRADE WINDS   7a (5.11d), 10 meters, 5 quickdraws★★★★
F.A. Greg Collum and Larissa Collum, December 1992
Retrobolted: December 1999

If you like 'em short, do this one. Its start is virtually the same as *Silkat's*, but then it moves out right.

12. TOM YUM   7a+ (5.12a), 12 meters, 6 quickdraws★★★★
F.A. Alex Wenner and Mark Maffe, April 1993
Retrobolted: December 1999

Another good one. This starts 2.5 meters right of route 11.

13. ON THE TERRACE   6b+ (5.10d), 20 meters, 10 quickdraws★★★
F.A. Greg Collum and Larissa Collum, December 1992
Retrobolted: February 1998 and perhaps 2004

Climb the ladder, then traverse up and right to the broad ledge. Technical corner. Be careful lowering someone here so they don't drop to the beach! In 2004 and 2005, about a zillion bolts were placed a third of the way up this climb to hold a few wedding parties on the wall. Yes, you read that right. At the time of this writing, the bolts had not been removed, and even if they are, it will be a mess.

The Roof Routes

14. FOR YOU AND FOR ME   6a+ (5.10b), 8 meters, 6 quickdraws
F.A. Dean Saydom, July 1994

This route, if you can call it that, goes up in the back of the cave behind the ladder and then traverses out to a dangerous natural anchor. Don't bother.

15. RIESEN BABY   7a+ (5.12a), 8 meters, 5 quickdraws★★
F.A. Volker Schoeffl, Gerd Schoeffl, and Sam Lightner Jr., December 1993
Retrobolted: December 1999

We put this up as a joke during a horrid rainstorm, and somehow it has gotten popular. The start fluctuates in difficulty, depending on how much sand is deposited during the monsoon. Look for this one about 6 meters right of the back of the cave.

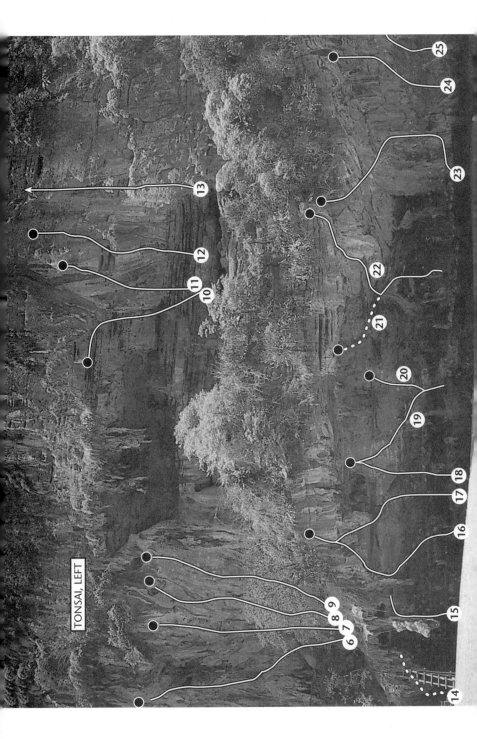

TONSAI, LEFT

16. SEAFOOD MONOS FRITAS   7c+ (5.13a), 14 meters,
                                     7 quickdraws★★★★

F.A. Carlos Brasco, January 1997

This is the first route from the left to go out the roof.

17. OLD CHICKEN MAKES GOOD SOUP   8a (5.13b), 14 meters,
                                            9 quickdraws★★★★

F.A. Rolando Larcher, January 1995
Retrobolted: April 1998

A pretty good route, if you like roofy boulder problems. Goes out the roof just right of the cleft and pulls over the lip to share an anchor with *Seafood Monos Fritas*.

18. HANG TEN   7c (5.12d), 9 meters, 5 quickdraws★★★

F.A. Will Hair, January 1994

This route starts out the cleft and then pulls right to share an anchor with *Tidal Wave*. As far as I'm concerned, this is a squeeze job on the classic to the right, but people like it.

19. TIDAL WAVE   7b+ (5.12c), 9 meters, 5 quickdraws★★★★★

F.A. Greg Collum and Larissa Collum, February 1993
Retrobolted: January 1997

This route starts on the tidal ledge below a couple of small stalactites, then traverses up and left to an anchor at the base of the horizontal roof. The easiest way to find it is to go to the line of people and rope bags and drop your gear. This is an all-time classic. Put on your elbow pads and get in line. Greg Collum was quite a prophet when he named this route. This climb is not only shaped like a tsunami but it's also the same size as the wave was when it hit the crag...the water was frothing up to the anchors of this great route.

20. BABY GORILLA   7c (5.12d), 7 meters, 4 quickdraws★★

F.A. Will Hair, December 1993
Retrobolted: December 1999

A highball boulder problem with bolts. Goes straight up from the start of *Tidal Wave*.

21. LEO'S LINE   7c+ (5.13a), 10 meters, 1 quickdraw and guts★

F.A. Leo Houlding, January 1999

About 9 meters right of *Tidal Wave*, look for an off-width roof crack. Take on the start of *Tantrum* to reach the crack, then wiggle your way to a nasty anchor. Not recommended.

22. TANTRUM   8a+ (5.13c), 12 meters, 8 quickdraws★★★★
F.A. Alex Catlin, March 1994
Retrobolted: January 2000
The start of this route is a boulder problem at the base of the big off-width roof. If routes this hard can be fun, then this one is.

23. CAFÉ ANDAMAN   7b (5.12b), 10 meters, 6 quickdraws★★★
F.A. Greg Collum and Trevor Massiah, March 1994
Retrobolted: January 1997
About 9 meters right of *Tantrum* is an overhanging route of tufas and sloping jugs. Reach it by climbing onto the tidal shelf and then traversing a couple meters right.

Central Tonsai

24. MEETING FRIENDS WITH STONES   8a (5.13b), 12 meters, 7 quickdraws★★★
F.A. Coco Drillo and Marie Monos, January 1997
Retrobolted: January 2000
About 6 meters right of *Café Andaman* is this powerful route. It ends in a big roof. The name comes from the fact that the first ascensionists almost killed a few people while aiding through the roof. It has since cleaned up nicely.

25. LOVE OF TRAVELING   7a+ (5.12a), 12 meters, 8 quickdraws★★
F.A. Kong, April 1999
This route requires some Chubby Checker dance moves. It starts just right of *Meeting Friends* in the tidal bulge and works up to a large chunk of tufa material, then on up the face.

26. JUST DUSIT   7c (5.12d), 12 meters, 6 quickdraws★★★
F.A. Will Hair, February 1994
This starts 3 meters right of *Love of Traveling*. Go up and then hang a left toward the tufas and large holds.

27. GERMANS IN TIGHTS   7b (5.12b), 12 meters, 7 quickdraws★★★
F.A. Will Hair, February 1994
Same start as *Just Dusit*, then slightly right and up.

28. SECOND HOME TONSAI 7a+ (5.12a), 12 meters, 9 quickdraws★★★★★
F.A. Kong, March 1999
This starts on the same ledge used to reach *Stalagasauras*, but just left, then

CENTRAL TONSAI

26

27

28

29

30

31

32

33

34

goes pretty much straight up. It is a great route, but Kong went cheap on bolts. They had been replaced once at the time of this writing.

29. STALAGASAURAS   7a (5.11d), 13 meters, 6 quickdraws★★★★★
F.A. Will Hair, February 1994
Retrobolted: December 1996
This once-classic route has recently suffered a nasty blow. For years it was ascended by climbers pushing out on and then climbing up on a huge but fragile stalactite. After years of this, the stalactite broke, almost killing a number of people at the base. What is left has gone from 6a to 7a and erased the world's steepest 5.10a.

30. BABES IN THAILAND   7a (5.11d), 13 meters, 6 quickdraws★★★★★
F.A. Will Hair, February 1994
Retrobolted: December 1996
This great route ascends the rock about 2.5 meters right of *Stalagasauras*. The usual start is from directly below it and requires a spotter.

31. SEX POWER   8a (5.13b), 13 meters, 6 quickdraws★★
F.A. Kong, April 1999
Starts 3 meters right of the start of *Babes in Thailand*. Scary bolts.

32. LA BAB   7a+ (5.12a), 13 meters, 6 quickdraws★★★★★
F.A. Ian Turnbull, February 1995
Retrobolted: January 1998
This reachy start is accessed by climbing up to the tidal ledge and then slightly left. Work your way up into the tufa material on pumpy climbing.

33. ELEPHANT   8a (5.13b), 13 meters, 6 quickdraws★★★
F.A. Kong, April 1999
About 6 meters above the beach and 3 meters right of *La Bab* is a stalactite that looks like an elephant's head. Climb to it and beyond.

34. CREAM OF SUM YUNG GAI   8a+ (5.13c), 14 meters, 6 quickdraws★★★★
F.A. Sam Lightner Jr. and Shamick Byszewski, March 1998
This route goes out the roof just right of the *Elephant* and a couple meters left of the gray tufa rock. Powerful start. Be accurate.

35. ANT JUMP   probably 8b+ (5.13d), 14 meters, quickdraws
Starting about 2.5 meters right of the gray tufa, this was Kong's project. He was willing to protect it with his life, until it almost cost him his life! We are not sure if it has had an ascent yet.

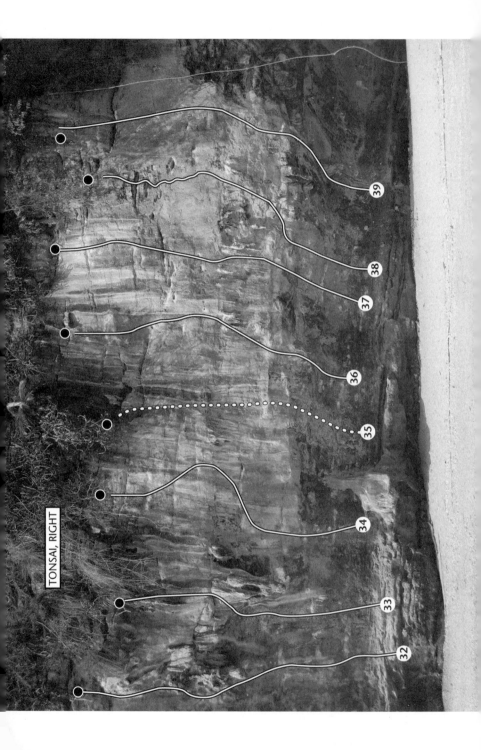

TONSAI, RIGHT

36. VOODOO DOLL   7c+ (5.13a), 15 meters, 7 quickdraws★★★
F.A. Max Dufford, February 1995

Go out the steep tufas in the roof to a single hard move.

37. BHET MAK MAK   7c+ (5.13a), 15 meters, 8 quickdraws★★★★★
F.A. Max Dufford and Divinder Singh, December 1992
Retrobolted: December 1996

This is the third from the last route on the buttress. It is the best route of its grade in Asia. The name means "very spicy," but its original name was *Mai Me Rang*, or "No Have Power." Sadly, another climber has tried to get in on the greatness of this climb by leaning off the first and second bolts and placing a couple of his own to create *Cara Congresso* to the right. This was later retrobolted without much thought and is somehow now a variation between *Bhet Mak Mak* and *Gaeng Som Plaa.*

38. CARA CONGRESSO   8b+ (5.14a), 15 meters, 7 quickdraws★★★
F.A. Either Carlos Brasco, or a visiting Czech climber, date unknown
Retrobolted: January 2000

Gerd Schoeffl enjoying an ascent of Bhet Mak Mak *(7c+) on a typical day in 1994.*

THE ASIAN TWO-STEP

The grunts in Vietnam referred to one snake, the bamboo viper, as the "Asian Two-Step" because supposedly its bite killed you after you took just two walking steps. This is a bit of an exaggeration (unless you take 45 minutes per step), but the snake is one of the more deadly animals in Southeast Asia and its venom can cause serious tissue destruction. In 1994, Volker and Gerd Schoeffl and I found one in the clipping jug for bolt 5 on *Gaeng Som Plaa*. Enjoy the route, and try to ignore this little tidbit of info when you're about to dyno for that hold!

39. GAENG SOM PLAA   7c+ (5.13a), 15 meters, 7 quickdraws★★★★★
F.A. Max Dufford and Divinder Singh, December 1992
Retrobolted: December 1996

Another classic by Max. This and *Bhet Mak Mak* were the first on this buttress. It is the route farthest right on the wall.

DUM'S KITCHEN

Sun exposure: During the dry season, this area is in the shade in the morning. The routes that are a few meters back from the beach and under the canopy can get shade all day, depending on the level of foliage hanging in front of them, which varies from year to year.

Wall angle and difficulty: Most of the wall is overhanging, but not quite so severely as the Tonsai buttress. These climbs can have stopper moves, but they tend to be a bit more endurance-oriented. The exceptions to this are two of the routes under the canopy that are extremely steep.

Hazards: Being the center of the scene, these climbs receive more retrobolting maintenance than any others in Thailand. You can expect that they will be the first to get re-retrobolted with titanium, but until then, the stainless-steel glue-ins are suspect.

Approach: With routes running the whole distance along the beach, the distinction between Tonsai and Dum's Kitchen has been blurred. Technically, Dum's Kitchen starts under the canopy of jungle that separates the two main beachside walls.

1. SOCIETY OF GRAVITATIONAL STUDIES   7c+ (5.13a), 11 meters,
                                                 5 quickdraws★★★
F.A. Sam Lightner Jr., Volker Schoeffl, and Gerd Schoeffl, December 1993
Retrobolted: March 1999

Of the routes back under the canopy of jungle, *Society* is the leftmost route, about 7.5 meters left of the obvious dihedral that is *Wake and Bake*. Hang a long sling on the out-of-place retrobolt. Sorry.

2. ART AND SPORT   8a+ (5.13c), 15 meters, 9 quickdraws★★★★
F.A. Gerd Schoeffl, Volker Schoeffl, and Sam Lightner Jr., December 1993
Retrobolted: January 2000

Start this route in the corner, then traverse out on sloping jugs. If you don't have a big reach and you want to do this one, I suggest you stretch your arms. The name reflects the two vocations one may cite to get permanent residency in Thailand. A direct boulder start (2a) was added by, I believe, some visiting British climbers. This supposedly added a letter to the grade.

3. WAKE AND BAKE   7a+ (5.12a), 16 meters, 7 quickdraws★★★★
F.A. Cyro Glad, December 1992
Retrobolted: January 2000

This is the steep corner that looks a little like something from New River Gorge. This route was originally climbed by Cyro on gear, but our understanding was that Cyro wanted it bolted but lacked the bolts. We did it for him and then later found out he did not want it bolted. However, there seems to be no going back and he is okay with it. That's good, 'cause it's a nice route.

4. BY WAY OF DECEPTION   7b (5.12b), 16 meters, 7 quickdraws★★
F.A. Volker Schoeffl, Sam Lightner Jr., and Gerd Schoeffl, December 1993

Three meters right of *Wake and Bake* is a roof crack with jugs. Climb out it and then up the ledgy wall to the former's anchor.

DUM'S MANOR

There was a time when nothing, or almost nothing, or nothing that is fit to print in a family-oriented guidebook, took place on Tonsai Beach. Back then, we called the place Dori-Land because Dori, one of our more colorful *farang* locals, lived in a small house back where the Tonsai Bungalows are now located. No one except a few climbers paid any attention to this beach, so it was easy to camp here. Of course the bungalows on Railay were so cheap then that no one bothered to camp, save Dum. Dum and friends lived in the cave between *Gaeng Som Plaa* (last route on Tonsai) and *Society of Gravitational Studies* (first route on what's now Dum's Kitchen). They spent at least a year there, making do with what a boatman's wages could provide and living a general party-hearty lifestyle. Somehow, we began calling this area Dum's Kitchen, though really it was his kitchen, living room, bathroom, and bedroom.

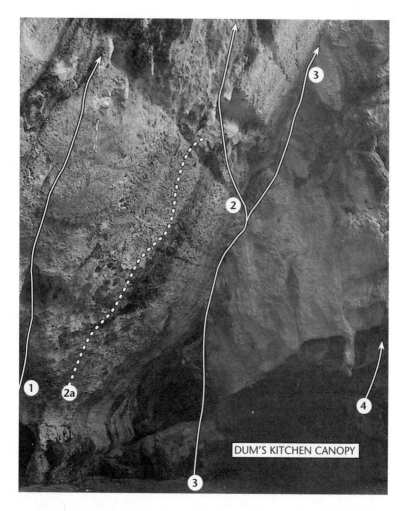

DUM'S KITCHEN CANOPY

5. JUMPING FOR JUGS   6c (5.11b), 15 meters, 8 quickdraws★★★
F.A. Cyro Glad, January 1993
Retrobolted: January 2000

This begins just right and around the corner from *By Way of Deception* and goes to an anchor straight up. To make the start, stand on something and jump.

6. NAIR NON   7b (5.12b), 15 meters, 8 quickdraws★★★
F.A. Ernesto Lopez, March 1995

Approach the same as *Jumping for Jugs,* then move up and right to the anchor of *Som Tam.* The moves are fun, but sandwiched routes forced between two good climbs won't get many stars from me.

7. SOM TAM   **7a (5.11d), 15 meters, 7 quickdraws★★★★**
F.A. Michael Hoffman, February 1992
Retrobolted: December 1997

This route goes over the bulges that *Jumping for Jugs* takes, but about 4.5 meters to the right, and then ends at an anchor above the higher roof where the foliage starts. However, you start it 6 meters right of this and traverse in. Best to remove the gear at the start as you pass by. Be careful. The name, sticking with the ever-present food theme, translates to "green papaya salad." Very tasty.

8. THE DAY AFTER   **7b (5.12b), 15 meters, 7 quickdraws★★★**
F.A. Christian Neumeyer and Reinhold Scherer, February 1997

DUM'S KITCHEN, LEFT

A little sharp. Start with *Som Tam* and then stay right after the bulge. In early 2005 another route was squeezed in just right of this. It goes at 6c+ (5.11c).

9. AUNT MARY-JOHANNA AND TWO GIRLS   6c (5.11b), 27 meters, threads, a handful of quickdraws
F.A. Nick Germang, January 1993

I will not disgrace the star by putting it next to this *kee*.

10. ROD YAK   6b (5.10c), 15 meters, 6 quickdraws★★★
F.A. Michael Hoffman, February 1992
Retrobolted: December 1996

Standing out on the beach, this is the first route on the left. Start right and work left.

11. DON QUIXOTE DE LA MANCHA   7a+ (5.12a), 15 meters, 5 quickdraws★
F.A. Ernesto Lopez and Pili Liatas, March 1995

Did these guys do anything with their own anchor? Thinking this was a worthy line was an exercise in windmill chasing.

12. PAHN TAA LOD   6a (5.10a), 15 meters, 6 quickdraws★★★★
F.A. Michael Hoffman, date unknown
Retrobolted: December 1996

The start can be desperate, depending on sand depth, but even so it is the easiest climb on the beach. Starts about 2.5 meters right of *Rod Yak*.

13. REMINISCENCE   7a+ (5.12a), 22 meters, 8 quickdraws★★★
F.A. Sam Lightner Jr. and Todd Skinner, January 1992
Retrobolted: March 2000

The climb goes up the tufas 4.5 meters right of *Pahn Taa Lod*. The bottom of this route is often dirty and wet, but the top is good. It was the first climb on Tonsai Beach.

14. MAI MEE FAHN   7a+ (5.12a), 13 meters, 6 quickdraws★★★★
F.A. Michael Hoffman, February 1992
Retrobolted: February 1998

Follow the tufa above the roof 2.5 meters right of *Reminiscence*. Difficult start. The name translates to either "No Have Teeth" or "No Have Girlfriend," depending on the pronunciation. *The Naja Traverse,* a boulder problem (V4), begins here.

15. THE LION KING   7a (5.11d), 13 meters, 5 quickdraws★★★★
F.A. Volker Schoeffl, Sam Lightner Jr., and Melanie Schoeffl, February 1996

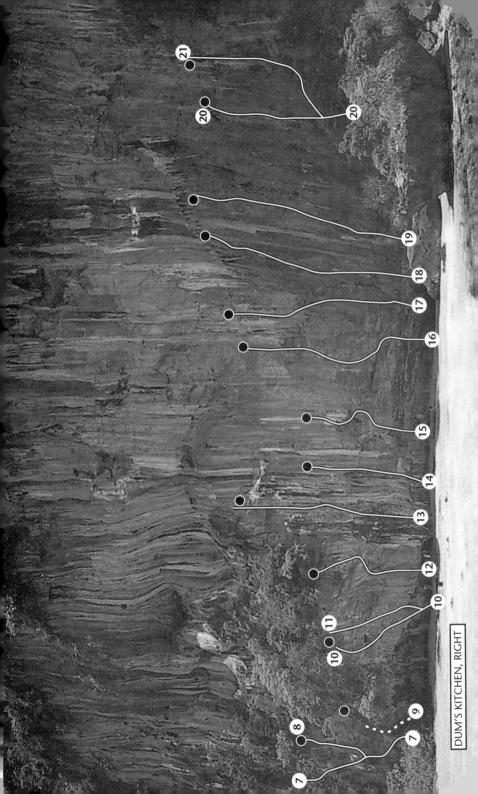

DUM'S KITCHEN, RIGHT

Retrobolted: December 1996 and again in 2004

Fun pump, but don't fall while clipping the third bolt or you might hit the corner. The belayer should never yank in rope on a fall in the crux because it will pull the leader into the wall and possibly break his or her legs.

16. JAI DOM   **8b (5.13d), 25 meters, 8 quickdraws★★★★★**
F.A. Sam Lightner Jr. and Alex Catlin, February 1997

Perhaps the best, and certainly the most natural, of the harder routes, this starts at a small roof about 7.5 meters from the end of the beach. The literal translation of *Jai Dom* is "Black Heart," but the meaning in English would be more along the lines of "pitiless." Many have had that feeling pumping off just below the anchor!

17. OF POPES AND POWER 8b+ (5.14a), 25 meters, 9 quickdraws★★★★
F.A. Alex Catlin and Sam Lightner Jr., January 1996

Starts about 3 meters from the end of the beach. The bolts have mostly fallen out of this one. It can't be done without being rebolted unless you want to get the forced-flash. *The Naja Traverse* ends at the base of this climb.

18. GREED   **8c (5.14b), 30 meters, 10 quickdraws★★★★**
F.A. Alex Catlin, February 1997
Retrobolted: February, 2005

Beginning on the gray horizontals just behind the big boulder, this is a pumper. Lots of V5–V8 with no rest. It is currently the hardest route in the country.

19. OPEN PROJECT   **grade unknown, 30 meters, 12 quickdraws**

This was bolted by a couple of Czech climbers but was never redpointed. Not much natural here, and the bolts are quite questionable.

THE NAJA TRAVERSE

When I first set foot on Tonsai Beach, there were no routes. Before we could get out the drills, we just had to pull on the overhanging wall, just to make sure it was real. Running from *The Lion King* to *Greed* is a horizontal crack that makes a nice warmup in the morning. I climbed up to it and began the traverse, but something tickled my fingers on the inside. I glanced in and saw a bit of rice paper flitting in the breeze. Farther on in the traverse, maybe two more moves, there was more of that tickling. I looked in to see more rice paper and this time pulled it out to get a better look. It turned out to be 2.5 meters long, and it was not rice paper ... it was a cobra skin.

20. ASIA'S SHADOW PLAY   8a (5.13b), 20 meters, 8 quickdraws★★★★
F.A. Sam Lightner Jr., Gerd Schoeffl, and Volker Schoeffl, December 1994
Retrobolted: December 1996
This route is just above the beach on a boulder at the start of the trail to Railay Beach. It is a classic in steep, technical climbing, and it is very photogenic.

21. THE SIT SPINS   6b+ (5.10d), 25 meters, 8 quickdraws★★★
F.A. Sam Lightner Jr., Volker Schoeffl, and Gerd Schoeffl, January 1995
Retrobolted: February 1999
We put this up to take pictures of its big sister and found we had established possibly the dirtiest rock climb in Asia. The name refers to how we felt, as though we'd had bad *Som Tom* the night before. Still, people flocked to it, cleaning it quite a bit, and now it's popular! I'm at a loss.

TYROLEAN WALL
Sun exposure: Like Dum's Kitchen, this wall gets afternoon sun but is cool in the morning.
Wall angle and difficulty: The climbing is powerful and requires a fair bit of endurance. Basically, these grades aren't giveaways.
Hazards: Routes 1–5 have had some loose rock, but they seem to have cleaned up well. Also, try not to block the trail when you drop your rope because it will, inevitably, get stepped on.
Approach: Down and left of Tiger Wall's big routes is the Tyrolean Wall.

Nearly a dozen one-pitch sport climbs can keep you entertained here. It's a dusty place and has its share of mosquitoes in the morning, but some of the routes are very good.

1. LOIS   6c+ (5.11c), 18 meters, 8 quickdraws★★★
F.A. Christian Neumeyer and Reinhold Scherer, February 1997
This is the leftmost route of the wall, starting with a powerful bulge and ending at an anchor in the roof with a vine curtain behind it. It's quite stiff for the grade.

2. MISSING SNOW   6b+ (5.10d), 18 meters, 8 quickdraws★★★★★
F.A. Christian Neumeyer and Reinhold Scherer, February 1997
Rebolted: July 2005
To find this one, look for the burnt-orange crystal holds rising above the boulders on the trail. Steep start.

3. AER UND SCHTEIL   7b (5.12b), 18 meters, toprope ★
F.A. Christian Neumeyer and Reinhold Scherer, February 1997
This runs up the gray rock between *Missing Snow* and *Longes Feschtl*.

4. LONGES FESCHTL   6b+ (5.10c), 15 meters, 6 quickdraws★★★
F.A. Christian Neumeyer and Reinhold Scherer, February 1997
  "Longes Feschtl"? I'll have to take your word for it! Starts with a 3-meter
tufa to flat edges and a bulge. One of the clips is pretty hard.

5. KUAHTITTNSEPPL   6c+ (5.11c), 15 meters, 6 quickdraws★★
F.A. Christian Neumeyer and Reinhold Scherer, February 1997
  This, the rightmost route on this sector of the wall, can be wet. Look for the
darker rock 3 meters right of *Longes Feschtl*.

6. K1   7c (5.12d), 20 meters, 7 quickdraws★★★★
F.A. Christian Neumeyer and Reinhold Scherer, February 1997
  This is the leftmost route on the right sector of Tyrolean. Look for a line of
bolts going up through light gray, dark gray, and then off-white stripes.

7. TYROLEAN AIR   7c (5.12d), 20 meters, 8 quickdraws★★★★
F.A. Christian Neumeyer and Reinhold Scherer, February 1997
  Two and a half meters left of a small cleft in the wall, this route goes up

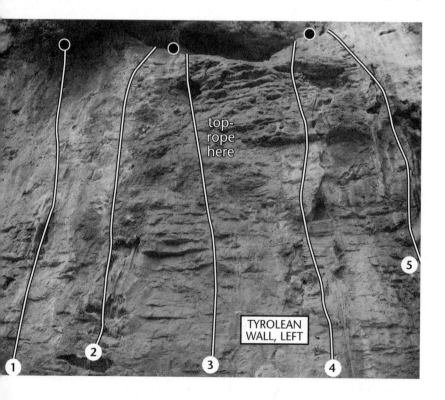

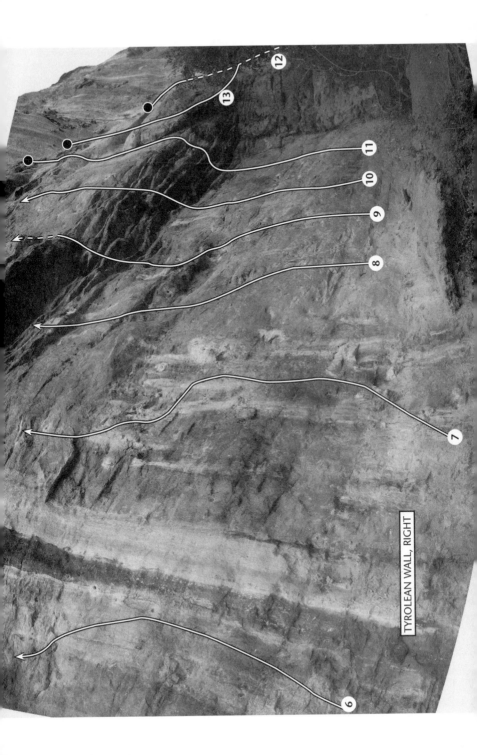

TYROLEAN WALL, RIGHT

about 4.5 meters through white tufa and then works back left and up to an anchor where the angle eases.

8. ZEPHYR   **7c (5.12d), 20 meters, 10 quickdraws★**
F.A. Ola Barhammer, February 2002
   This route is thin and protected by drilled V-threads. Considering our problems, it was good to think of something that did not require bolts. However, they need to be replaced regularly and they tend not to be.... Take care here.

9. NO HAVE   **7b+ (5.12c), 25 meters, 9 quickdraws★★★★**
F.A. Christian Neumeyer and Reinhold Scherer, February 1997
   This route is characterized by the weak dihedral that makes up part of its upper half. The base is about 4.5 meters right of *Tyrolean Air*.

10. JUST CALL ME HELMET   8a (5.13b), 25 meters, 9 quickdraws★★★★
F.A. Scott Cosgrove, February 1997
   Named for Scott's wonderful haircut, this route begins less than a meter right of *No Have*.

11. DEAF, DUMB, AND BLIND   **7b (5.12b), 25 meters,**
                                     12 quickdraws★★★★
F.A. Jaime Lombard III and his posse, November 2003
   This fun climb begins just a couple meters left of a dirty dihedral. It's a good pump.

12. LARS AND LARS   **7a (5.11d), 25 meters, 7 quickdraws★★★★**
F.A. Lars and Lars maybe, January 2004
   This climb begins on a steep slab about 7.5 meters right of *Deaf, Dumb, and Blind*. It's sporty to the first bolt but not too difficult.
   As we went to press another line went up just left of this one. It is *Affentanz* (route 13 on the overlay), a 7c established by Daniel Hetzschel, and actually shares the start of *Lars and Lars* and then goes up and left for 30 meters. You need like a dozen quickdraws.

TIGER WALL

Sun exposure: This wall goes into the sun just before noon and you don't want to be on it when it does!
   Wall angle and difficulty: These routes are very difficult and the most serious undertakings in this book.
   Hazards: *The Brit Line* is a very dangerous route due to the lack of protection and some loose rock. *Year of the Tiger* has its own list of dangers. The pitches are long and steep, making a descent whenever you feel like going down not

the easiest option. You must back-clip to get down off the last pitch, and if you don't you will be stuck in space. Also, timing this route is difficult. The sun hits the wall around 11:30 A.M. and its concave shape focuses the heat on the climbing party. Get up early for this.

Approach: Uphill from the Tyrolean Wall routes, perhaps 100 meters or so, you can find the start of one of the most difficult routes on the peninsula, near the crest of the hill on the Tonsai side.

As you enter Railay Bay on a longtail a number of faces might catch your fancy, but there is one that is hard to take your eyes off. In the center of the peninsula, on the west face of the massif that splits the area in two, is the Tiger Wall, an orange-, white-, and black-striped, almost perfect stretch of Thai limestone.

I say perfect and I mean it, because this wall actually has very few holds up high. There are two routes in the middle of the face, both very difficult but for

different reasons. *Year of the Tiger* is difficult by its grade, not to mention the *khay* it takes to take big whippers up high on it. At its grade, *Year of the Tiger* is a classic, but it's not something everyone should throw themselves at. *The Brit Line* is difficult 'cause in spots you have to climb 7a on bad rock while facing a 30-meter fall. (Yes, Leo Houlding has been to Thailand.) Still, if you feel up to it, this is a beautiful place to climb.

Another note: I did the first ascent but did not go to the obvious cave to end it. However, it seemed silly to put the anchor where I was when there was this obvious ending just above. I decided to put the anchor in the cave so the route could have a fitting end, but then I never went back to redpoint it through the last 6 meters. For that reason, I list two ratings: the one that I did, and one that I suspect it would be if you make it through the last bit (it's either really dirty there, which weakens the line, or it's a huge dyno...too big for me). This route took five weeks to equip because it had to be aided both up and down. It almost cost me my life in a 6-meter factor-2 fall. Don't tell me that you get to rename it because you did that last bit, 'cause there is a lot more to establishing a big route than simply redpointing it.

1. YEAR OF THE TIGER   8a+ (5.13c) A0/8b, 120 meters, 18 quickdraws and 2 60-meter ropes★★★★

F.A. Sam Lightner Jr., Nancy Feagin, Scott Morley, and Samporn Suebhait (King), March 1998

Pitch 1: 7b (5.12b), 30 meters, 13 quickdraws. This is a fine pitch in its own right. Quite technical. Ascend to the obvious ledge.

Pitch 2: 7c (5.12d), 51 meters, 18 quickdraws. This pitch defines the word "pumpy." Climb up and right for an absurd distance, then set up the hanging belay and get ready to log airtime. Some bolts on this pitch were glued in with hangers...rumor has it that a couple of the hangers came off. They are not the crux bolts.

Pitch 3: 8a+A0/8b (5.13c with aid), 40 meters, 15 quickdraws. Follow the bolt line up the wall. Sometimes they are a bit spacey. The last bit where the huge dyno or slightly dirty stalactite must be climbed was not done on the first ascent but only makes sense as part of the route.

Descent: Rappelling this route is dangerous. Do *not* attempt to rappel from the top of pitch 2 to the ground because it is more than 70 meters. There is a rappel station perhaps 12 meters below this belay. Be off by noon. King charges $200 per person for an afternoon rescue.

2. THE BRIT LINE   7b+ (maybe) (5.12c), 120 meters (possibly), gear, draws, slings, a clear head

F.A. started by Max the Kiwi, then myself, pushed up by Leo Houlding and friends, date unknown

I can only tell you what I know and found on this but cannot give a blow-by-blow rendition of it. This is a traditional route that ascends the obvious dihedral in the center of the wall. Max the Kiwi tried an ascent of it in the early '90s, then I pushed his line farther when working on route 1. Leo Houlding and friends took it a few steps beyond that. Starting on the lower-angle rock at the top of the hill, the route goes up to the dihedral and up it, then beyond my high point and onto very loose and run-out stone above and to its right. Thirty-meter falls are possible up there, and the rappels are desperate. This is a very dangerous route.

3. MORNING SONG   **7b (5.12b), 35 meters, 12 quickdraws★**
F.A. Sam Lightner Jr., Volker Schoeffl, and Gerd Schoeffl, November 1994
   This route is in the sun at all times and is thus not popular. The bolts have mostly rusted away and we have let the route all but disappear as climbing on it was upsetting the falcons on the wall to its right.

DIAMOND CAVE
Sun exposure: In the dry season, the lower wall of Diamond Cave gets some tree-filtered sunlight, but the higher wall is generally in the shade. In the rainy season, the whole wall can get morning light. Afternoons are always in the shade.
   Wall angle and difficulty: The climbs are just under vertical to slightly overhanging, with some multipitch sport climbs. Most of the routes are easy to moderate by Phra Nang standards.
   Hazards: Like all walls at Phra Nang, this one has more than its share of bad bolts. Not much has been rebolted here. Also, it's good to keep in mind that the Thai guides tend to overwhelm this area for much of the day.
   Approach: Go up the concrete walkway toward the cave and national park headquarters, passing them on your left, and continue on for about 100 more meters. Look for the first of the climbing just around the corner of the wall on your left. The lower left wall is shown here, and the upper wall is just 20 meters or so farther. Routes 8–14 are at the right side of the north face, about 20 meters past the first five routes.

At the north end of Railay East is the Diamond Cave and the national park headquarters. Diamond Cave is a good beginner's crag, although it is limited in the total number of routes. It's generally a quiet place because the droning longtails are nowhere in sight. The routes aren't as steep as many places but they have the usual big holds. The climbs rise out of an old rubber plantation that has been replaced by bungalows. The climbing used to extend all along the wall behind the park headquarters building and on either side of the cave, but for reasons unknown to the national park employees, these routes were closed. Nevertheless, we must heed the rules.

Over the years, the lower left wall has become a gridwork of slings and such. This is because the four original routes have proven not to be enough for the guides, and they have added threads and anchors any place that might help them to guide more clients on the wall.

1. NAME UNKNOWN   **5 (5.8), 15 meters, some quickdraws★**
F.A. Unknown

This route is the leftmost on this face. It does not go all the way up to the ledge. All of the protection is via threads.

2. NAME UNKNOWN   **5 (5.8), 20 meters, 6 quickdraws★★**
F.A. Unknown

It just appeared one day, but it gets climbed a lot. Goes over the small roof to an anchor just left of the small tree (down and right of the big one).

3. CHOK DEE   **5 (5.8), 20 meters, 6 quickdraws★★★**
F.A. Dean Saydom, January 1995

Shares the anchor for route 2.

DOLF'S COMMODE

A few movies have been filmed in the Krabi area, most notably *The Beach* and *The Man with the Golden Gun*. One that you might have missed, or at least should have missed, was *Men of War*. This cinematic masterpiece didn't win many awards. Actually, I don't think it was released except on video in the states, and even the teenage Thais who were seconds in the film thought it lacked a coherent plot. Still, it is remembered on Tonsai Beach for a stately landmark that has only recently been removed. A number of the shoot-'em-up scenes were done on Tonsai Beach, and the lead actor, a certain oversized Swede who has done a lot of films that won't be getting Academy Awards, apparently did not go for the local facilities. Who's to blame him? There were none then. A foundation was laid two-thirds of the way down the beach, a tank put in the ground, and a blue toilet was mounted there, next to the knelling waves and soft sand. The toilet came with a nice view of the Thaiwand and Tiger Wall but limited reading material. The thatch walls that provided a degree of privacy and the blue toilet have recently disappeared, but the concrete it rested on still stands as Phra Nang's monument to *Men of War*.

4. KEEP THE JAM, MAN   **7a (5.11d), 70 meters,**
10 quickdraws plus gear★★★★

F.A. Nick Blaise and Martin Carstens, January 1995

Pitch 1: 5 (5.8), 20 meters, 8 quickdraws. Goes to an anchor at the tree. A bit sharp and the bolts are bad.

Pitch 2: 6a (5.10a), 15 meters, 5 quickdraws, 1 60-meter rope. You can reach the ground from here with one rope.

Pitch 3: 7a (5.11d), 35 meters, various bits of natural gear. This is a gear pitch, with limited threads. Personally, I backed off!

5. NAME UNKNOWN   5 (5.8), 20 meters, 6 quickdraws★★★
F.A. Unknown

This goes straight up, then angles right to an anchor near the small tree. The bolts are bad.

6. NAME UNKNOWN   6a+ (5.10b), 20 meters, 8 quickdraws★★★★
F.A. More of the Unknown

Pretty much straight up. Anchor either the tree or old hardware.

7. NAME UNKNOWN   6a+ (5.10b), 20 meters, 8 quickdraws★★★★
F.A. Unknown

Continue on that theme...

8. NULL AKTION   6a (5.10a), 20 meters, 7 quickdraws★
F.A. M. Hoffman, February 1995

On the left side of this wall is a low-angle slab that angles out left, then turns steep. Follow it and then back right to the anchor. This gives you access to *Diamonds are Forever*, but *Les Petites* is the better of the two.

9. DIAMONDS ARE FOREVER   6b+ (5.10d), 25 meters, 11 quickdraws★
F.A. Marel Eckhardt, January 1995

This is basically the second pitch of *Les Petites Oreilles*. One 60-meter rope may not reach the ground from this anchor, and the bolts are bad.

10. LES PETITES OREILLES   6b+ (5.10d), 20 meters, 8 quickdraws★★★★
F.A. Stefan Schmidt, January 1995

Take the well-used line of threads and bolts just right of *Null Aktion*.

11. SEVEN, SEVEN, SEVEN 6c (5.11b), 55 meters, maybe 9 quickdraws★★★★★
F.A. Stefan Schmidt and friends, January 1995

This route has recently been rebolted, thus I do not know how many quickdraws you need for each pitch.

Pitch 1: 6b (5.10c), 20 meters. Starting on gray and white rock in the middle of this face, this pitch takes the left line around the shrubs on the ledge 20 meters up.

Pitch 2: 6c (5.11b), 20 meters. Something technical and different for Thailand! Very fun. Scary bolts, including the hanging belay. A long sling makes this belay unnecessary because you can combine pitches 2 and 3 into one long pitch.

Pitch 3: 6c (5.11b), 15 meters, Great climbing on excellent rock. Scary bolts. Connecting this pitch with pitch 2 makes it 6c+, which can easily be done. Be kind to the cycad palm (*plong* in Thai) at the top: it is very fragile.

12. NAME UNKNOWN   6b (5.10c), 20 meters, 7 quickdraws★★★★
F.A. Paul Brunner, date unknown

Start this one with the start to *Seven, Seven, Seven*, then trend right on good holds. Going through the bulge, it's a little sharp but fun.

13. ALMOST HEAVEN   7a+ (5.12a), 25 meters, 12 quickdraws*★★★★
F.A. Tom Cecil and John Rosholt, February 1995

A fine pitch going straight up from the anchor at the top of route 12 or 14. You are stretching the 60 meters to reach the ground lowering off this route. Tie a knot or rappel.

14. NAME UNKNOWN   6c (5.11b), 21 meters, 7 quickdraws★★★
F.A. Paul Brunner, date unknown

Start this one at the very edge of the vines hanging on the wall's right side. Scary threads and bolts.

GENERATOR WALL

Sun exposure: During the dry season, this wall is in the shade pretty much all day. You might catch a ray or two very early but nothing but shade from early morning on.

Wall angle and difficulty: The climbs here are all quite difficult. Also, on most of the routes there are very few intermediate holds...you have to make big pulls on steep rock to climb here.

Hazards: The protection used here, for the most part, is sections of rope tied in loops through the rock. It's something akin to the abalakov used in ice climbing. You might want to bring some old rope up here to replace what is in the threads. You will need one of those nasty little hooks used to thread abalakovs to do this because the holes are pretty tight (a sharpened coat hanger works as well). How the rope reacts to repetetive strain in the rock is yet to be determined. Also, in my experience, this is a very "snaky" crag: watch where you step and what you grab. Finally, there are a lot of wasps here, and they sting hard!

Approach: To reach this crag, walk up the Tonsai Road toward the pass between Tonsai Beach and Railay East. After about 15 minutes from the beach, you will come to Tiew Khaow Bungalows. Take a right into their establishment, walking up a long line of steps. There are ninety-five of them, so be prepared to bivy! At the end of the steps, go up a path to the generator. The wall is another 30 meters on and quite obvious. This will put you at the base of routes 1–4.

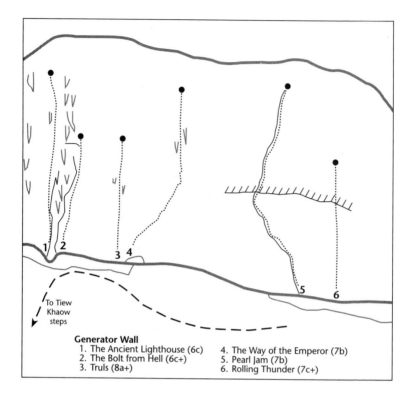

Generator Wall
1. The Ancient Lighthouse (6c)
2. The Bolt from Hell (6c+)
3. Truls (8a+)
4. The Way of the Emperor (7b)
5. Pearl Jam (7b)
6. Rolling Thunder (7c+)

The Generator Wall has some of the best rock on the penisula. It is exceptionally compact, similar in character to Koh Phi Phi's Drinking Wall, but far steeper.

1. THE ANCIENT LIGHTHOUSE   6c (5.11b), 30 meters, 14 quickdraws★★★★★

F.A. Ola Barhammer, May 2002

This route starts on the left side of the obvious large column. It ascends the left side of the wall on the left side of a large stalactite system and is an excellent climb. Be leery of critters in the larger huecos!

2. THE BOLT FROM HELL   6c+ (5.11c), 25 meters, 10 quickdraws and a can of Raid!★★★★

F.A. Ola Barhammer, May 2002

This route ascends the right side of the stalactite system, starting about 3 meters right of route 1 and ending on the top of said stalactites. Also very fun climbing, but popular with some very grumpy hornets. Also, the bolt mentioned in the name is bad, barely in the wall, and hell to clip (probably was hell to place, too).

3. TRULS   8a+ (5.13c), 25 meters, 8 quickdraws★★★★
F.A Ola Barhammer, May 2002

This ascends the beautiful face about 4 meters right of route 2. This is excellent rock...be ready for slopers and big pulls.

4. THE WAY OF THE EMPEROR   7b (5.12b), 30 meters,
                                      12 quickdraws★★★★★
F.A. Ola Barhammer, May 2002

Find the start to this one on a ledge of vines just right of *Truls*. This is an outstanding rock climb. If the emperor climbed, this is what he would want. Its only fault is that a large pocket at about the sixth bolt is the ugly home of QUITE A FEW HORNETS.

5. PEARL JAM   7b (5.12b), 30 meters, 14 quickdraws★★★★★
F.A. M. Auliot, January 2003

A great name for an outstanding climb. This climb rivals *Bhet Mak Mak* (route 37 on Tonsai) and *Cross-Eyed* (route 7 on the Melting Wall, North Peninsula) for best pitch in southern Thailand. It is a splitter hand crack up a wall way steeper than the boys in Yosemite and Moab are used to. It overhangs 10 meters in its length. Even though the crack is very smooth, you might want to tape because the backs of your hands will sweat and tear.

The crack starts on the ledge up and left from the clearing beneath this end of the wall.

6. ROLLING THUNDER   7c+ (5.13a), 25 meters, 12 quickdraws★★★★★
F.A. Aaron Gully, Sam Lightner Jr., and Michelle Garbert, November 2004

This beautiful climb goes up the wall and through the roof just right of *Pearl Jam*. It's as good as it looks.

Chapter 7

NORTH PENINSULA CLIMBS

In the last few years, Tonsai (Thai for "Pine Tree") Beach has become the main hangout for climbers. The walls at the north end of this beach offer a wide variety of climbing and consistently go into the sun in early afternoon. Some of the best routes in Thailand can be found here at places like Melting Wall, Wild Kingdom, and Cat Wall. For those who want to get up off the deck, there are multipitch climbs at many of the crags, varing in difficulty from *The Wave*, a 6a+ (5.10b) at Beauty and the Beast crag, to *Kitty Porn*, a 7c+ (5.13a) at Cat Wall.

MARLEY WALL

Sun exposure: This wall goes into the shade in early afternoon, although it holds heat for a while because the morning sun gets a clear shot at it.

Wall angle and difficulty: These are steep climbs of an intermediate level.

Hazards: Some of the bolts are the best we have, but the bolts on the multipitch route are aging fast. There are lots of mosquitoes up here, so bring bug repellent.

Approach: You get here from the Tonsai Road at the 90-degree turn near the Nest by taking the trail toward Jungle Hut; this is about 100 meters toward Dream Valley and Krabi Mountain View Resort. Walk up toward Jungle Hut for about 250 meters. You will ascend some irregular concrete steps at this point. Look out left to a couple of large, blue water tanks and pass them on your way to the old concrete generator shed. Walk around the shed to find a trail that works up through the jungle, then out left to the wall. It's about 4 minutes from the generator shed. The trail takes you to *Catch a Fire*.

On the north side, this column of rock is one of the last lines of stone to the right (east) before the rock degenerates into rotten, yellow bands. It's a fun place to climb, with great views.

1. CATCH A FIRE   7a+ (5.12a), 22 meters, 13 quickdraws★★★★★
F.A. Tom Cecil, Justin Day, Josh Lyons, and the gang, date unknown

At the far right side of the wall, next to a boulder, this climb works its way up pockets and edges. It's a good endurance pump with excellent bolts for its

Marley
Wall

The Nest
and Wild
Kingdom

Monitor
Wall

Cat
Wall

Fire
Wall

Melting
Wall

Eagle Wall

Cobra Wall

The Point

NORTH WALLS

first 20 meters. As we went to press, two more pitches were added above this, at 6b and 6c. Nothing else was known.

2. EXODUS　　　　　　　7c (5.12d), 25 meters, 10 quickdraws★★★★
F.A. Brian Sweeney and Justin Day, January, 2005

This route was named as everyone left the peninsula after the wave.

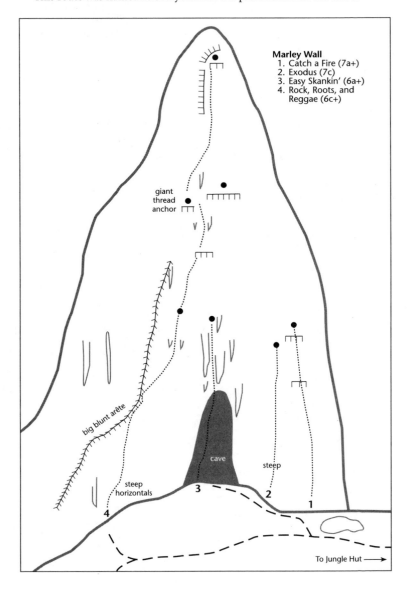

3. EASY SKANKIN'   **6a+ (5.10b), 25 meters, 12 quickdraws★★★★**

F.A. Tom Cecil and Justin Day, November 2004

This route promises to be fun climbing on ground that is crazy steep for the grade. Be leery of weak stalactites. Find the start in the cave to the left of *Catch a Fire* and work your way out and up on big holds, threads, and bolts. The anchor is at the lip.

4. ROCK, ROOTS, AND REGGAE   **6c+ (5.11c), 60 meters,**
                                                  12 quickdraws★★★★

F.A. Tom Cecil, Justin Day, and Josh Lyons, date unknown

This route starts on the white rock, under a steep bulge with horizontals, about 15 meters left of the cave. It's fun climbing, and I would have to say it is stiff for the grade. Be aware that as we went to press it had not been rebolted and was thus nearing its expiration date. The route was set up as three pitches, but I find it more pleasant to take some extra long draws and link pitches 1 and 2 into one 40-meter pitch.

Pitch 1: 6c (5.11b), 30 meters, 12 quickdraws. Climb over the bulge on horizontals to a fun face, then up to a slight arête and out a bulge. The anchor is better suited for lowering someone when doing this first pitch alone. Otherwise, it's sort of a hanging stance.

Pitch 2: 6a (5.10a), 10 meters, 5 quickdraws. Continue on up and right, moving past large tufas and stalactites and past a big ledge. There are two anchors for the last pitch. The better one is the lower left ledge, which is a bit smaller but sets you up better for pitch 3. The anchor is a giant tufa. Two 60-meter ropes will get you back to the ground from here.

Pitch 3: 6c+ (5.11c), 20 meters, 10 quickdraws. Climb up and right over the bulge and then past a dihedral to an anchor under a large overhang. It is easy to lower back to the previous ledge from here and then rappel from there.

WILD KINGDOM WALL

Sun exposure: This wall faces south and thus catches morning sun and afternoon shade. It gets some protection from the trees, but because those are quickly disappearing, so too is the shade.

Wall angle and difficulty: Wild Kingdom varies from gently overhanging to really steep. It's not Tonsai, but it's close. The routes vary in difficulty from 6a+ to 7b+.

Hazards: As usual, be leery of non-titanium glue-ins. Also, this area can be pretty buggy, and back when it was actually wild, you needed to watch out for ticks.

Approach: To reach this fun wall, walk to Paasook Resort, the bungalow operation where Tonsai Road makes a 90-degree turn. The climbs are on the obvious walls left of the bungalows. Politely walk past a few bungalows and up a little hill to Wild Kingdom.

The Wild Kingdom, so named for the monkeys, monitors, snakes, birds, and ticks that were found here during the first ascents, is a great climbing venue. Unfortunately, the name is now more ironic than descriptive, because the critters have been traded in for bungalows and generators.

1. MUTUAL OF OMAHA   6c (5.11b), 18 meters, 9 quickdraws★★★
F.A. Mark Miner and Cameron Fairbairn, January 2000
 This climb starts on the flowstone just right of route *Freedom Safari* and

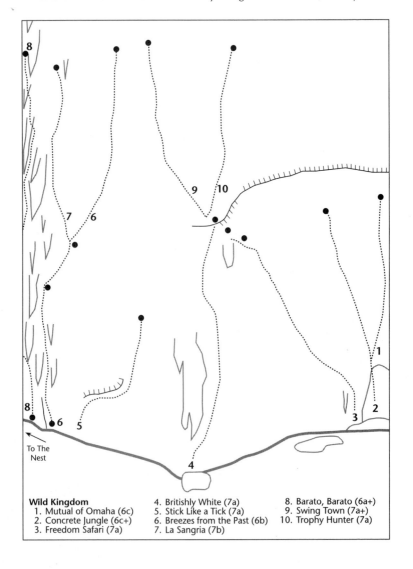

Wild Kingdom
1. Mutual of Omaha (6c)
2. Concrete Jungle (6c+)
3. Freedom Safari (7a)

4. Britishly White (7a)
5. Stick Like a Tick (7a)
6. Breezes from the Past (6b)
7. La Sangria (7b)

8. Barato, Barato (6a+)
9. Swing Town (7a+)
10. Trophy Hunter (7a)

then breaks right to the sharper stone, coming back to the anchor on the gray face up high. A serious accident happened here due to loose rock and a loose belay (see "Climbing Accidents" in Chapter 5, The Phra Nang Peninsula in Southern Thailand).

2. CONCRETE JUNGLE   6c+ (5.11c), 20 meters, 11 quickdraws★★★★
FA: Tom Cecil and Mark Miner, January 2000

This one shares a start with *Mutual of Omaha* but it goes straight up where *Omaha* goes right. It's pumpy for the grade. Fun climb.

3. FREEDOM SAFARI   7a (5.11d), 20 meters, 11 quickdraws★★★★
F.A. Paul Turecki and Kirsten Klemer, January 2000
Retrobolted: February 2005

Find this climb at the right end of the wall. Look for a crack between two pieces of flowstone leading to a steep white face. This fun climb traverses left over a lot of bulging rock. For those who like their routes to end at the end, during the retrobolting process we added an anchor on a ledge two meters beyond the original anchor. This increases the grade to 7a+, but at least you clip from a stance.

4. BRITISHLY WHITE   7a (5.11d), 20 meters, 8 quickdraws★★★★★
F.A. Tom Cecil, January 2000

This is an excellent climb found at the middle of the wall. You should stick-clip the first bolt and try to ignore the wasps near the top. They don't seem to sting...much.

5. STICK LIKE A TICK   7a (5.11d), 18 meters, 6 quickdraws★★
F.A. Paul Turecki and Kirsten Klemer, January 2000

Climb out the bulge and roof from the ramp just right of *Breezes from the Past.*

6. BREEZES FROM THE PAST   6b (5.10c), 18 meters, 8 quickdraws★★★★
F.A. Mark Miner and Tom Cecil, January 2000

This starts at the top of the ramp on the right side of the flowstone. There are three variations to this route, so prepare yourself for confusion! One option is continuing up and right past another bolt to a second anchor, making the route grade 7a because of one move. It's at this point that two variations begin. If you go straight up the steepest part of the wall you are on a 7b called *La Sangria*. However, if you continue up and right on the clean orange and white face, you will be on a great extension of this route (labelled 6 on the topo). This is a 7b established by Tom and Mark and it is one of the better routes of its grade around. A 60-meter rope will get you back to the ground.

7. LA SANGRIA   **7b (5.12b), 30 meters, 12 quickdraws★★★★**
F.A. Ernesto Lopez and friends, January 2000
   This route is the staight-up extension of *Breezes from the Past.*

8. BARATO, BARATO   **6a+ (5.10b), 35 meters, 10 quickdraws★★★**
F.A. Ernesto Lopez and friends, January 2000
   Pitch 1: 6a+ (5.10b), 15 meters, 8 quickdraws. This climb starts on the left side of the prominent piece of flowstone that separates Wild Kingdom from the Nest. There is a thread through the flowstone that can be used for a hanging belay. The threads on this route are fairly solid, but the bolts are bad.
   Pitch 2: 6a+ (5.10b), 20 meters, 10 quickdraws. Requires a double rope rappel to reach the ground safely. Also, a variation, which is called *Sorry, the Kitchen Is Closed* (route 1 on the topo for the Nest) at 7a+, veers off to the left just above the pitch 1 anchor.

9. SWING TOWN   **7a+ (5.12a), 12 meters, 8 quickdraws★★★**
F.A. Mark Miner and Cameron Fairbairn, January 2000
   This route can be found starting at the ledge above *Britishly White*. It is sharp. This climb moves up and left from the anchor. From the top anchor of this climb, it is possible to lower the leader to the ground with a 60-meter rope. The belayer would have to rappel from here.

10. TROPHY HUNTER   **7a (5.11d), 12 meters, 6 quickdraws★★★**
F.A. Tom Cecil, January 2000
   This route also can be found starting at the ledge above *Britishly White*. It is also sharp. This one goes up and right. Same deal as *Swing Town* for getting down.

THE NEST

Sun exposure: This wall faces south and thus catches morning sun and afternoon shade. It gets some protection from the trees, but because those are quickly disappearing, so too is the shade.
   Wall angle and difficulty: The Nest varies from gently overhanging to really steep. It's not Tonsai, but it's close. The routes vary in difficulty from 6a+ to 7b+.
   Hazards: As usual, be leery of non-titanium glue-ins. Also, this area can be pretty buggy.
   Approach: From Wild Kingdom, make a left turn and follow the trail 25 meters to the Nest…it's pretty obvious from Paasook Resort. You can access the Golden Bowl via *Dozer Days.*
   Descent: You need two ropes to get down from the Golden Bowl or you need to rappel to the lower *Dozer Days* anchor and go from there.

The Nest got its name from the bundle of vines you used to stand on to belay. Fortunately, they have disappeared. Routes 14–16 are located in the so-called "Golden Bowl," the beautiful brown stone above the Nest.

1. SORRY, THE KITCHEN IS CLOSED   7a+ (5.12a), 30 meters, 12 quickdraws★★

F.A. Ernesto Lopez and friends, January 2000

This climb breaks off left from the second pitch of *Barato Barato*.

2. BARATO, BARATO   6a+ (5.10b), 35 meters, 10 quickdraws★★★

F.A. Ernesto Lopez and friends, January 2000

Described as route 8 on the Wild Kingdom, above.

3. TECHNO BUG   6a+ (5.10b), 15 meters, 5 quickdraws★★★

F.A. Tom Cecil, Mark Miner, Drew Spalding, Josh Lyons, and Justin Dayaka, their orchestra, November 2000

Retrobolted: February, 2005

This climb starts on the steep tufas just left of the bulge that separates Wild Kingdom and the Nest.

4. BANANA HAMMOCK   6a+ (5.10b), 20 meters, 9 quickdraws★★★★

F.A. Tom Cecil, Mark Miner, and their orchestra, November 2000

Named for the popular German beach attire, this route starts to the left of *Techno Bug* and climbs up tufas. There is a lower station shared by *Techno Bug*, but these days people are bypassing it and going to a higher station on the giant tufa. Use this to access the anchor at the base of *Over It!*

5. PLA LEK   6b+ (5.11a), 15 meters, 7 quickdraws★★★

F.A. Tom Cecil, Mark Miner, and their orchestra, November 2000

This climb goes up the next line of tufas and pockets left of *Banana Hammock*. *Pla Lek* means "little fish."

6. JUNGLE LOVE   7a+ (5.12a), 25 meters, 11 quickdraws★★★★

F.A. Sam Lightner Jr. and Michelle Garbert, October 2004

This route starts in the cave and climbs out, right, onto the steepest part of the wall and then up the column above the ledge. It is soft for the grade. The expansion bolts will expire in the winter of 2006!

7. STRANGLE HOLD   6c+ (5.11c), 15 meters, 6 quickdraws★★★

F.A. Tom Cecil, Mark Miner, and their orchestra, November 2000

This powerful little climb goes up the right side of the tufas just left of the small cave.

8. KITTY TOE   6b (5.10c), 15 meters, 6 quickdraws★★★

F.A. Tom Cecil, Mark Miner, and their orchestra, November 2000
Retrobolted: February 2005

The next route left of *Strangle Hold,* this climb goes up the left side of stalactites and tufa stone.

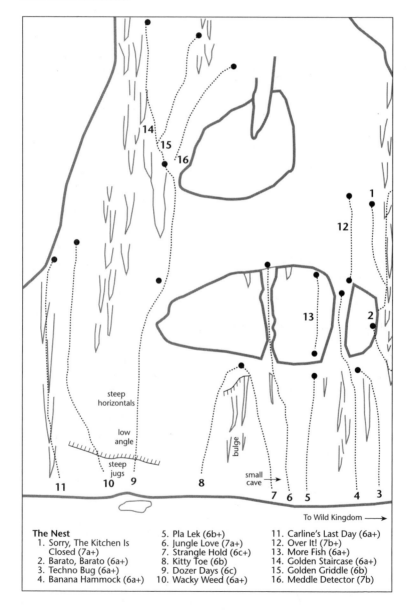

The Nest
1. Sorry, The Kitchen Is
   Closed (7a+)
2. Barato, Barato (6a+)
3. Techno Bug (6a+)
4. Banana Hammock (6a+)

5. Pla Lek (6b+)
6. Jungle Love (7a+)
7. Strangle Hold (6c+)
8. Kitty Toe (6b)
9. Dozer Days (6c)
10. Wacky Weed (6a+)

11. Carline's Last Day (6a+)
12. Over It! (7b+)
13. More Fish (6a+)
14. Golden Staircase (6a+)
15. Golden Griddle (6b)
16. Meddle Detector (7b)

9. DOZER DAYS   6c (5.11b), 35 meters, 15 quickdraws★★★★★

F.A. Tom Cecil, Mark Miner, and their orchestra, November 2000

Start off at a boulder left of *Kitty Toe* and traverse left on low-angled rock to steeper climbing. Power through excellent climbing up and eventually left past a large tufa. This is the climb to use to access the Golden Bowl. An anchor exists about 25 meters off the ground, but if you want to climb above, continue on (long slings might help with drag) to a ledge and anchor another 10 meters higher. Fun climbing.

KITTY TOE

In the mid-'90s, volleyball rivaled climbing as Railay Beach's true calling. There was only one court, the one in front of Sand Sea Bungalow and the Sunset Bar, but everyone played. Each evening, about 4 P.M. we'd run off the cats from the shady bit of beach, drag out the beer, turn up the tunes, and start bumping. Some days we would quit climbing early just so we could get back in time for evening volleyball.

That is, until we all started getting Kitty Toe.

At first we thought Kitty Toe was a worm. It looked like a worm, inching its way through the feet of virtually anyone who had played volleyball. The first symptoms came at night, when you'd wake up itching worse than a porn star in poison ivy. Scratch all you want; that little worm would not quit itching. Some of us couldn't sleep. It got so bad for Dickie B. that he eventually went off to Bangkok to see what could be done about it.

At the tropical disease ward of one of Bangkok's better hospitals, Dick found that our problem was actually a bacteria that colonized the skin in squiggly lines. There was medicine for it, which had to be taken orally and limited one's evening libations.

Sand Sea Bungalow changed to Sand Sea Resort, which of course meant there could be no volleyball out front because that was not something finer "resorts" allowed, and it spelled the end of the volleyball scene. However, Kitty Toe had already taken a lot of the wind out of our sails.

Seemingly unrelated, it was about that same time a python moved into the woods down by the Railay Beach Club and took a serious whack at the cat population. Years went by and the cat population rebounded; as it did, a few climbers living on the beach began to pick up Kitty Toe once more. Another trip to the hospital was warranted and this time we found out the key to the spread of the vile Kitty Toe: cats, which treat the beach like a giant litter box, carry and spread this bug in their feces. Somehow, that made getting Kitty Toe even worse.

Volleyball in front of Sand Sea

10. WACKY WEED   **6a+ (5.10b), 25 meters, 8 quickdraws★★★**
F.A. Tom Cecil, Mark Miner, Paul Turecki, Kristen Klemer, Brian Warshow, and Josh
    Lyons—aka their orchestra, November 2000
    This climb begins with a small roof to low-angled rock and then continues
up through tufas.

11. CARLINE'S LAST DAY   **6a+ (5.10a), 25 or 40 meters, 10 quickdraws***
F.A. Unknown, April 2003
    This route goes up throught the tufas on the far left of the crag. It's best to
top-rope it off the anchors of route 10 because the anchors on *Carline's Last Day*
are very bad. There is a second pitch that also has bad anchors.

12. OVER IT!   **7b+ (5.12c), 15 meters, 8 quickdraws★★★★**
F.A. Tom Cecil and his orchestra, March 2003
    This route goes out the big roof above *Banana Hammock* and *Techno Bug*. Big
moves. Questionable bolts as of the time of this writing. One 60-meter rope
reaches back to the ground.

13. MORE FISH   **6a+ (5.10b), 15 meters, 8 quickdraws★★★★**
F.A. Mark Miner, Tom Cecil, and their orchestra, March 2003
    Absurdly steep for the grade, this goes out the right side of the big tufa
above *Pla Lek* and left of the *Banana Hammock* extension. Very fun. Bolts are
breaking down fast.

14. GOLDEN STAIRCASE   6a+ (5.10b), 23 meters, 10 quickdraws★★★★
F.A. Greg Collum and Mike Ho, November 2000
   This is the left route going straight up off the belay for *Dozer Days*.

15. GOLDEN GRIDDLE   6b (5.10b), 25 meters, 10 quickdraws★★★★
F.A. Greg Collum and Mike Ho, November 2000
   This climb goes up and right from the belay for *Dozer Days*.

16. MEDDLE DETECTOR   7b (5.12b), 20 meters, 10 quickdraws★★★★
F.A. Greg Collum and Mike Ho, November 2000
   This climb goes up and hard right over the mouth of the cave that is right of
the belay for *Dozer Days*. Getting back to the belay is a bit of a workout! Make
sure you tie a knot in the end of the rope.

MONITOR WALL (AKA ASPHYXIATION WALL) AND MONKEY WORLD

Sun exposure: Morning sun and afternoon shade. The rock can hold the heat
for a long time.

Wall angle and difficulty: This wall is actually very steep, but the climbs
tend toward the easiest lines up the wall, making them easier than the angle
would suggest.

Hazards: The bolts are old and very bad. On top of that, this is a very big
wall that requires big, overhanging rappels to descend. More than one party
has been stranded on their rappel lines because they did not back-clip or tried
to come down on ropes that were too short. Finally, the generator at the base of
this wall is not always on. If it comes on while you are climbing, you are in big
trouble. It pumps out a lot of carbon monoxide and thus poisons you (hence
the moniker "Asphyxiation Wall"). Make sure to ask the bungalow operators
when they plan to have it on and be down before it's running.

Approach: To find these routes, follow the Tonsai Road at the north end of
Tonsai Beach. About 200 meters in from the beach is a huge alcove. A short trail
goes up to the start of routes 1, 3, and 4. Farther left and moving up through
vines and over a couple slabs is a trail to the base of the *Ninth Life* (route 8).
   About 100 meters west of the 90-degree turn on the far side of Tonsai Road,
about halfway between the Nest and Monitor Wall, is the buttress with *Beauty
and the Beast* (route 13) on it. This was set up as an access route to Monkey World
(see below) but has become a fun climb on its own. The buttress extends almost
right down to the road, with the climb starting no more than 4.5 meters from
the electrical wires that run along the road. When we went to press, it was best
to reach the base by going about 30 meters closer to the beach, climbing up to
the wall, then going into the big cave that runs the entire base of this wall. Walk
through the cave to a point where it opens at the base of the route.

It's hard to say where Monitor Wall begins and the Cat Wall ends. Both are on a buttress originally dubbed the Sleeping Indian Wall, but that name has long since been lost. For this book, we call anything around the huge alcove the Monitor Wall; to the left of the alcove is Cat Wall. Monkey World is the beautiful tan wall up and right of the buttress, but, sadly, due to a lack of proper equipment, it is not climbable. When it gets fixed up, we will get all the correct information to you.

These climbs are on a very steep wall. However, the wall is a maze of ledges, overlapping roofs, tunnels and caves, and giant stalactite corners. Thus, most of the longer climbs have been established so that they follow the ledges and corners and are easier than the angle of the wall would indicate. On the longer routes, it is often more important to try and follow the route as dictated by the rock rather than trying to find the line of bolts. If you follow the line of least resistance, some form of protection will probably present itself.

It also means that getting down is often more difficult than getting up. In some spots, you might have to down-climb in the caves that allow the route's ascent. The rappels off the longest routes are exceptionally difficult. It is best to fix ropes behind you and thus have a means to rap back to the previous station because back-clipping down the wall is often very, very difficult. In other words, this place is dangerous.

Just to add to that, *The Ninth Life* and *The Monitor* were originally done on glue-ins, but nothing else has been rebolted with titanium. As we went to press, some of the routes were being retrofitted with bolts and anchors were being adjusted here and there. For that reason, pitch length is not given here. Look for it in the next edition. It's an adventure up there. *Chok dee!*

1. SHAFT OF LIGHT   7a+ (5.10d), 100 meters, 12 quickdraws★★★★
F.A. Tom Cecil and Mark Miner, January 2001

This climb, which has a first pitch that was originally bolted as *Red-Eyed Cowboy*, has become the general access for the rest of the wall. The upper pitches of routes 1–7, 10, and 11 are all accessed via *Shaft of Light's* first pitch.

Pitch 1: Go to the left when inside the cave, not to the right. Once that's done you are at the mouth of a cave at an anchor on its left side. Climb up and left past the multiple anchors to a second anchor on the large ledge. A bolt has recently broken off this pitch.

Pitch 2: 6b+ (5.10d) This pitch leads to a ledge.

Pitch 3: 5- (5.8) Move up to a ledge and then traverse across it to the arête belay on *The Monitor*.

2. WHIPPER SNAPPER   6b+ (5.10d), 30 meters, 11 quickdraws★★★
F.A. Mark Miner and Tom Cecil, December 2000

From an anchor just above the one halfway up pitch 3 of *Shaft of Light,* this route climbs up steep and fun rock to an independent anchor.

3. RED-EYED COWBOY   6c (5.11b), 25 meters★★★
F.A. Ian Turnball and J. Beverage, February 1995

This has become the access pitch for the entire upper wall. It is possible to use the original start to *Snake, Ganga,* and *Rastaman,* which comes up left of the top-rope anchors, but that pitch is not as enjoyable and requires a bunch of traversing.

4. THE MONITOR   7a (5.11d), 100 meters,12 quickdraws★★★★

F.A. Tom Cecil and Mark Miner, December 2000

This climb follows the left side of the large stalactite system. I would really like to recommend it because the climbing is fun. However, it has way too many problems. There is a lot of rope drag, and getting down off this thing is just a nightmare. Finally, the last pitch is belayed from a hanging stance that has great exposure, but is two meters left of a perfect ledge. In my opinion, it's not a good setup. However, if you have lots of long runners and are pretty good at getting down a severely overhanging wall, the climbing is very fun.

Pitch 1: 6c (5.11b) The first pitch of this route is also the old line for *Snake, Ganga, and Rastaman*. It starts down and right of the other routes and goes up over stalactites to just below the tunnel-cave that *Shaft of Light* accesses.

Pitch 2: 5- (5.8) Move up easy ground through the tunnel-cave to a belay on the right side of the cave exit. This is spelunkers' right, but climbers' left...you are facing out when you find it.

Pitch 3: 7a (5.11d) Climb up and right onto a large stalactite and belay on a ledge. Use long slings at the start.

Pitch 4: 6b (5.10c) Climb up and right, past an alcove, and up the face. Don't trend too hard right to the rappel anchors in a cave. The end of this pitch is also the top of the traverse pitch on *Shaft of Light*. Lousy belay stance.

Pitch 5: 6a (5.10a) This pitch is shared by *Shaft of Light*.

Descent: Rappel this route to get down. It is very steep in places, so the best way to get down from the top is to trail a rope and then leave one end of it fixed at the top of pitch 3. Tow the other end up to the top and then you have two lines to get down, one of which you can use to pull yourself into the anchor. From here, the first ascentionists got down with one big 60-meter rappel. However, my 60-meter cords didn't reach, forcing us to back-clip in on the steepest descent. It was most uncomfortable.

5. Project

You might notice bolts and slings partially protecting this route. It has not been properly equipped yet, but is included on the overlay so that you do not confuse it with another route.

6. Anchors for various top ropes

These anchors are in very bad condition and are poorly linked together.

7. SNAKE, GANGA, AND RASTAMAN   6c (5.11b), 75 meters, bad bolts
and threads

F.A. Peter Lutz, Hany Lutz, and Dan Brunner, March 1994

This climb, the first on the wall, is actually wedged between *The Monitor* and *Praying Mantis* and weaves its way up both sides of the large stalactite system.

It is not shown on the overlay. The gear is old and rotten, so it's best to stick with the other routes to be safe.

8. THE NINTH LIFE   7a+ (5.12a), 7 pitches, 150 meters, 12 quick-draws and long slings★★★

F.A. Sam Lightner Jr. and about a dozen people, 2000

Don't climb the route when the generator is running. This climb might actually mark the cusp between the Cat Wall and Monitor Wall, because it is accessible from both (see the route overlay photo for Cat Wall for another view of this climb). It has some excellent climbing and some loose rock, with an interesting ending position. The route is definitely an adventure climb. The bolts are glue-ins and very solid—but not always nearby! Start near the back of the cave above the horrid generator. This is the longest climb on the Phra Nang Peninsula.

Pitch 1: 6b+ (5.11a) Requires a bit of climbing then a big traverse left under the Spear, the huge roof that juts out over the alcove.

Pitch 2: 6c+ (5.11c) Go up onto the left side of the Spear and then traverse right to the belay.

Pitch 3: 7a+ (5.12a) Steep and pumpy, this one goes more or less straight up the bulging face. There is some loose rock. A project, partially completed, is the line going up and right toward a faint arête.

Pitch 4: 6b (5.10c) This can be broken into two pitches to lessen rope drag. Or use some long slings in the appropriate spots. This pitch can be pretty dirty.

Pitch 5: 4- (5.4) A traverse through the cave.

Pitch 6: 7a (5.11d) This goes up steep ground behind a stalactite and then out onto the face. Belay on a large, comfortable ledge.

Pitch 7: 6b (5.10c) This is pretty runout 6b. Not for the faint of heart. Ends at a belay next to a dark, windy cave at the top of the wall.

Descent: To get down this one, you rappel the route. This requires some back-clipping and some down-climbing in the big cave in the middle of the wall. One 60-meter rappel will reach the ground from the top of pitch 2.

9. FORGOTTEN WALL

This wall has seldom been climbed since the first ascents and thus has had no repairs. In other words, bad gear here. The half dozen or so climbs are all 5s and easy 6s.

10. PRAYING MANTIS   7a (5.11d), 120 meters, 14 quickdraws★★★★

F.A. Drew Spalding and Thai, December 2004

This is a fun route on the right side of the stalactite system out right of the old *Snake, Ganga, and Rastaman*. To reach it you go out the right cave rather than the left cave, as you do for *Shaft of Light*. Be prepared to back-clip to get down on the steeper pitches. The climb that heads left out of the window is called *Snake Skin*. Both climbs are supposed to be excellent but have an expiration date of 2006!

Pitch 1: 6c (5.11b) Ascend the first pitch of *The Monitor.*

Pitch 2: 4- (5.6) Ascend through the tunnel to the huge Monitor Cave—at the top of the tunnel ramp, go right for about 10 meters (headlamp useful) to another part of the cave that has two huge windows.

Pitch 3: 7a (5.11d) Climb out the left side of the cave on a long, steep wall to an anchor on a ledge.

Pitch 4: 6b+ (5.10d) Continue up and right through a bulge onto lower-angle rock and belay at a small cave.

Pitch 5: 6a+ (5.10b) Climb pretty much straight up on lower-angle rock to a belay just below the vegetation.

11. SNAKE SKIN   6b (5.10c), 80 meters, 10 quickdraws★★★
F.A. Tom Cecil, Justin Day, and Brian Cornwell, December 2004

The name comes from the decoration (huge snakeskin) found by the first ascensionists in the first huge jug on the third pitch. Climb the first two pitches of *Praying Mantis* to reach the start of this route.

Pitch 3: 6b (5.10c) Climb out the right side of the cave on brown and white rock, past a large cave, to an anchor on a ledge.

Pitch 4: 5 (5.8) This is a short and easy traverse out right to an anchor on the ledge.

Pitch 5: 6b (5.10c) Climb straight up to an anchor.

Descent: To get back down, you have to down-climb pitch 4 and then rappel to the cave where *Mantis* and *Snake Skin* share an anchor.

12. THE WAVE   6b (5.10c), 100 meters, 12 quickdraws★★★★
F.A. Catherine Stedham and Tom Cecil, December 26, 2004

A fun climb, named for the obvious event.

Pitch 1: 6a+ (5.10b) Climb the beastly first pitch of *Beauty and the Beast.*

Pitch 2: 6a+ (5.10b) From the ledge, climb left on better rock to an anchor on a ledge.

Pitch 3: 6b (5.10c) Climb straight up on slightly steeper rock to an anchor.

Pitch 4: 6a+ (5.10b) Continue straight up on good rock in a corner system of sorts.

Pitch 5: 6a+ (5.10b) Climb up and to the left onto white rock and up to an anchor where the vegetation begins…an airy finish.

Descent: You can get off this route with one 60-meter rope…don't forget to tie a knot in the ends.

13. BEAUTY AND THE BEAST   6b+ (5.11a), 75 meters, 14 quickdraws★★★★
F.A. Tom Cecil, Justin Day, Brian Cornwell, Mike Ho, and Dute, November 2004

This route starts on sharp rock at the mouth of a cave about 3 meters above the road. After the first pitch, it goes right and into a large alcove that cannot be seen on the topo. However, if you can find the base and go right at the top of the first pitch, you won't get lost.

Pitch 1: 6a+ (5.10b), 30 meters, 14 quickdraws. This is the "beast" part of the route. It's quite sharp. There is a small ledge at the top of this pitch.

Pitch 2: 6a+ (5.10b), 15 meters, 8 quickdraws. The climbing is getting better. Trend up right to a belay station below the overhanging bowl of excellent rock.

Pitch 3: 6b+ (5.11a), 30 meters, 14 quickdraws. Now you're at the "beauty." Follow the line of gear on beautiful rock up the steep wall. You can lower back to the anchor with a long rope. An incomplete project extends off the top of this pitch.

Descent: You can get back down doing three rappels with a single 60-meter rope.

CAT WALL

Sun exposure: This wall faces south and thus catches morning sun. The only thing that provides minimal shade for the rock is its own steep angle, thus the stone tends to hold heat well into the afternoon.

Wall angle and difficulty: Cat Wall is steeper than it looks. When you first see it you think, because of the angle of the approaching rock, that it is gently overhanging. Once you climb on it, you realize how overhanging it is. For this reason, and because the climbs are long, this is an advanced climbing crag. Only one route under 6c+ exists here.

Hazards: Because of the intense heat that this crag gets in the morning, the bolts here take a horrid beating from the elements (remember that the breakdown process is sped up with heat). Also, be aware that it is possible to lower someone off the end of the rope because the routes are long and start from a ledge 30 meters above ground level. The multipitch climbs have the usual warnings, and here they are even more pronounced. Beginners should not learn to do multipitch climbing on a wall this steep. Finally, the routes on the right side of the wall have loose rock, so please keep in mind there are people and buildings below you.

Approach: To get to the wall, look for a trail off the Tonsai Road between various ever-evolving buildings at the north end of Tonsai Beach...it's about 80 meters in from the beach. Follow the trail, pulling on vines, ropes, and dirt, to a spot where two choices in previously hung ropes exist.

Routes 1–7 are accessed by following the trail to its end, then climbing about 10 meters up low-angle rock to a large ledge. A rope often hangs here, though it sees a lot of ultraviolet light. Routes 3–6 are best started, and belayed, from the ledge beneath the middle of the wall. It's a dusty place, but after a few pitches it will feel like home. There may be fixed ropes getting you up the slab from here. Also, it is good to clip in to a fixed rope (when available) at the base of the wall and traverse to the first bolt of your particular pitch...but don't put too much faith in an old line.

Routes 8–10 can be accessed by climbing up into a cave above and right of the trail perhaps 10 meters before its end. These routes are accessed by climbing up through the cave and out its obvious opening. Don't put too much faith into the fixed line unless someone has checked it.

The single-pitch climbs here are all classics, and if you can, you should do them. The shorter sport climbs tend to be quite steep with big holds. There still is a bit of loose rock, especially on the higher routes, so be careful near the base.

1. THE CAT AND THE COBRA   6b (5.10c), 20 meters, 7 quickdraws★★★★
F.A. Shamick Byszewski and Mary Lee, March 1997

The best place to belay this is on a smaller ledge up and left of the main ledge. Be careful getting there.

2. KITTY PORN   7c+ (5.13a), 95 meters, 17 quickdraws★★★★★
F.A. Sam Lightner Jr. and Volker Schoeffl, February 2000

This climb, one of the better "hard" multipitches in Thailand, starts just right of the obvious big tufa and stalactite system on the left side of the wall. The two upper pitches of this route are stellar. The first is a bit dirty.

Pitch 1: 7b+ (5.12c), 25 meters, 8 quickdraws. From the left end of the ledge, climb up through powerful moves to a ledge on the obvious large stalactite.

Pitch 2: 7c+ (5.13a), 30 meters, 12 quickdraws. Continue up, then go slightly left above the steepest part of the wall.

Pitch 3: 7b (5.12b), 40 meters, 17 quickdraws. Straight up the arête to a hanging belay at the very top of the wall.

Descent: Rappelling off it can be done in two raps with two 60-meter ropes, but it puts you pretty far out from the wall. Best is to do it in three raps by back-clipping your way down the second pitch.

3. APRIL FOOLS   7b (5.12b), 30 meters, 10 quickdraws★★★★★
F.A. Shamick Byszewski and Richard Prohaska, April 1996
Retrobolted: February 1998

This climb starts just right of *Kitty Porn*. Like the rest of these, start from the ledge and climb the slab to the base of the business. Make sure you tie a knot in the end of the rope before lowering someone. An excellent climb.

4. GILLESNOLIMITS   7c (5.12d), 30 meters, 12 quickdraws★★★★★
F.A. Steve Amstutz and Joel Burli, February 2000

Another great one; 4.5 meters right of *April Fools*.

5. BLACK CAT 7c (5.12d), 45 meters, 12 quickdraws★★★★★

F.A. Shamick Byszewski and Richard Prohaska, April 1996

Retrobolted: February 1998

Pitch 1: 7a (5.11d), 30 meters, 12 quickdraws. This climbs the corner and then left onto the face at the right side of the wall.

Pitch 2: 7c (5.12c), 15 meters, 8 quickdraws.

6. KING CAT   **6c+ (5.11c), 25 meters, 10 quickdraws★★★★★**
F.A. Shamick Byszewski and Richard Prohaska, April 1996
Retrobolted: February 1998

This climb goes out the crazy-steep bulge right of *Black Cat*. Put a long sling on the first bolt (shared by *Black Cat*) to lower drag.

7. HEART OF DARKNESS   **7a (5.11d), 110 meters, 15 quickdraws★★★★★**
F.A. Shamick Byszewski and company, March 2000.

This climb goes straight up on very exposed ground. Beautiful climbing. Be careful on sharper rock up high and be prepared to be above your bolts! Hanging finish. Make sure you know how to back-clip: getting down is the crux. The route was bolted with more anchors than necessary for the ascent. This can make getting down easier if you don't like back-clipping full pitches.

Pitch 1: 7a (5.11d), 25 meters, 10 quickdraws. Start from a small alcove just below the main ledge for the preceding routes. Stay right of *King Cat*.

Pitch 2: 6c (5.11b), 15 meters, 8 quickdraws. Climb up and right to an anchor shared by *Road to Damascus*.

Pitch 3: 6c (5.11b), 15 meters, 9 quickdraws.

Pitch 4: 6c+ (5.11c), 20 meters, 9 quickdraws. Continue on and thread the eye of the needle!

Pitch 5: 7a (5.11d), 35 meters, 15 quickdraws.

Descent: This route must be back-clipped to be rappelled, and you must rethread the needle on pitch 4. It is possible to do it in three big raps, though the steepness makes it hard to get back onto the ledges.

8. ROAD TO DAMASCUS   **7b+ (5.12c), 32 meters, 12 quickdraws★★★★★**
F.A. Richard Prohaska and Shamick Byszewski, April 1996
Retrobolted: February 1998

This climb starts right as you exit the cave...kind of a spectacular spot. Lowering off this line can kill you, because the start is 30 meters off the deck. Make sure you are ready to rappel or have an extralong rope.

9. HOT TIN ROOF   **7b (5.12b), 15 meters, 7 quickdraws★★★**
F.A. Sam Lightner Jr. and Elaine Catlin, January 2000

It is easiest to belay this route from the alcove 10 meters above the cave mouth (start of route 8). Two bolts on route 10 will get you there semisafely. You can rappel off from the obvious superthread anchor at the back of the alcove. The route is a bit loose but will clean up in time. The angle is to die for. This could be called a poor man's *Tidal Wave*.

10. MUSONG   **7a (5.11d), 100 meters, 15 quickdraws★★★★**
F.A. Sam Lightner Jr. and Scott Morely, January 1998

Rappelling this route is difficult. This is the problem with overhanging multipitch climbs, and it really makes you realize what a gift *Lord of the Thais* is! Do not be fooled by the grade. If I had to rate by the rappels, I'd call it 7c. By the way, *Musong* means "civet cat" in Thai.

Pitch 1: 6a (5.10a), 20 meters, 3 quickdraws. Starting from the cave opening (*Road to Damascus's* start), climb up and to the far right side of the alcove to a set of glue-in anchors. Be sure to clip in to the thread anchor to protect your second in the traverse.

Pitch 2: 7a (5.11d), 25 meters, 10 quickdraws. Go up and right through the bulge, then up the brown face. Some loose rock can be found at the top of this pitch.

Pitch 3: 6b+ (5.10d), 35 meters, 15 quickdraws. Climb up and across flaky rock to the tufa, then up it and out the bulge above. You will encounter loose rock on the first half of this pitch and it is directly above the trail. Be careful.

Pitch 4: 7a (5.11d), 30 meters, 15 quickdraws. Climb left out of the cave and up the steep face, then through "the womb." When you have "birthed," you can belay on an anchor or you can go for another 10 meters with rope drag (not recommended).

Pitch 5: 6b+ (5.11a), 10 meters, 5 quickdraws. This is an optional pitch if you decide to stop pitch 4 at the end of the womb. One bolt that is out of line is a bit of a pain. The huge cave at the top, which looks small from the beach, has some great views.

Descent: From the top, you must do a short rappel to the top of the womb. Rap the womb, back-clipping every bolt. It's a team effort to get the second down. If you don't back-clip every bolt, you will not make it back to the top of pitch 3. Cleaning it is harder, so the stronger climber should go second on the rappel and should be helped "in" by the first, who will be waiting at the pitch 3 anchor. Rapping pitch 3 to pitch 2 needs at least a couple back-clipped bolts. From pitch 2 you can get to the ground with a 60-meter rope, or you can just go to pitch 1 and rap from there.

11. THE NINTH LIFE

This is route 8 on the Monitor Wall, also shown here for additional perspective.

FIRE WALL

Sun exposure: Like everything else on this side of the bay, this wall faces southeast and thus catches morning sun. As the rainy season approaches, it sees more shade.

Wall angle and difficulty: Fire Wall comes at you from all angles...and all difficulties. On the lower right side it is vertical, but the middle of the wall and upper left have some very steep routes.

FIRE WALL, RIGHT

Hazards: The bolts here take a horrid beating from the elements.

Approach: To find this wall go to the end of the beach, then proceed up one of two trails. To reach route 16, directly from the end of the beach, take a trail that goes up over some rocks to the base of *Groove Tube*. To reach routes 7–13, behind some large, oddly eroded boulders in the bay, perhaps 15 meters from the main beach, take another trail that comes up to the large cave in the middle of the wall. These access trails are the same ones used to reach the Melting Wall.

Descent: A number of the routes are longer than 30 meters, thus necessitating a rappel. People have been seriously injured here when lowering off climbs that were more than 30 meters in length.

At the north end of Tonsai Beach are three major walls. The rightmost is the Cat Wall; the left one with the really long stalactites is the Melting Wall. In the middle, with dark red stone running through its center, is the aptly named Fire Wall.

1. THE GROOVE TUBE   6a (5.10a), 35 meters, 12 quickdraws★★★★★
F.A. Ray Bernard, March 1995

This is a Railay classic. Find the obvious half pipe running up the rock about 9 meters up the right side of the wall.

Climb to the half pipe and then up to an anchor on a small ledge.

Optional pitch: (6b/5.10c, 10 meters, 8 quickdraws). A second pitch was added by Shamick Byszewski. This pitch puts you well out of range for reaching the ground with a single rope, so take two. *Do not lower from the second anchor with a 60-meter rope.*

2. THE BOOB TUBE   6b (5.10c), 30 meters, 12 quickdraws★★★
F.A. Shamick Byszewski and a pair of friends, April 1999

This starts a couple meters left of *The Groove Tube* on tufas and stalactites. You need a 60-meter rope to safely reach the ground.

3. FOR HAIGA   6a (5.10a), 30 meters, 12 quickdraws★★★
F.A. Shamick Byszewski and Heidi, April 1999

This begins a couple meters left of *The Boob Tube* and goes to a nearby anchor. You need a 60-meter rope to safely reach the ground.

Optional pitch: (7a/5.11d). A second pitch (7 meters) goes out the orange bulge that hangs over all these routes.

4. WHITE HOT HERNIAS   6b+ (5.10d), 16 meters, 7 quickdraws★★★
F.A. Gavin Punnell and Sharyn George, date unknown

This climbs the tufas just around the corner from *For Haiga*. It shares an anchor with *Fire Starter*.

5. FIRE STARTER   6c+ (5.11c), 16 meters, 8 quickdraws★★★★
F.A. Ray Bernard and Trevor Hobbs, January 1996
   Starts up the face left of the corner and works right and up. Fun and powerful.

6. FIRE SHOW   6c+ (5.11c), 16 meters, 10 quickdraws★★★
F.A. Drew Spalding and Julie Petersen, April 2001
   Climbs the face 3 meters left of *Fire Starter*.

7. FLAME THROWER   7b+ (5.12c), 27 meters, 8 quickdraws
F.A. Alex Catlin and Sam Lightner Jr., January 1997
   This route is accessed by climbing onto a loose ledge to the right of the cave.
The bolts have all but fallen from the wall, so it should not be climbed until
they are replaced. It is not shown on the overlay.

8. PLAYING WITH FIRE   7c (5.12d), 35 meters, 9 quickdraws★★★★★
F.A. Greg Collum and Trevor Massiah, February 1995
Retrobolted: 2000
   Pitch 1: 6b (5.10c), 20 meters, 8 quickdraws. This pitch traverses from the
mouth of the *Burnt Offerings* cave to below the center of the wall. It's not that
much fun, but it must be done to reach the goods on pitch 2.
   Pitch 2: 7c (5.12d), 15 meters, 8 quickdraws. This pitch proceeds straight
up from the belay.

9. BURNT OFFERINGS   7a+ (5.12a), 13 meters, 8 quickdraws★★★★
F.A. Greg Collum and Trevor Massiah, February 1995
   This route goes out the jugs from the back of the cave to an anchor above and
on the right. It is considered a classic by many, but it has a fair bit of loose rock
in one section. **An extension** (8a+/5.13c) of it done by Alex Catlin adds another
15 meters of good climbing. If you do this, it requires a 30-meter rope.

10. CHICKEN SKIN   7b+ (5.12c), 40 meters, 16 quickdraws★★
F.A. Greg Collum and Larissa Collum, January 1996
   About 12 meters left of the cave is a smooth bit of wall with just enough
holds to get you up to a traversing fracture in the rock. You need two ropes
to get down.

11. TUNA MUSCLE   6b (5.10c), 35 meters, 12 quickdraws★★★
F.A. Greg Collum and Larissa Collum, January 1996
   This route gets you really far off the ground in a big hurry. It is a neat exposure but is way overdue for new bolts. Start it from the tree just up and around
from *Chicken Skin*. You must have two ropes to reach the ground when doing
this climb. The anchors could be bad.

(MORE) FIRE WALL, RIGHT

12. TUNA MELT   **7a+ (5.12a), 25 meters, 12 quickdraws★★★★**
F.A. Greg Collum and Larissa Collum, January 1996
    A great climb. It shares a start with *Tuna Muscle*.
    Tuna Melt-Down variation: (7b+/5.12b). Another start to *Tuna Melt* goes
slightly left, then regains the main route with a very hard move after a few
bolts.

13. BURN OUT   **25 meters, balls**
F.A. Greg Collum and Trevor Massiah, February 1995
    I note this "route" so that when you see some ancient relic of a bolt out
on the wall, you know *not* to go there. This pitch is only there as a means of
accessing the *Playing with Fire* anchors.

SHADOW CLEFT

If you enjoy boring movement on razor-sharp rock with poorly placed gear,
plus lots of pulling on bushes, swatting mosquitoes, and a general setup that
cries out for an accident, then this is your crag. And if that's what you want,
then you should go buy one of the other guidebooks, because this one does
not cover such *kee*!
    Shadow Cleft is in the cirque between Fire Wall and Melting Wall. Most of
the dozen or so routes range between grade 4 and 6a, with one, which we used
for years to access the top of the Melting Wall (but never reported because it was
just too nasty), a 6b. With all the beautiful crags on the Phra Nang Peninsula,
it might be best just to skip this place.

MELTING WALL

Sun exposure: This wall, like the Fire Wall, faces south, but it gets shade a bit
earlier due to its overhanging nature and the number of giant stalactites that
shroud it. Unfortunately, those same features block any breeze, so it can be a
bit like a sauna even an hour after the sun has moved on.
    Wall angle and difficulty: The routes here are slightly overhanging to very
steep, depending on the grade. There are some lower grade 6s, but most of the
routes are 7a or harder.
    Hazards: The usual bolt problems are pandemic here, and one route, the
Climb of the Ancient Mariner, is destined to kill someone (see below). We have
recently been able to retrobolt *S.O.S.,* which should make it a much safer climb.
We have hopes of getting to *Ancient Mariner* soon as well, but until then, take
care! One thing to note about this crag is that it gets very bad airflow. No one
comes here without sweating like Nixon, so prepare yourself. Also, bug dope
is helpful.
    Approach: Proceed along the trail past the Fire Wall, through a short bit of
jungle, and through a cave with some nice formations (known as the Smoking

Room). Very suddenly you are at the Melting Wall and the base of routes 1–7. Climbs 8–9 are on the left end of the Melting Wall. You access them by climbing up to the ledge on *Cross-Eyed* (route 7) and then traversing out the ramp to where the routes turn up the face

This cliff is limited in scope but home to one of the world's best single pitches of climbing: *Cross-Eyed.*

1. SMOKING ROOM   6c (5.11b), 20 meters, 9 quickdraws★★★★
F.A. Mark Miner and Tom Cecil, January 1996
Retrobolted: February 1998
    Start this climb from the ledge outside the upper exit in the Smoking Room Cave.

2. *BON SOIR*   7a+(5.12a), 14 meters, 5 quickdraws★★★★
F.A. Sam Lightner Jr. and Greg Collum, January 1996
    This climb starts just outside the Smoking Room Cave and proceeds up a steep line of tufas to the left of *Smoking Room.*

3. RIGHT HAND OF BUDDHA   6b (5.10c), 14 meters, 5 quickdraws★★★
F.A. Greg Collum and Tom Cecil, January 1996
Retrobolted: December 1997
    This is the rightmost route on the Buddha Buttress, the large column of flowstone that forms the prow of the wall here.
    A couple of extensions go off from above this, both put in by Ray Bernard. The left one, 6b, is fairly short. The one going right is ungraded, because it is an open project (route 10). The bolts are quite old up here and neither route is recommended.

4. CAPTAIN HOOK   6b (5.10c), 14 meters, 6 quickdraws★★★
F.A. Tom Cecil and Chris Carr, January 1996
Retrobolted: December 1997
    Goes up the center of the Buddha Buttress.

5. CLIMB OF THE ANCIENT MARINER   6a (5.10a) (7a/5.11d if you do
                                         the upper half) 14 (30) meters,
                                         6 quickdraws★★★
F.A. Chris Carr and Tom Cecil, January 1996
    This route, in my opinion, is fun but very dangerous. A long, thin, often-swaying stalactite hangs down behind it and is tempting to stem to. If it breaks, you will fall and yank the belayer into the crash zone. The belayer will certainly be killed. I propose that the upper half, which becomes 7a, should not be done, and instead you should lower from the anchor at the top of the Buddha Buttress.

MELTING WALL

Shadow
Cleft

6. AFFENHITZE   **7b (5.12b), 30 meters, 12 quickdraws★★★**

F.A. Mark Hoffman and M. Huber, February 1997

This route starts on *Cross-Eyed* and traverses over the upper part of the *Climb of the Ancient Mariner* (everyone wants a piece of this brilliant wall, even if it is crowding the other lines). If you don't do the upper parts of *Mariner*, which you shouldn't (see above), then this makes an alternative to get on that bit of wall. One thing: The bolts here look like glue-ins, but they are not. They are actually quite weak, so I wouldn't put a lot of faith in them.

7. CROSS-EYED   **7b (5.12b), 30 meters, 13 quickdraws★★★★★**

F.A. Greg Collum and Chris Carr, January 1996

Retrobolted: December 1997, July 2005

There is a God, and, obviously, he climbs. Access this climb at the left side of the Buddha Buttress. Climb up the easy ground to the cave-ledge, then up a column and onto the clean wall. (Route 6 breaks out right at the top of this column.) A 60-meter rope will lower you, with some care, onto a ledge out left of the wall. Tie a knot in the rope to make sure.

Doctor, My Moot Hurts variation: (6b/5.10c). It is possible, if you are so inclined, to continue up the wall from the *Cross-Eyed* anchor on tufas, bushes, and snakeskins. *Doctor, My Moot Hurts* provides access to *Cockroach Beach's* high anchor (established by Sam and Volker). I don't recommend it, because there is no fixed protection and limited natural gear.

8. COCKROACH BEACH   **6c+ (5.11c), 66 meters, 14 quickdraws ★★★★★**

F.A. Sam Lightner Jr., Volker Schoeffl, and Gerd Schoeffl, February 1996

Retrobolted: June 2005

Pitch 1: 6c (5.11b), 25 meters, 8 quickdraws. The original line climbed up to just before the "business" of *Cross-Eyed* begins, then traversed left for approximately 15 meters to a stance belay. This was 6a, about 20 meters long, and required 8 quickdraws. The better and newer option, put in during the rebolting of 2005, goes up from directly below the route. To access it, go to the Melting Wall via Fire Wall approach and then descend down, or climb up to Cobra Wall, and then traverse along the wall to the right until you are under the route. This first pitch is a bit reachy.

Pitch 2: 6c+ (5.11c), 26 meters, 14 quickdraws. Proceed straight up and over the bulge to a comfortable ledge.

Pitch 3: 6b+ (5.11a), 20 meters, 10 quickdraws. Continue straight up, stemming and pulling, until a small cave is found. It's easiest for the leader to lower back down to the belay and then allow the second to top-rope it.

Descent: This route requires two ropes to rappel and you must back-climb the traverse (if you do it the original way).

9. S.O.S.   **7a+ (5.12a), 70 meters, 16 quickdraws★★★★★**
F.A. Sam Lightner Jr., Volker Schoeffl, and Gerd Schoeffl, February 1996
Retrobolted: June 2005

This route has recently been rebolted and, in the process slightly altered (for the better). It is now done as the final pitch of *Cockroach Beach*, going up and left from the 3rd pitch's belay point. The original route climbed on some dubious rock, left of *Cockroach Beach*, before getting to the goods. Its new incarnation is much better, though it's now only a single final pitch alternative.

Pitch 1: Same as *Cockroach Beach*.

Pitch 2: Same as *Cockroach Beach*.

Pitch 3: 7a+ (5.12a), 25 meters, 10 quickdraws. From the belay ledge, move up and left onto the pretty, clean face.

10. PROJECT

See variation to *Right Hand of Buddha*.

11. THE NORTHERN BIRD   **6a (5.9), 20 meters, 7 quickdraws★★★**
F.A. Nuu, Sam Lightner Jr., and Louise Whitehead, June 2005

This fun little climb starts below and left of the main Melting Wall crag. You can reach it either from the main wall by climbing down and finding the trail, or by walking up along the wall from Cobra Wall. The anchor is a very large tree growing from the wall.

COBRA WALL

Sun exposure: Like all the other walls over here, this one is in the sun in the morning and shade in the afternoon. It faces a bit more east than the rest, though, so it might get shade just a little earlier.

Wall angle and difficulty: These are easy to moderate climbs on a wall that is just beyond vertical, with two routes on the Cobra's Hood.

Hazards: The hardware takes a beating, so all of the protection is suspect. Also, watch for loose rock in spots.

Approach: Access to them is limited to when the tide is a little low, unless you don't mind wading. You climb up to the base from the reef about 24 meters right of where the climbs actually ascend the wall.

These climbs are new and quite popular.

1. MAE BIA   **7b (5.12b), 25 meters, 12 quickdraws★★★★**
F.A. Sam Lightner Jr., Wee Changrua, and Michelle Garbert, November 2004

Long, but still a boulderer's delight because its one really hard move takes it from 7a to 7b. Access this one by going to the end of the ledge past *Cobra Head,* then up a couple meters and out an exposed ledge to a bolt belay. The

Dangerously close to a crab-eating macaque

A Dusky langur on the Phra Nang Peninsula

Though it rarely bites, the yellow-lipped sea snake is perhaps the most poisonous snake on Earth.

A long-nosed whip snake looking for a damp warm place to loll away the afternoon. Don't forget to shake your shoes before you slip them on! (Volker Schoeffl)

A large water monitor searches through a pile of leaves for a bite to eat.

A sign of the times: a long-tail boat's anchor line that is U.I.A.A. certified!

The classic Caveman *(7a), on the Thaiwand.* (Bobby Model)

High over Railay Bay, this is Pitch 5 of Lord of the Thais *(7b), one of the best multi-pitch routes you will ever do.* (Bobby Model)

Melanie Schoeffl on Stalagasauras *(6c+), at Tonsai.* (Dr. Volker Schoeffl)

Following page: Hot Tin Roof *at the Cat Wall, one of the steeper 7b's on the peninsula.* (Bobby Model)

A quiet morning on one of the streets of Phi Phi Town before the tsunami

Previous page: The unique Groove Tube *(6a), on the Fire Wall.* (Jim Gudjonson)

A quiet morning on one of the streets of Phi Phi Town a few days after the tsunami

Volker Schoeffl doing the second ascent of Orange Tears *(7a+) at Muai Thai* (Frank Dicker)

Lisa McKay climbing the beautiful Mai Pen Rai *(6a+) in the Defile, Phra Nang Beach* (Joe McKay)

Michelle Garbert on the 3rd pitch of Rev De Phi-Phi-Dom *(7b) on Tonsai Tower*

Chris McNamara on the summit of the Oyster Blade with Tonsai Bay and Phi Phi Don in the background

Meghanne Reburn focused on Humanality *(6b+) above the bar at Tonsai.* (Joe McKay)

The beautiful climb, Emerald Blue *(7c+) on Koh Tabon in Trang Province.* (Bobby Model)

Opposite: The route 007, *a 7a+ above the marine village of Koh Panyi in Pha Nga Bay.* (Somporn Suebhait (King))

Wat Chedi Luang at Sunset, Chiang Mai, Thailand

Seeing the sights, like the Golden Buddha in Wat Phan Tao, is what takes most of us to Thailand.

"One banana for mom, and one for baby.... Get me more bananas, quick!" The elephant sanctuary 90 minutes south of Chaing Mai

Pulling hard out of a **Barrel Roll** *(8a) at Tham Nam Them near Vang Vieng, Laos*

The Thaiwand from Railay Beach at Sunset

COBRA WALL

name means "cobra hood." A somewhat easier variation to this was established as this book went to press. It goes left where *Mae Bia* comes back right (at the hard move).

2. COBRA HEAD   6a+ (5.10b), 20 meters, 8 quickdraws★★★
F.A. Wee Changrua, January 2001
This is the leftmost of the routes on the lower ledge. It climbs the tufas and blocks just a couple meters left of *Snake Whiskey*.

3. SNAKE WHISKEY   6a (5.10a), 22 meters, 8 quickdraws★★★★
F.A. Wee Changrua, January 2001
This climbs up the center of the little buttress on fairly solid stone about a meter right of *Cobra Head*.

4. SOMETHING SNAKE   6a+ (5.10b), 22 meters, 9 quickdraws★★★★
F.A. Wee Changrua, January 2001
Starts on the prominent bit of rock between *Baby Snake* and *Snake Whiskey*. More steep rock with big holds.

5. BABY SNAKE   7a (5.11d), 22 meters, 9 quickdraws★★★★
F.A. Wee Changrua, January 2001
This climb starts about 3 meters right of *Snake Whiskey* and goes out a dirty roof to a red face. There is a powerful move at the lip, so the belayer needs to be ready for a fall down low.

6. OLD SNAKE   6b (5.10b), 22 meters, 8 quickdraws★★★
F.A. Wee Changrua, March 2002
The lowest sling on this can be seen 5 meters right of *Baby Snake,* but the best start is from inside the cave next to *Super Snake*.

7. SUPER SNAKE   6b+ (5.11a), 25 meters, 10 quickdraws★★★★★
F.A. Wee Changrua and friends, August 2004
An excellent climb that looks like it should be much more difficult, this goes out the right side of the cave through some very steep terrain.

EAGLE WALL
Sun exposure: This wall faces southeast, so in the dry season it sees sun all morning. The closer you get to the rainy season, the more shade you get. Afternoons are always nice.

Wall angle and difficulty: For the most part, this is a gently overhanging wall. There is one steep 8a+ here, but most of the routes are 7b and below on slightly overhanging ground.

Hazards: There has been at least one very serious accident due to rockfall at the far left end of the wall. Also, being southeast-facing means it gets lots of heat, thus speeding up the harmful chemical reactions on the bolts. Bring lots of bug repellent.

Approach: The Eagle Wall, located between the beach and the eagle's nest, is reached by first getting to the beach. To do that, you can either go by boat when the tide is high or walk when the tide is low. Keep in mind that getting out of here at dusk with a high tide can be difficult. From the beach, follow the trail back through the forest to the right end of the wall. Climbs 1–16 start from the right, where the trail ascends to the wall. Farther along the wall near a large dihedral are routes 17–20. There has been some very serious rockfall here, so be careful. Climbing these routes might have led to the eagles' departure, so I have never bothered with them. It was bad karma for the things to go in at all.

At the far north end of Railay Bay, just before the cape you have to pass to go to Ao Nang, is a large gray wall split by a dark cleft. In the cleft stands a huge tree, and near the very top of that tree one can see a Mir-size clump of branches, leaves, fish bones, twine, and broken eggs. This is the former home of Railay's resident sea eagles, and it was theirs for as many years as I can remember. Down and to the right of this wall is a small swath of tan sand known to many locals as Ruth's Beach (see sidebar "The Swiss Miss"). This beautiful place, backed by jungle and settled betwixt folds in the cliff, is the access point to the wall named after its most notable former residents. The eagles have flown the coop, perhaps because of the overdevelopment of the place, perhaps because they just got old, or perhaps because climbers got too close. I only hope it wasn't because of the latter.

East Wall

1. THE ANNIHILATOR   6c (5.11b), 22 meters, 8 quickdraws★
F.A. Cecil and Todd Offenbacher, December 1998
This climb starts out right of where the trail ascends. It's a bit hard to get to and not really worth the effort. Also, the bolts are bad.

2. SPEAKING OUT LOUD   6b+ (5.11a), 30 meters, 13 quickdraws★★★★
F.A. Tom Cecil and R. D. Smith, December 1998
This route name sounds like a Bushism! The climb starts from a cleft between the obvious big, flat boulder and the wall. It is best to anchor the belayer to the large tree so that he or she isn't pulled out right and below these routes. Climb out and right to a dihedral, then up to an anchor in a cave. You must have a 60-meter rope to lower from this.

THE SWISS MISS

Years ago...Dick and friends were doing their thing, thrashing through the jungle in hopes they would find a cave or a snake or a big bunch of ants or whatever it is one looks for in the jungle. Dick's nephew found the day's prize. Behind a few ferns and under an elephant ear palm, he found a Swiss girl.

Yes, you read that correctly: a Swiss girl. Now on a remote beach in southern Thailand, with limited access and rarely a visitor, a Swiss girl is quite a find. No doubt many of you reading this have gone looking for Swiss girls since you got here and have come up short. Finding one in the jungle, with no *Yaa Baa* ("crazy drug," an amphetamine) or whiskey as an aid, and in the middle of the day, is very good fortune.

She was cowering, covered in bug bites and dirt, and looking fairly healthy if not a bit out of place. According to hearsay, she was "a bit out of it." They took her home and did the obvious: they gave her a shower. She cleaned up nicely but seemed even more out of it. Lots of crying. Lots of complaining about armies of bugbears chasing her on top of the water, or something like that.

Anyway, they got her name, Ruth, and found out she was Swiss. A quick phone call proved the Swiss Embassy, being Swiss and thus nothing if not thorough, knew of her. She had apparently run away from a hospital for the mentally troubled and had somehow afforded a ticket on Swissair to Thailand (only the insane *from Switzerland* can afford this). She then made her way to Phra Nang, where she stopped taking her medication and promptly noticed an army of bugbears was chasing her. She hid in the jungle behind what's now known as Ruth's Beach...pretty much at the base of the Eagle Wall. Monuments to her were constructed by visiting climbers.

---

3. SEA MONKEYS   6b+ (5.11a), 30 meters, 12 quickdraws★★★★★
F.A. Tom Cecil and R. D. Smith, December 1998

Start this one on the ramp left of *Speaking Out Loud*. Anchor your belayer. Climb up and right, then straight up the middle of the wall to an anchor that is shared with *Speaking Out Loud*. It's an excellent, pumpy climb.

4. FOUR-TWENTY   6a (5.10a), 15 meters, 6 quickdraws★★★
F.A. Mark Miner, Todd Offenbacher, and Tom Cecil, December 1998

Same starting moves as *Sea Monkeys,* then go left on easier ground.

Afterburner variation: (7a/5.11d). An extension goes up another 10 meters.

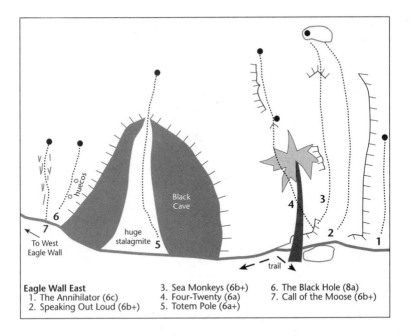

Eagle Wall East
1. The Annihilator (6c)
2. Speaking Out Loud (6b+)
3. Sea Monkeys (6b+)
4. Four-Twenty (6a)
5. Totem Pole (6a+)
6. The Black Hole (8a)
7. Call of the Moose (6b+)

---

5. TOTEM POLE　　　　6a+ (5.10b), 25 meters, 6 quickdraws★★★

F.A. Paul Turecki and Kristen Kremer, December 1998

This route, which looks like a WI 6 ice climb, ascends on threads up the fanglike pillar in front of the large cave. It is a bit dirty and, like an ice climb, a little run out.

West Wall

6. THE BLACK HOLE　　　8a (5.13b), 12 meters, 4 quickdraws★★

F.A. Kevin Swift and Elviv Rund, February 1999

A difficult boulder problem of a climb 6 meters left of the *Totem Pole* and the cave.

7. CALL OF THE MOOSE　　6b+ (5.11a), 15 meters, 7 quickdraws★★★

F.A. Kevin Swift and Elviv Rund, February 1999

This climb goes up the crack and broken tufas 7.5 meters left of *The Black Hole*.

8. MENTALLY DERANGED AND HIDING　　　6c (5.11b), 17 meters,
8 quickdraws★★

F.A. Paul Turecki and Kristen Kremer, December 1998

This climb starts in a chimney 3 meters left of *Call of the Moose*. See the sidebar "The Swiss Miss" for an explanation of the route name.

9. YAA BAA   7a+ (5.12a), 15 meters, 6 quickdraws★★★
F.A. Mathais Skafar and Sam Lightner Jr., March 1999

Powerful start just 2.5 meters left of *Mentally Deranged and Hiding.* Clipping the second bolt can be a bit spicy. The name translates to "crazy drug," an amphetamine known to make people who regularly use it lose touch with reality. *Yaa Baa* was a very popular mixer for party-punch at a number of the bars.

10. 5D MAK MAK   6c (5.11b), 12 meters, 6 quickdraws★★
F.A. Wee Changrua and Him, December 1998

Look for a line of bolts that go over a small roof left of *Yaa Baa.* It's a little sharp.

11. SANG TIP   7b+ (5.12c), 14, meters, 5 quickdraws★★★
F.A. Paul Turecki and Kristen Kremer, December 1998

This is another powerful route with bad feet at the start. It's just left of *5D Mak Mak.*

12. AMAZING THAILAND   7a (5.11d), 25 meters, 9 quickdraws★★★★★
F.A. Todd Offenbacher and Tom Cecil, December 1998

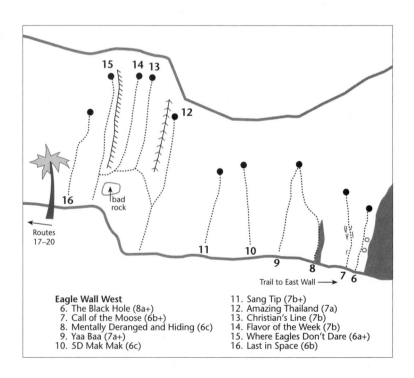

Eagle Wall West
  6. The Black Hole (8a+)
  7. Call of the Moose (6b+)
  8. Mentally Deranged and Hiding (6c)
  9. Yaa Baa (7a+)
 10. 5D Mak Mak (6c)

11. Sang Tip (7b+)
12. Amazing Thailand (7a)
13. Christian's Line (7b)
14. Flavor of the Week (7b)
15. Where Eagles Don't Dare (6a+)
16. Last in Space (6b)

This climb starts with a face and then goes up an obvious arête about 9 meters off the ground. The start is about 18 meters left of *Call of the Moose* and 6 meters right of *Flavor of the Week*, but it is easy to find if you just look for the arête. It's an excellent climb.

13. CHRISTIAN'S LINE   7b (5.12b), 28 meters, 10 quickdraws★★★
F.A. Christian Nuemeyer, January 2000

This face is climbed by doing the first third of *Amazing Thailand* and then traversing a few moves left and straight up the face. It's a bit of a squeeze. It can also be reached, with a bit more drag, from *Flavor of the Week*.

14. FLAVOR OF THE WEEK   7b (5.12b), 28 meters, 9 quickdraws★★★★★
F.A. Sam Lightner Jr. and Mathais Skafar, February 1999

This fun and technical climb starts with the slab moves of *Where Eagles Don't Dare* and then moves out right onto the face. A 60-meter rope is needed to lower from the anchor.

15. WHERE EAGLES DON'T DARE   6a+ (5.10c), 30 meters,
                                      10 quickdraws★★★★
F.A. Todd Offenbacher and Mark Miller, December 1998

This goes up the faint but large dihedral higher up the wall. It starts on low-angle rock 6 meters right of the big tree. It's a good climb, but the rock up high is not the most solid. Be leery while belaying, and warn others.

16. LAST IN SPACE   6b (5.10c), 20 meters, 7 quickdraws★★★
F.A. Wee Changrua, December 1998

This climbs the face to the left of *Where Eagles Don't Dare*. Rumors of a couple routes to the left, both being in the 6a range, seem greatly exaggerated... it's a jungle out there.

17. MADE IN SPAIN   6b+ (5.11a), 32 meters★
F.A. Laurent Sarthe and Rosa Alnakez, December 1998

18. SPIDERMAN   6b (5.10c), 32 meters★
F.A. Laurent Sarthe and Rosa Alnakez, December 1998

19. DESAYUNO DE MONO   6a (5.10a), 31 meters★
F.A. Laurent Sarthe and Rosa Alnakez, December 1998

20. ALTA RUTA   6a+ (5.10b), 20 meters★
F.A. Laurent Sarthe and Rosa Alnakez, December 1998
The name means "High Route."

THE POINT

It is impossible for a climber to miss the sharp, double overhung arête that juts out over the water at the northwest end of Railay Bay. Sadly, this obvious climbing crag is never given much shade. The south-facing routes, those you can see from Tonsai and Railay Beaches, are in the sun until late afternoon; the west-facing routes go into the sun in late morning. In the rainy season, this wall is in the shade, but the waves keep the boatmen from taking anyone ashore. All of these conditions have made it so that this would-be climbing crag is seeing very little, if any, climbing. That which has been done has not been reported to me as anything other than "we tried to make it go, but it was just too hot." The threads and bolts that are there are in disrepair and do not add up to a completed route.

AO NANG TOWER

Sun exposure: Ao Nang Tower goes into the sun in early afternoon. You will be climbing in the morning when there is shade, but you can still get a lot of glare off the water, and it's not uncommon to get stuck on the wall well into the blazing afternoon.

Wall angle and difficulty: The routes here are mostly vertical, with a few powerful bulge moves.

Hazards: Bad bolts, of course. Make sure you bring sunscreen for these climbs.

Approach: Getting here (and away) is not difficult, but it requires a boatman who is willing to bring his boat close to the wall. In the rainy season this is almost impossible, so don't expect much help. In the dry season you should be able to get a boat for whatever the half-day price is at the time (it fluctuates). It's best to get the boatman to stick around instead of taking off, unless you are sure he will come back. Also, if you have an accident, you will need him to get you out of there. Flagging down one of the passing boats is often harder than it would seem.

Halfway between Railay Beach and the hamlet of Ao Nang, a solitary tower stands out of the water. The Ao Nang Tower is that lone spire in a sea of sapphire water that you dreamed of when you left home, and it has a couple of fine routes. It has its downside, too (see below), but the climbing on the island's west face is quite good.

1. ORANGE CHANDELIERS   6c (5.11b), 75 meters, 12 quickdraws★★★★★
F.A. Will Hair, Dean Saydom, Paul Brunner, and Trevor Massiah, February 1994–98
Retrobolted: January 2000
   Pitch 1: 6b (5.10c), 32 meters, 11 quickdraws. The first pitch on the spire was established by Will and Dean. Getting out of the boat is the first crux. It's best to get the boat in close, let one climber off who ties in to the rope, then

AO NANG TOWER

pull the boat away and belay that person to the start of the anchor roughly 10 meters left of the point you climb onto the wall (the start of *Ao Nang, Ao Nang*). Pull the boat in again and get the second belayed up. The pitch itself is pretty straightforward.

Pitch 2: 6b+ (5.10d), 18 meters, 8 quickdraws. Go up and over the bulge. Excellent climbing and severe exposure. The upper two pitches were put in by Trevor and Paul.

Pitch 3: 6c (5.11b), 25 meters, 12 quickdraws. Continue on with some sustained climbing to a hanging belay. Swallow that lump in your throat and bring up your partner.

Descent: You can rappel from here to the top of pitch 2, back-clipping a bolt or two, then from there to the waiting boat 50 meters below. Unless you are really lucky, your ropes will get wet when you pull them (the "downside").

2. AO NANG, AO NANG   6a (5.10a), 20 meters, 8 quickdraws★★
F.A. Will Hair and Dean Saydom, February 1994

Follow the procedure in pitch 1 of *Orange Chandeliers* to get onto the wall, then climb straight up to a big ledge.

3. NAME UNKNOWN   7c★
F.A. Kevin Swift, date unknown

A harder climb continues on from a few feet right of *Ao Nang, Ao Nang*'s top anchor past the big cave partway up the wall. I understand it to be very powerful, but I have not done it. Good luck.

4. CLIMBS LOST IN TIME AND TO THE ELEMENTS

VINLAND AND PHIA PHLONG BEACH
Sun exposure: Vinland faces northwest and tends to stay in the shade until midafternoon. The closer you get to the rainy season, the earlier the sun hits it.

Wall angle and difficulty: This wall is gently overhanging, though there are routes, such as *Snake Story,* that have very steep sections.

Hazards: The protection up here is good, but the wall does not see as many climbers as many other places, so the climbs may not be cleaned off as well. Watch out for loose rocks, especially on the left side. Also, the trail can be a bit spooky, mostly because of the unsavory creatures that frequent the jungle here (note the route names). Make sure the vine you pull on is a vine!

Approach: Vinland is up and right of the beach. Before construction began, you could access Vinland via a climber's trail that was on the private property. The trail went back into the jungle at the south end of the beach, then went up toward the cliff far to the left of the Vinland Wall. When you hit the rock, you cut back right and traverse the wall, watching for the easiest ground, until you reached the crag. All of this is subject to change, depending on the whims of this resort.

Just south of Ao Nang, back in a bay behind Ao Nang Tower, is the beautiful Phia Phlong Beach (*phia phlong* means "section of bamboo"). The potential here for new routes is limited really by only one factor: the land behind the beach is the site of a future high-end hotel that probably won't want climbers on its property. Currently, the only wall with any route development here is Vinland.

1. THE HECTORING   **6b+ (5.11a), 30 meters, 10 quickdraws★★★**
F.A. Hector Keeling, Greg Collum, and Mike Ho, February 2001
   This line follows the tufas up the left side of the wall.

2. RIPE FRUIT   **7a (5.11d), 25 meters, 10 quickdraws★★★**
F.A. Mike Ho and Greg Collum, February 2001
   Go up the gray wall to a large ledge (watch the giant detached block), then up the steep rock to the anchor.

THAT DEAFENING ROAR

If there is a bane of Railay Beach, it is the noise from the longtail boats, and no single place in all of southern Thailand is louder than Ao Nang Tower. The reason this crag stands out as the loudest point is that it is in the middle of the boat route from Ao Nang to Railay, and the Ao Nang boatmen refuse to use mufflers on their boats. Granted, most of the boatmen from Krabi and Nam Mao have been reluctant to stick a muffler on the back of their boats, but it's the Ao Nang boys who have absolutely refused. Local businesses have complained only to find that they then can't get a ride anymore. Politicians have passed laws, but who's out there on a day-to-day basis to enforce it? Even the big resort, formerly owned by the Dusit Corporation, got involved by buying the boatmen mufflers and promising to replace them as needed. Nope, the extra three horsepower was too much of a loss, especially when they are racing each other to the beach. I have tried to explain to the guys that a proper muffler, matched to their engine, will actually give more power, but they don't buy it. So we get this abominable noise. Paradise has its downsides, and these guys are absolutely responsible for this one. Let them know you hate it.

VINLAND

3. HOLLYWOOD AND VINE   7b (5.12b), 20 meters, 7 quickdraws★★★★
F.A. Mike Ho and Greg Collum, February 2001

On the clean white wall, there are two routes next to each other. This is the left line. Fun climbing.

4. CORNUCOPIA   7b+ (5.12c), 20 meters, 7 quickdraws★★★★
F.A. Greg Collum and Mike Ho, February 2001

This is the line to the right of *Hollywood and Vine*. Powerful little thing!

5. THE VIPER'S GUEST   7a (5.11d), 30 meters, 12 quickdraws★★★★
F.A. Mike Ho and Greg Collum, February 2001

You can get to this via one of two ways: climb *Cornucopia* and traverse right to the anchor, or climb *Vanishing Breeder* and lower to the anchor. A bolt has been added on the face left of *Vanishing Breeder* to aid you in getting there. The climb itself is fun. You can imagine, if you saw how much jungle thrashing had to be done initially to get to this climb, how it got its name. Ditto for *Snake Story*.

6. VANISHING BREEDER   6b+ (5.10d), 30 meters, 12 quickdraws★★★★
F.A. Greg Collum and Mike Ho, February 2001

A long, fun climb up the middle of the wall just right of the gray streaks.

7. SNAKE STORY   7c (5.12d), 30 meters, 12 quickdraws★★★★★
F.A. Greg Collum and Mike Ho, February 2001

Greg has put up some brilliant lines, and this could be the best (competing with *Cross-Eyed* on the Melting Wall). Climb *Vanishing Breeder* to a large ledge, where you will find the lower anchor for this climb. Make sure you're warmed up.

Chapter 8

SOUTH PENINSULA CLIMBS

The southeast corner of the Phra Nang Peninsula is really where Railay Beach started as a climbing area. The very first routes were put up in Phra Nang Cave, but the quality of rock at two little cliffs, 1, 2, 3 and Muai Thai, on what was then dubbed Nam Mao Beach, drew climbers here and became the first concentrated climbing venue. It all grew from here.

MUAI THAI AND 1, 2, 3 AREA

Sun exposure: In the dry season, these walls are in the shade for almost all of the day. Rainy season can be sunny, and the walls are known to seep.

Wall angle and difficulty: These routes tend to be vertical to slightly over-hanging, with the odd slab climb thrown in to keep things relaxed. It's an easy to moderate area, with a couple very difficult routes here and there for spice. Above 1, 2, 3 is all very difficult....It's also very dangerous because the bolts are Precambrian in origin.

Hazards: The usual bad bolts can be found, but 1, 2, 3 has its own peculiari-ties. Anything, from carabiners to actual climbers, can be dropped on the belay area. Having people step on your rope is not just common, it's the norm. Make sure you don't get into an argument with a guide over something silly...this is the area where those little arguments can get taken very seriously, and you have not had enough kickboxing practice to win. Also, a few of the most popular routes are more than 25 meters in length, so a 50-meter rope will not reach the ground when lowering off.

Approach: Located at the south end of East Railay (the Nam Mao Beach) near the Phra Nang Lagoon path.

These two sectors have the highest concentration of moderate-level climbs. Just the same, they can be intimidating in their own way. The Thai guides use this as the instruction area, so between their work and the general appeal of the routes, access to the most popular climbs can often be difficult. The best times to get on the climbs are before 9:00 A.M. and after 4:00 P.M. because most of the guiding is not taking place then.

Muai Thai

1,2,3

Hidden World

The Duncan's Boot
Slot

Jungle Gym

The Keep

Castle Crag

To Low Tide
and Hueco Wall

SOUTH WALLS

THE MONEY MAKER

Once upon a time, there were only three, maybe four Thais earning a living by "guiding." Guiding then was simpler than now. They would get up early, break up with whomever they'd gotten up with, have breakfast, then make for Phra Nang Cave. Once there, they would climb *Money Maker,* a 6a route 30 meters left of the shrine. They would establish a top rope, put out a sign that said "Top Rope 100 Baht," and wait for the money to roll in. Meanwhile, they talked and bouldered around the base to "soft rock," planning the route they wanted to "redpoint" that evening. The money did roll in, and they lived well.

Muai Thai

This is the first wall you see when you step onto this end of the beach. The name is the Thai word for Thai boxing, or "kickboxing." Routes 8–14 are around the corner from Muai Thai. None of them, except *Chicken Head,* are really worth the trouble, and they all have bad bolts.

1. MONEY MAKER II   5- (5.8), 12 meters, 5 quickdraws★★★
F.A. Sam Lightner Jr., January 1994
Retrobolted: March 1997

It is at the very far left side of the wall.

2. IDAPACCAYADA   6b+ (5.11a), 13 meters, 6 quickdraws★★
F.A. Volker Schoeffl and Frank Dicker, December 1990
Retrobolted: March 1997

This goes up *Money Maker II* and then traverses out right. The name is a Buddhist term meaning "dependent origination." To understand that, you need to check in to a monastery and not speak for a month!

3. SHOOTING THRU   7b (5.12b), 12 meters, 7 quickdraws★
F.A. Phil de Joux, date unknown

This route is little more than a contrived sandwich between *Idapaccayada* and *Orange Tears.*

4. ORANGE TEARS (AKA NAM DAH SEE SOM)   7a+ (5.12a), 13 meters,
                                              7 quickdraws★★★★
F.A. Francois Brunier and Dominique Potard, December 1990
Retrobolted: February 1997

Up the difficult orange bulge and to the high left side of the wall. This is a must-do, but be careful lunging for holds that might bring tears to your eyes!

5

6

6

4

5

8–14

1–3

MAUI THAI

7

5. NUAT HIN   6b (5.10c), 15 meters, 7 quickdraws★★★

F.A. Volker Schoeffl and Frank Dicker, December 1990
Retrobolted: February 1997

This climb ascends the clean rock to the cave in the middle of the wall. The name means "massage the rock" in Thai. It has gotten more difficult over the years as it has polished up like fine china.

6. PATTICA SAMUPADE   6b+ (5.11a), 14 meters, 7 quickdraws★★★

F.A. Volker Schoeffl, Frank Dicker, and Sam Lightner Jr., January 1991
Retrobolted: February 1997

Start on *Nuat Hin*, then hang a right through the bulge. The first bolts on this route were hand drilled, and the tapping of the hammer brought a swarm of bees out of one of the pockets. Every one of them must have stung us and died, 'cause they're all gone now. An extended and silly waste of pitch continues on the dagger rock at 6a for four bolts.

7. MUAI THAI   6b+ (5.11a), 15 meters, 6 quickdraws★★★★

F.A. Francois Burnier and Dominique Potard, December 1990
Retrobolted: March 1997

Muai Thai means "Thai boxing" in Thai, referring to the odd positions the route contorts you into. This starts on the right side of the buttress, the last climb you get to straight off the beach.

8. CHICKEN HEAD   6c+ (5.11c), 13 meters, 5 quickdraws★★★

F.A. Ralph Tenbrink and Louis, 1992
Retrobolted: March 2005

9. REACHING LIKE A MONKEY   6c (5.11b), 13 meters, 4 quickdraws★

F.A. Wee Changrua, June 1996

10. DEBORAH   6b (5.10c), 8 meters, 4 quickdraws★

F.A. Jack, February 1996

11. HELLO CHRISTINE   6a (5.10a), 15 meters, 8 quickdraws★

F.A. Wee Changrua, August 1997

12. VALENTINE   6a+ (5.10b), 12 meters, 6 quickdraws★

F.A. Jack, February 1996

13. ALONE   6b+ (5.10d), 12 meters, 7 quickdraws★

F.A. Jack, February 1996

14. TAKE IT EASY   5+ (5.9), 8 meters, 5 quickdraws★
F.A. Wee Changrua, August 1997

1, 2, 3 Area

This venue is just a few steps farther along the beach from Muai Thai.

1. SAMEBOY   6a+ (5.10b), 12 meters, 6 quickdraws★★
F.A. Wee Changrua, June 1997
   Found at the far left of the wall. You'll want tough hands for this one.

2. SELEE   6a (5.10a), 12 meters, 5 quickdraws★★
F.A. Wee Changrua, June 1997
   Another sharpy on the dagger rock at the left end of the crag.

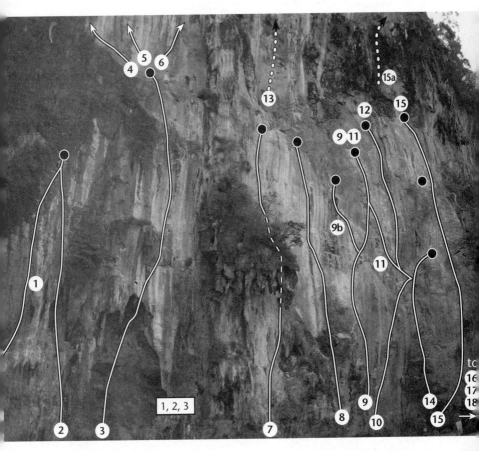

3. KRATOY   6c (5.11b), 26 meters, 8 quickdraws★★★
F.A. Alex Wenner, Somjit Nigwari, and Vitsanu Rachsang, date unknown
Retrobolted: January 1998

This goes up through the largest cave about 6 meters off the ground. The glue-in bolts here seem to be holding, but the people who did the replacement did not clean the holes to the manufacturer's specs. Still, they've held for this long.... Also, make sure you keep an eye on the end of the rope when lowering someone.

4. ONE THOUSAND KNIVES 6b+ (5.11a), 25 meters, 10 quickdraws★★
F.A. Pep Masip, January 1995

One Thousand Knives, as well as *La Riba* and *Triana*, begins on the ledge above *Kratoy* and *We Sad*. There is a lot in the name, which appropriately describes the holds. Also, the bolts are pretty questionable, including the anchors.

Pitch 1: 6b+ (5.11a), 10 quickdraws.
Pitch 2: 6b+ (5.11a), 7 quickdraws. The second pitch climbs way out left before going up.

5. LA RIBA   7c+ (5.13a), 20 meters, 8 quickdraws★★
F.A. Pep Masip, January 1995

Again, start on the high ledge. Very bad bolts. You cannot safely lower to the ground from the higher anchor.

THE KRATOY GAME

We could all see she was gorgeous. She was hotter than the sun, and she was giving my friend, who shall remain nameless, the eye. Usually when a beautiful Thai girl is giving a *farang* tourist the eye, it means a business proposal is in the making. However, the two of them hit it off with no discussion of compensation ever taking place. They left the bar and I assumed the best.

Nope. It was the worst.

Just inside the door of my friend's bungalow, heated passion took over and clothes flew across the room. It was only then did he realize she was, well, a he. Screaming, yelling, and no more panting. His date left immediately and he began contemplating the unintentional homosexuality!

But feel for him. Some of the most beautiful women in Thailand are actually men. You doubt me? You think you can always tell? Go to one of the cabaret shows on Koh Phi Phi or, better yet, check this website: *www.paradise-thai.com/EN/top.html.* It's shocking ...but not as shocking as it was for my friend!

6. TRIANA   **7b+ (5.12c), 28 meters, 12 quickdraws★★**
F.A. Pep Masip, January 1995
This one goes up and right off the ledge. You cannot lower off with a standard rope. Bad bolts.

7. WE SAD   **6a+ (5.10b), 8 bolts, 25 meters★★★★**
F.A. Barry Chamber, Leni Reeves, and Vitsanu Rachsang, March 1993
Retrobolted: March 1997
This climb ascends the right side of the big tufa system. If you need a boost at the start, you're in the majority. It's a no-feet thing and it's the hardest bit of climbing.

8. KNIGHTS IN WHITE SATIN   **7b+ (5.12c), 25 meters, 8 quickdraws★★★★**
F.A. Volker Schoeffl, Dominique Potard, and Francois Burnier, December 1990
Retrobolted: March 1997
This starts on the right side of the steep bulge just off the beach. The business is up in the clean rock. It has gotten a bit polished over the years.

9. MAKE A WAY   **6b (5.10c), 27 meters, 12 quickdraws★★★★★**
F.A. Cyro Glad, January 1993
Retrobolted: March 1997
A classic at Railay East. Start a couple meters right of *Knights in White Satin* and climb up the juggy corner right onto the face. There is a **variation** that is harder and not quite as good (shown in the photo as route 9b). It is known as *Flying to the Stars* 7a+, and can be done by going left through the main bulge just after the obvious rest.

10. QUARKS   **7b (5.12b), 14 meters, 4 quickdraws★★★**
F.A. Francois Burnier and Dominique Potard, January 1992
This tweaky nightmare is popular, so I give it some stars. Personally, it's not my thing, and it is as polished as the marble steps in the Vatican.

11. CONFUSION   **6b+ (5.11a), 27 meters, 13 quickdraws★★★★**
F.A. Francois Burnier and Dominique Potard, December 1990
Climb the *King Cobra* corner, then up the face to the *Make a Way* anchor. Some bolts are bad, and a longer sling on the bolt where you leave the corner is helpful for dealing with rope drag.

12. ORIENTALES   **6b+ (5.11a), 27 meters, 12 quickdraws★★★★★**
F.A. Ralph Tenbrink and Louis, January 1992
Retrobolted: March 1997
Go up *King Cobra*, then follow the line up the right side of the tufa and

prepare to get pumped!

13. GANDALF   8a+ (5.13c), 28 meters, 14 quickdraws
F.A. Rolando Larcher, February 1995

This route has bad bolts. It starts from the ledge above the *Make a Way* anchors and is impossible to safely lower from with a standard rope. Anyone below it when a climber is approaching the anchor should be leery, because there is a very weak stalactite that could easily break away if the climber were to step on it. All in all, not recommended.

14. KING COBRA   5- (5.8), 13 meters, 6 quickdraws★★★
F.A. Sam Lightner Jr. and Jolande Van Marle, January 1991

Short and easy. Up the corner to the anchor on the ledge.

15. MASSAGE SECRET (AKA 1, 2, 3)   6a+ (5.10b), 30 meters,
9 quickdraws★★★★★
F.A. Francois Burnier and Dominique Potard, December 1990
Retrobolted: March 1997

This is a classic. It was originally put in as three short pitches and is now done as either two pitches or one big one.

Pitch 1: 5+ (5.9), 13 meters, 5 quickdraws.41

Pitch 2: 6a+ (5.10b), 18 meters, 9 quickdraws.

15 a. Another pitch (6a+), put in by Dean Saydom in '94, goes right from the cave anchor at the top but is rarely done. It is on old rotten threads and goes up dirt rock; it is dangerous and not worth the risk.

Descent: A 60-meter rope only barely reaches when lowering the leader. Pay attention here.

Routes 16–18 are not shown on the overlay.

16. SHORT AND SAVAGE   6b (5.10c), 6 meters, 3 quickdraws★★
F.A. Unknown
Retrobolted: March 1997

Find this just right of *Massage Secrets*.

17. GIGERRING FOR CLIMBING   5+ (5.9), 12 meters, 5 quickdraws★★
F.A. Pep Masip, January 1995

This one is just right of *Short and Savage*.

18. LING NOI   5+ (5.9), 10 meters, 4 quickdraws★★
F.A. Dean Saydom, April 1994

Ling Noi means "little monkey" in Thai.

The Pinnacle

The detached block in front of 1, 2, 3 is known simply as the Pinnacle. There are three short routes on it.

19. LONG LIVE THE HERM   5+ (5.9), 8 meters, 4 quickdraws★★
F.A. Sash Nukuda and Brendan Robertson, December 1994
   Take the left line.

20. BE CAREFUL   6b (5.10b), 6 meters, 3 quickdraws★★
F.A. Jack, January 1996
   Take the middle line.

21. CASH FLOW   5+ (5.9), 10 meters, 4 quickdraws★★
F.A. Unknown
   Take the right line.

DUNCAN'S BOOT

Sun exposure: In the dry season, these walls are shady for all but the earliest risers. In the rainy season, they can get hit with filtered sunlight.

   Wall angle and difficulty: The climbs are very steep at Duncan's Boot. It's all moderately difficult and there are no easy climbs here.

   Hazards: Lowering off and cleaning a route at Duncan's Boot can be dangerous because you could swing into the wall and jungle behind you. Clean with care. As always, beware of the bolts, and for a special note on that, take a look at the sidebar, Duncan's Bolts. The wall can seep a lot during the rainy season. Bring bug repellent.

   Approach: To reach Duncan's Boot, look for a trail through some scraggly bamboo about 80 meters past 1, 2, 3. Ten meters up this trail is a fork. Going left drops you into a sink and to the base of Duncan's Boot. The routes are listed here from left to right, which corresponds with best to not-so-best. Down and left of *Lost Lek* (route 1) is a short overhang known as the Toilet Wall. There are a couple of threaded routes here, although they are sharp, short, and often wet. They aren't fun and, as the name implies, it's hard to find a clean place to set your rope down. Remember, it's best to poop away from the walls.

Tucked away in the jungle about 80 meters past 1, 2, 3 are a couple of fun cliffs that are usually shady and cool. Duncan's Boot, the first one you come to, is characterized by short, steep climbs. Above it is Hidden World. Both areas are very popular with mosquitoes.

1. LOST LEK   7a (5.11d), 18 meters, 9 quickdraws★★★★★
F.A. Max Dufford and Divinder Dufford, December 1992

This climb starts on the slab at the far left end of the wall. It goes up and left toward the jungle, then cuts back right to the high point of the wall. If I had a baht for every classic Max Dufford has established, I'd have, like, a dollar.

2. MAKE A BOW   7a+ (5.12a), 14 meters, 9 quickdraws★
F.A. Thomas Arnold, February 1998

This starts 3 meters right of *Lost Lek*. Climb up left on a smooth wall to an anchor just below the jungle. Good bolts, bad climb. Sort of an overhanging slab.

3. THE DARK SIDE   7b (5.12b), 14 meters, 7 quickdraws★★★
F.A. Duncan, February 1994

This one starts at the most prominent bulge in the rock. Bad bolts, good climb (see sidebar "Duncan's Bolts").

4. THE VOICE OF DOOM   6c (5.11b), 14 meters, 7 quickdraws★★★★
F.A. Duncan, February 1994

Just right of *The Dark Side* trending right, is a steep, fun bit of rock with lots of wild twisting and leg-pulling through tufas. It takes the steepest bit of the wall before angling back right.

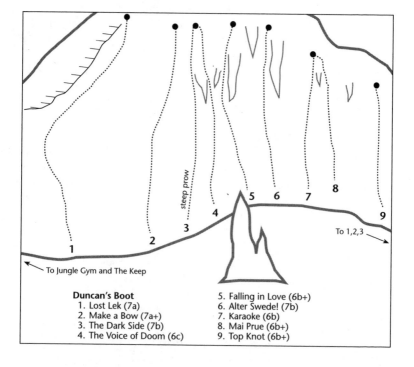

To Jungle Gym and The Keep

Duncan's Boot	
1. Lost Lek (7a)	5. Falling in Love (6b+)
2. Make a Bow (7a+)	6. Alter Swede! (7b)
3. The Dark Side (7b)	7. Karaoke (6b)
4. The Voice of Doom (6c)	8. Mai Prue (6b+)
	9. Top Knot (6b+)

5. FALLING IN LOVE   6b+ (5.11a), 13 meters, 9 quickdraws★★★★

F.A. Stefan Pisburek and Markus Wiesenfarth, February 1998

Another fun and steep route, just right of *The Voice of Doom*. This one goes through the biggest of the stalactites. You'll be impaled if you swing off from the first bolt while cleaning.

6. ALTER SWEDE!   7b (5.12b), 10 meters, 6 quickdraws★★

F.A. Thomas Arnold, January 1998

Starts 3 meters or so right of *Falling in Love.*

7. KARAOKE   6b (5.10c), 8 meters, 5 quickdraws★★

F.A. Dean Saydom, date unknown

Go up the cleft in the rock, trending right.

DUNCAN'S BOLTS: GLUE-INS SANS GLUE

Duncan put up some excellent climbs here, and no one would argue that he placed bolts in the wrong place or that he over- or underbolted a route. Also, he spared no expense in his efforts to give the climbing world a better Phra Nang Peninsula: he used Petzl glue-in anchors, the best on the market at that time.

However, it's just hearsay, but perhaps because of too much party time while doing his climbing work, he placed them incorrectly. A glue-in bolt of 10 mm diameter needs a hole that is a minimum of 12 mm diameter. That way, there is room in the hole for the steel of the bolt plus the glue that holds it in. A 10 mm steel glue-in placed in a 10 mm hole will squeeze all the glue out of the hole, leaving nothing to bond it to the rock.

Well, sadly, that's just what Duncan did. The weeks after his routes first went in saw some interesting almost-accidents. In one case, a climber clipped in a quickdraw, and with it and the weight of the rope, the bolt pulled from the wall. In another, the climber clipped in to the anchor and then watched as the rope pulled out each of the bolts from the concave wall below him. Fortunately, the anchor was on a slab so he was okay.

Now some of these bolts seem to be okay . . . somehow, they had enough glue to hold them in and have been tested by a number of years of climbing. I understand from a visiting Australian that Duncan thinks we all hate him, which is definitely not true. He made a mistake, or six dozen mistakes, and that happens. But you, the visiting climber, should be aware that Mother Nature is not the only one messing with the quality of your protection. Please be aware of this mistake so you don't confuse a new glue-in with extra glue to an old one with none.

8. MAI PRUE   6b+ (5.10d), 8 meters, 5 quickdraws★★
F.A. Dean Saydom, date unknown
   Go up the right side of the cleft, trending left.

9. TOP KNOT   6b+ (5.10d), 8 meters, 3 quickdraws★★
F.A. Wee Changrua, December 1996
   At the far right, go up the short face to the tree with the anchor.

HIDDEN WORLD

Sun exposure: Hidden World is not quite as steep as Duncan's Boot. However, it's one of the shadiest places on the peninsula.

Wall angle and difficulty: The slightly overhanging climbs at Hidden World are good for moderate to advanced climbers.

Hazards: Generally the stone is excellent, but there has been some loose rock reported here, including one serious injury from a large block coming out of the conglomeratelike rock in the middle of the wall. Some bolts are dubious, and *Rocket Head* has a hard clip with potential for a nasty fall.

Approach: To reach Hidden World, go up through the bamboo as if going to Duncan's Boot, but instead of going left, work your way up the right fork and scramble up a bit of dirty rock to the very right end of the cliff.

With longer sport climbs on excellent rock, this wall has one standout climb, *Tom's Pitch*. This 7a+ is one of the better routes at its grade in Thailand, and *Red Dwarf*, the 7a to its left, is also quite popular. All of the 6s in the middle are worthy of an afternoon, but the 6a+ on the right end of the cliff, *Satanic Alliance*, is lousy. It should have been left for the ever-present monkeys.

1. BANANA SHIP   7b+ (5.12c), 20 meters, 9 quickdraws★★★
F.A. Mario Waser and Thomas K, January 1998
   This climb is behind the big tree at the left end of the wall. It shares a start and an anchor with *Red Dwarf*.

2. RED DWARF   7a (5.11d), 20 meters, 9 quickdraws★★★★
F.A. Ian Turnbull and S. Beverage, January 1998
Retrobolted: January 2000
   The first few bolts on this line are shared with *Banana Ship*. The climb goes right around the bulge, where *Banana Ship* goes left. They share an anchor. Pumpy!

3. TOM'S PITCH   7a+ (5.12a), 25 meters, 10 quickdraws ★★★★★
F.A. Mario Waser and Thomas K, January 1998
Retrobolted: January 2000

Da kine!!! This is the route to the right of *Red Dwarf*; it's up the middle of the wall, trending slightly left up high. Getting polished.

4. NAME UNKNOWN   **6c+ (5.11c), 28 meters, 12 quickdraws★★★★★**
F.A. Unknown
Retrobolted: February 2002

Excellent climb. It starts just below broken conglomerate and passes through this and up the left side of a tufa system, then up and left through steep rock near stalactites.

KARMA FOR SURFING

I stepped onto the beach in front of where the old Sunrise Bungalows were, only to find a group of fishermen kicking sand on a leopard shark. The animal was in its death throes, flopping around on the beach, and the fishermen were just laughing. I asked them where it was going, thinking it would be steaks in a couple hours. It wasn't going anywhere, I was told. They were unable to sell it and were just going to kill it for the pleasure.

I got pissed and yelled at them, something one should never do. Perhaps they had some twinges of guilt, 'cause when I told them to help me get it back in the water, they helped. The shark was about 2 meters long and weighed at least 60 kilos, so I needed that help. I took it near the gills and two others grabbed behind. I walked into the water and let go. Sadly, the fish lacked the strength to swim off.

I grabbed its dorsal fin in one hand and a pectoral in the other and walked toward deeper water. The animal stared up at me, its big brown and yellow eyes blinking like a puppy's. I walked out and toward the point, as though I were cutting across toward Duncan's Boot. After about five minutes the shark kicked a bit, so I let go, but he just hovered there, not getting to deeper water and allowing no water to pass over his gills.

I grabbed hold again and walked into deeper water. We went for about 10 more minutes, all the while the big fish staring at me with those big sad eyes. It made one big thrash and stopped. I let go and the shark swam a bit. It went about 2 meters from me, then slowly swam around me, just close enough that I could still see one of its eyes looking at me. The shark did two laps, very slowly, then paused a moment. I stared, the shark stared, then with a twitch it was off to deeper water.

I'm told by old surfers that I can surf anywhere I want and never have to worry now.

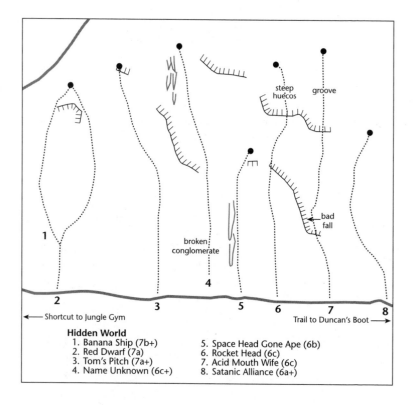

steep huecos

groove

bad fall

1

broken conglomerate

4

2

3

5

6

7

8

← Shortcut to Jungle Gym

Trail to Duncan's Boot →

Hidden World
1. Banana Ship (7b+)
2. Red Dwarf (7a)
3. Tom's Pitch (7a+)
4. Name Unknown (6c+)
5. Space Head Gone Ape (6b)
6. Rocket Head (6c)
7. Acid Mouth Wife (6c)
8. Satanic Alliance (6a+)

5. SPACE HEAD GONE APE   6b (5.10c), 12 meters, 6 quickdraws★★★
F.A. Ian Turnbull and S. Beverage, February 1993
Retrobolted: February 2002

This climbs the right side of the tufa system in the middle of the wall.

6. ROCKET HEAD   6c (5.11b), 20 meters, 9 quickdraws★★★★
F.A. Duncan, February 1994

This goes up a clean face just right of *Space Head Gone Ape* and then takes on the huecoed bulge up high. It's thuggy up there.

7. ACID MOUTH WIFE   6c (5.11b), 20 meters, 8 quickdraws★★
F.A. Duncan, February 1994
Retrobolted: February 2002

This route goes next to the dihedral to an anchor high on the wall and in a groove. It is dangerous and difficult getting to the third clip.

8. SATANIC ALLIANCE   6a+ (5.10b), 18 meters, 6 quickdraws★

F.A. Duncan, February 1994

"Evil Temptation" would have been a good name because this route is hell. Hopefully the nearby vines will take it back soon.

JUNGLE GYM

Sun exposure: If you've got a sunburn, this is your wall. It gets little or no sunlight and is generally cool.

Wall angle and difficulty: Most of the climbing here is vertical to only slightly overhanging. There is only one "easier" route here, a few moderates, and a few open projects with unspecified grades.

Hazards: The usual bad-bolt warning holds, and keep a watch for loose blocks up high. Note that on some of these you won't reach the ground with a 60-meter rope.

Approach: If you traverse along the base of Duncan's Boot and up through the jungle past *Lost Lek* (route 1 on that wall), after 50 meters or so you will come to a cirque of walls known as the Jungle Gym. A huge canyon cuts this area in two and leads to The Keep.

1. FOCUS ON YOUR ABDOMINAL BREATHING   6a (5.10a), 23 meters,
                                              9 quickdraws★★★★

F.A. Fang, Gerda Trutnovsky, and Mario Waser, January 1998

This goes up the dagger rock on the far left, but it's better than it looks.

2. CLIMBER'S VIEWPOINT   6c+ (5.11c), 35 meters, 12 quickdraws★★★

F.A. Mario Waser, January 1998

Pitch 1: 6c+ (5.11c), 25 meters, 12 quickdraws. Pitch 1 is sharp but interesting. Watch out for a large detached block just below the anchor because it will kill anyone it hits below.

Pitch 2: 6a (5.10a), 10 meters, 5 quickdraws. I haven't done pitch 2 (nor has anyone else I know), so the rating is not firsthand.

3. ADALING   7b (5.12b), 25 meters, 10 quickdraws★★★★

F.A. Mario Waser, January 1998

This is thin, technical, fun climbing, with very good contact friction! The route shares an anchor with *Climber's Viewpoint*.

4. VIOLA   7a (5.11a), 22 meters, 10 quickdraws★★★★

F.A. Mario Waser, January 1998

There are a couple of sharp holds, but this is a good climb with gymnastic moves. There is a second pitch but it is anything but inviting. Just come down from the first anchor and avoid the miserable dagger rock above.

5. OPEN PROJECT

Bolted by Mario Waser, 1998. The bolts are in bad shape. The route is actually in the first bits of the Slot.

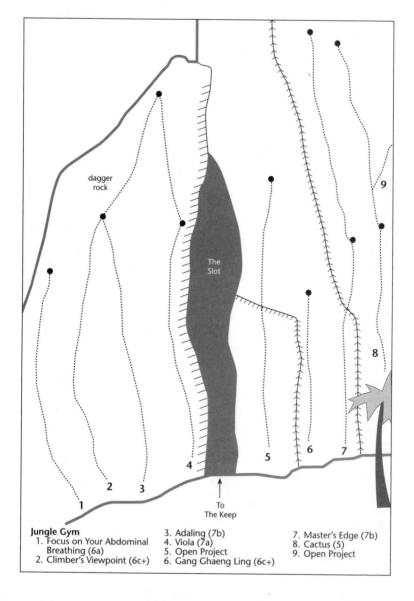

Jungle Gym
1. Focus on Your Abdominal Breathing (6a)
2. Climber's Viewpoint (6c+)
3. Adaling (7b)
4. Viola (7a)
5. Open Project
6. Gang Ghaeng Ling (6c+)
7. Master's Edge (7b)
8. Cactus (5)
9. Open Project

6. GANG GHAENG LING   6c+ (5.11c), 15 meters, 6 quickdraws★★
F.A. Dean Saydom, April 1994
The name means "monkey's pants" or "monkey's underwear" in Thai.

7. MASTER'S EDGE   7b (5.12b), 30 meters, 8 quickdraws★
F.A. Mario Waser, January 1998
The name alone is perhaps the most overused label in the climbing world, and the climbing is so bad that I'd rather be serenaded to sleep by a symphony of unmuffled longtail boats than ever touch it again.
Pitch 1: 7b (5.12b), 15 meters, 7 quickdraws.
Pitch 2: Open project.

8. CACTUS   5 (5.8), 32 meters, 12 quickdraws★
F.A. Mario Waser, January 1998
The bolts are questionable, as always, and the name is well chosen, considering the stone.
Pitch 1: 5, 14 meters, 5 quickdraws.
Pitch 2: Open project by Mario.
The second pitch of this also features a project, shown as route 9 on the topo.

THE KEEP

Sun exposure: The Keep goes into the shade in late morning during the dry season. However, the closer you are to the rainy season, on either side of the calendar, the more sun it gets.

Wall angle and difficulty: The wall is slightly overhanging, with medium-length sport climbs that are easy to moderate. There are a couple of harder climbs in the center of the wall.

Hazards: Due to the popularity of the climbing here, the bolts are being replaced as often as anywhere. All of these climbs were scheduled for a titanium update as this book went to press. Clip the titanium bolts if they are there! Still, be leery of fixed protection. Also, remember that some routes are rather long, so watch the end of the rope when lowering your partner. Finally, the down-climb to the ledge can be a bit slick and would be a nasty fall. Weaker folks might want a belay, even though it's only about 3 meters high.

Approach: After walking past the routes on Duncan's Boot to the Jungle Gym, you will see the trail go up a steep and skinny slot canyon that splits the Jungle Gym crag. Follow this for perhaps 50 meters, or to its end, where you'll reach the "keyhole" and a blast of wind that cools you from the strenuous walk. Stretching away to the south is a sloping ledge partially shrouded in palms and stubby ficus trees, almost tailormade for belaying from. Carefully climb down the rock from the keyhole, remembering your shoes are a bit muddy, using the old rope that hangs there only when all else fails.

After you down-climb to the ledge, you might notice four climbs to the right (facing the wall) of the keyhole. These climbs (routes 9–12), which are technically on the back side of the Jungle Gym tower, are a good place for splicing ropes, cutting webbing, and tearing open that only pair of shoes you brought. All are 6s that come with Ginsu-like holds, so just skip 'em and head out the ledge to the real McCoy.

The Keep is one of the most popular walls on the Peninsula.

1. MONKEY'S BUM   6b (5.10c), 18 meters, 8 quickdraws★★★
F.A. Greg Collum and Trevor Massiah, January 95
   This is the first route you come to, ascending broken tufa ground to a dagger rock anchor. Not a classic, but okay.

2. BABO DOES THAILAND   6c (5.11b), 27 meters, 13 quickdraws★★★★
F.A. J. Yoder and M. Ford, January 1996
   This is the long, fun pitch up solid rock just left of *Monkey's Bum*.

3. MEDUSA'S LOVER   6c (5.11b), 26 meters, 9 quickdraws★★★★★
F.A. Greg Collum and Trevor Massiah, January 1995
Retrobolted: March 1999
   Start this one from the large boulder on the ledge. This is one of the reasons you came to Siam.

4. NUT CRACKER   6c (5.11b), 25 meters, 8 quickdraws★★★★★
F.A. Greg Collum and Trevor Massiah, January 1995
Retrobolted: December 1997
   Another must-do! This climb starts about 6 meters left of *Medusa's Lover* and then works right.

5. BOTTOM FEEDER   7c (5.12d), 18 meters, 8 quickdraws★★★
F.A. Alex Catlin, February 1996
Retrobolted: March 1999
   This climb starts barely left of *Nut Cracker* and goes up to a seriously hard move near the anchor. The name implies that the first ascent was snatched from the folks who bolted it... not a nice thing to do. An anchor has recently appeared below the hard move, making the lower bit a short 6b.

6. LOM MON   7a (5.11d), 31 meters, 11 quickdraws★★★★
F.A. Greg Collum and Trevor Massiah, January 1995
Retrobolted: December 1997

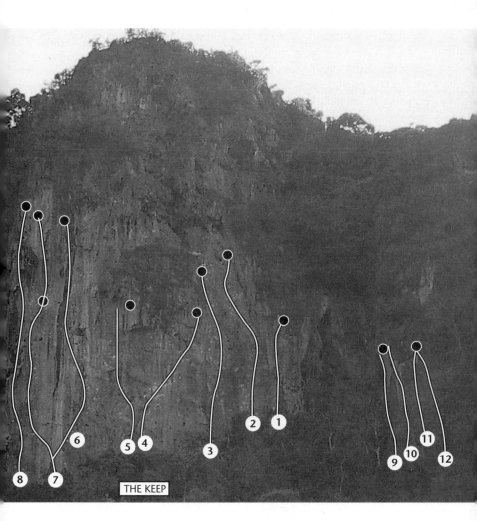

THE KEEP

This long climb goes up and right of *Tongue Thaid*, then straight up to a high anchor. *Lom Mon* means "cyclone" in Thai. Beware of rope length and that big void behind the belay ledge!

7. TONGUE THAID   7a+ (5.12a), 20 meters, 8 quickdraws★★★★★
F.A. Greg Collum and Trevor Massiah, January 1995
Retrobolted: December 1997
   This climb goes left, then to an anchor on a ledge between it and the next route, *Genghis Bond*. An extension, making the route a 7b (5.12b), can be done; it adds about 11 meters and requires 5 additional quickdraws.

8. GENGHIS BOND   **6b (5.10c), 31 meters, 14 quickdraws★★★★★**
F.A. Greg Collum and Trevor Massiah, January 1995
Retrobolted: March 1999
   This fun climb ascends the steep tufa system at the end of the wall. Note the length: You can lower someone from this anchor on a full 60-meter rope with stretch, but it's a *real* stretch. Make sure you tie a knot in the end first. On the way up, look for an anchor that can be used to do a second lower from if your rope is under 60 meters.

CASTLE CRAG

Sun exposure: Castle Crag gets early morning sun but spends most of the day in the shade.
   Wall angle and difficulty: This is a more or less vertical area with three moderate climbs.
   Hazards: Castle Crag has never been rebolted and very much needs to be. These routes are very dangerous.
   Approach: As you walk along the tidal pools toward Low Tide, you come across this little buttress below the Keep.

This is an okay bit of rock, but the routes are not worth risking your life.

1. STALACTITE DANGER   **6b+ (5.10d), 20 meters, 6 quickdraws★**
F.A. Duncan, February 1994
   Find this one on the left side of the crag.

2. HARD-HEADED WOMAN   **6b (5.10c), 25 meters, 9 quickdraws★**
F.A. Duncan, February 1994
   Hard-headed Woman and *Bad and Beware* share a start and quite a few holds, almost making them the same route. *Hard-headed Woman* has the dubious distinction of creating more rope drag.

3. BAD AND BEWARE   **6b (5.10c), 25 meters, 9 quickdraws★**
F.A. Duncan, February 1994
   There is a lot in a name.

LOW TIDE

Sun exposure: For almost all of the year, this wall is in the sun until midafternoon. Timing the sun with low tide is hard to do. It holds the heat for a while, too.
   Wall angle and difficulty: All of these routes are slightly overhanging and of a moderate to advanced level.
   Hazards: The bolts here have been replaced four times now and are asking

CASTLE CRAG

Strider (7b)

for it again. This is one of the worst walls for steel corrosion, so be careful. Also, it is one of the more remote places. It can take a while to get help if you have an accident here. A very serious accident happened here in 1999 when a climber failed to properly tie his knot. I've seen a lot of sea snakes on this trek, so don't play with anything long and slippery when wading back!

Approach: At low tide, you can walk to—d'oh!—Low Tide by going past 1, 2, 3 and simply following the water and rock around until you reach the pretty beach with the big pink wall above it. It's about 600 meters beyond 1, 2, 3. At high tide, you can hire a boat from the boat stand in front of Ya Ya's for something along the lines of 20 baht (US 50 cents) per person. However, if the tide is high, you might find that belaying and staying dry are impossible to do at the same time. Also, don't count on the boat to come back for you if the tide is too high to walk back; some do, some don't.

If you were enticed to come to Thailand by magazine articles, slide shows, or friends who all raved about beautiful walls streaking above secluded beaches, then you will want to climb at Low Tide (originally dubbed Frodo's Wall). If you're lucky, you get the Robinson Crusoe–meets-Buoux sensation by having this place to yourself. The wall is made of pink, white, and orange flowstone, something you rarely find anywhere but in caves and on Ratburi karst formations. It has a limited number of routes, but those that are here are some of the best in Thailand. The jungle hangs over the beach, the waves lap onto the sand, and the strange and colorful stone makes this one of the more perfect climbing venues in *Sawan*.

Perhaps 80 meters up and left of Low Tide is Jurassic Park, a wall with two multipitch climbs: *One of Our Dinosaurs Is Missing* and *The Land Time Forgot* are both 6b+ and have three pitches of dagger-rock climbing. To paraphrase Dr. Ian Malcolm from the movie, "That's one big pile of *kee*."

1. A WALK IN THE PARK   6a (5.10a), 13 meters, 6 quickdraws★★★★
F.A. Glen Tempest, B. Everett, K. Everett, and S. Mason, April 1993
Retrobolted: May 1998, July 2005
    This climb is on the left side of the wall between the stalactites. It is sporty to the first clip, with an ugly landing…don't make this your first lead.

2. THE NARSILION   7a (5.11d), 22 meters, 10 quickdraws★★★★★
F.A. Sam Lightner Jr., Jacob Valdez, and Ingo Kube, February 1992
Retrobolted: February 1997, July 2005
    This one is just right of the big stalactites. It goes up, then right over the bulge. Be careful up there; a ledge could make falling a nasty proposition. The name refers to "The Song of the Moon and Sun" in J. R. R. Tolkien's *Lord of the Rings*.

3. DEFINITELY MAKES YOU WHINGE 7c+ (5.13a), 30 meters,
                                            14 quickdraws★★★★★
F.A. Mike Tupper and Todd Skinner, December 1992
Retrobolted: May 1998
    This one goes up the middle of the wall. Don't whine about the reachiness…Lynn flashed it.

4. STRIDER   7b (5.12b), 30 meters, 13 quickdraws★★★★★
F.A. Sam Lightner Jr. and Jacob Valdez, February 1992 e
Retrobolted: February 1997, July 2005
    This climb begins near the middle of the wall just left of a tufa corner. It used to go all the way to the ledge, but we lowered the anchor so one rope would reach (barely). This is arguably the best single pitch in Thailand. I admit to being biased, but it's definitely in the top five!
    A highball direct start, done without gear by Alex Catlin, comes in from the right (shown as 4a in the photo) and makes the route 8a+.

5. LOW TIDE   6b+ (5.11a), 50 meters, 10 quickdraws, extra
                                      tie-off slings★★★★
F.A. Somporn Suebhait (King) and Ralph Tenbrink, March 1994
Retrobolted: partially February 1998
    The gear on this route is a bit dodgy because it wears out fast and is not regularly replaced. Take slings to back up threads, and be prepared for some scary belays.
    Pitch 1: 6b+ (5.11a), 23 meters, 9 quickdraws. This climb has a bouldery start, to the left side of the big tufa system, then on to gray dagger rock.
    Pitch 2: 6b (5.10c), 27 meters, 10 quickdraws.

6. HIGH TIDE   6b+ (5.11a), 53 meters, 10 quickdraws★★
F.A. Paul Brunner, December 1997

1

2

3

4

4a

5

6

To Hueco
Wall

To
1, 2, 3

LOW TIDE

This route is not done very often, mostly due to scary pro, sharp holds, and loose rock.

Pitch 1: 6b (5.10c), 28 meters, 10 quickdraws. It starts about 4.5 meters right of Low Tide.

Pitch 2: 6b+ (5.11a), 25 meters, 7 quickdraws.

HUECO WALL

Sun exposure: During the dry season, this wall gets sun in the morning but is shady and cool for more of the day than is Low Tide. In the rainy season, Hueco gets sun until the early afternoon.

Wall angle and difficulty: Hueco Wall is slightly overhanging to rooflike, depending on the difficulty. The routes vary from one extreme to the other, with not much in between.

Hazards: These bolts are very bad, and as of the time of this writing, they had not been replaced. We need more time, money, and volunteers, folks!

Approach: Reach Hueco Wall by walking beyond Low Tide, through the beach boulders, and to the obvious wall perhaps 100 meters away. All the routes start from the ledge that is accessed from the beach. Routes 1 and 2 require some fairly committing moves to get across the very small part of the ledge and reach their bases.

1. VIOLENCE IS GOLDEN   8a+ (5.13c), 7 meters, 6 quickdraws★★★
F.A. Todd Skinner and Mike Tupper, January 1993
    This roofy thing is sort of a boulder problem in the sky. Very hard on individual fingers! It starts at the left end of the ledge.

2. LOVE AND PERFORMANCE   7c+ (5.13a), 15 meters, 9 quickdraws★★★
F.A. Mike Tupper and Todd Skinner, January 1993
    Look for a line of horribly rusted hardware about 6 meters right of *Violence Is Golden.*

3. YOUTH IN ASIA   7b (5.12b), 20 meters, 8 quickdraws★★★
F.A. Todd Skinner and Mike Tupper, January 1993
    This one accesses the clean wall via a large stalactite. It's a bit contrived because you can go back and forth from easy ground to the bolts in the more difficult ground. The climbing, if done as intended, is characterized by big pulls on solid rock. The route shares a start with the next one, *Travels.*

4. TRAVELS WITH THE BLUDGEON BROTHERS   6a (5.10a), 15 meters,
**   7 quickdraws★★★★**
F.A. Melissa Quigley and the Bludgeon Brothers, January 1993
    This fine route might actually have enough threads (instead of bolts) to be

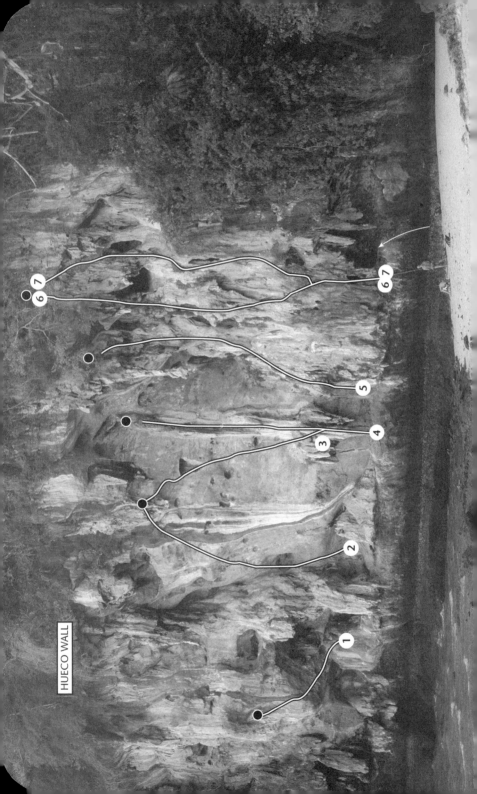

HUECO WALL

safe, if you replace the threads. It goes up the stalactite and tufa system just right of *Youth in Asia*.

5. SAM I'M NOT — 6a (5.10a), 23 meters, 9 quickdraws and a couple slings★★
F.A. Todd Skinner, Sam Lightner Jr., and the Girl-of-Dispute, January 1993

Again, this is all threads and might be safe enough if you replace a few. Use some long slings instead of quickdraws to eliminate drag. (By the way, Todd, she wasn't worth the hassles!)

6. PLAGIARISTS — 6a (5.10a), 23 meters, 8 quickdraws★★
F.A. Unknown

This climb goes straight up the wall from the beach to the same anchor as *Gecko Babe*. At one point, it may have been an extension of *Sam I'm Not,* but this is how it is climbed now. It shares its starting moves with *Gecko Babe*.

7. GECKO BABE — 6a (5.10a), 23 meters, 4 quickdraws★★
F.A. Michael Woodrow and Adrienne Johnson, January 1997

This one starts from the cave-ledge entrance. Lots of pulling on sharp stone. Critter avoidance is sometimes needed to reach the anchor.

THE DEFILE
Sun exposure: The Defile is one of the coolest and shadiest places on the peninsula.

Wall angle and difficulty: The low-angle slab here is what most people climb, but there are steeper routes. The area actually has a bit of everything.

Hazards: Because the area is damp and in Thailand, all of the bolts here are highly suspect.

Approach: The Defile area is accessed via Phra Nang Beach. To reach Phra Nang Beach, walk down Railay East toward 1, 2, 3 and Muai Thai, then go right and follow the Monkey Bite Trail, which goes from one beach to the other between the resort's fence and the rock walls. It's a great little trail, except the macaques often stand guard at the resort and have been known to exact a toll from those on the trail. This trail opens up in Phra Nang Cave about 100 meters from the main shrine honoring the Princess. To reach the Defile, go to the shrine and then past it, hugging the wall until you enter a boulder-strewn canyon at the very south end of Phra Nang Beach. Climbs 1–6 on the wall in the photograph here are on the right side of the canyon.

When you step into the Defile, it is difficult to discern the best position for taking in the view. Standing with the silky sand washing around your feet,

TAM MOT DAENG

Dick and I were looking for the back way into the Prince's Lagoon. Granted, there was no evidence that there *was* a "back way," but a quest to find it would no doubt bring about a jungle adventure. We decided the gully up and right of the Hueco Wall was as good a spot to search as any, and it was about as far as we could get from humanity on that end of the peninsula. So off we went.

Thrutching up through the thorns and palms was, as usual, uncomfortable, but it was the first pitch of climbing where the real ugliness began. For days, Dick had been talking about *tam mot daeng,* or "spicy red ant salad" in English. Yes, the people of northeast Thailand are known to eat pretty much anything, and red ant salad had wound up on Dick's dinner plate when some construction workers from the northeast had put a new deck on his place. Dick raved about it, saying the little eggs were delicious: "like crunchable rice grains" is I believe how he put it. Well, about halfway up the first pitch, he was wishing he'd never heard of the stuff.

There, passing over a bulge of vegetation, he pulled a nest of the evil little bastards down on his head. The ants went nuts, biting him as much as they could. I lowered Dick as he slapped his head and shoulders, then went about whacking him a few times myself. We spent the next hour plucking ants out of his beard and hair. Dick got a bit sick from this run-in with the infamous *mot daeng* and vowed to never eat *tam mot daeng* again. It was that meal, obviously, that had damaged his karma and brought the nest down two weeks later.

you will find the shapes of the walls around you mesmerizing. The red walls, stretching as much as 180 meters above, are riddled with caves. Massive stalactites, some perhaps 45 meters long, dangle above the aquamarine water. The postcard views out either end of the canyon have inspired *The New York Times* to name Phra Nang Beach—the toenail strip of blond sand that begins at the north end of the Defile—the most beautiful beach in the world.

Then there's the view up your proposed climb. Late in the day, when the sun is setting out over Phuket Island, it's sometimes hard to believe how well the fiery red of the main wall so perfectly contrasts with the pale blue of the tropical sky. A climber on *Mai Pen Rai,* perhaps the first route on the Phra Nang Peninsula, is bathed in an orange and yellow light reflected from this most impressive of walls. It is the most beautiful spot in southern Thailand, and that is a very big claim. Give it a try, and if you honestly think I'm wrong, come let me know at the bar.

1. CRYSTAL PRISON   7c (5.12d), 40 meters, 20 quickdraws★★★
F.A. Todd Skinner and Mike Tupper, January 1993
This climb is on the overhanging wall to the left of the photo. Stick-clip the first bolt (if it's still there), and remember you will need a trailing rope to get down. That's if you can brave the climb to get to the top. The bolts are terrible, and the wall is often wet. If it weren't for the constant mist, this would be a classic.

2. THANK YOU, SOPHIE   7b (5.12b), 10 meters, 5 quickdraws★★★
F.A. Sam Lightner Jr. and Ted Youngs, June 1993
Retrobolted: January 2000
This powerful little bulge is just right of the large cleft between the boulder route 1 is on and the boulder routes 2, 3, and 4 are on.

3. "KRABI! KRABI!"   6c (5.11b), 25 meters, 12 quickdraws★★★★
F.A. Pep Masip, January 1995
Retrobolted: January 2000
This climb goes up the middle of the wall. It used to have its own anchor, but at the time of this writing it shared one with *Mai Pen Rai*...we're on a budget with the rebolting.

4. ALLO, LA TERRE   7b (5.12b), 40 meters, 11 quickdraws★
F.A. Francois Burnier and Dominique Potard, December 1990
This is done as three pitches, all of them short.

THANK YOU, SOPHIE

Years ago, the community guidebook was nothing more than a file of notes on napkins, beer labels, and pages from various diaries that was kept in the Sunset Bar. Every climber had to read it, and half of them had to scratch something out and make a note (and half of them had to put their name next to their note). This was leaving the community guidebook in tatters, so something had to be done.

Egk asked a girl, a very attractive Swedish girl named Sophie, to rewrite everything. She mostly sat and watched volleyball, so she didn't mind the job. What Egk gave her for compensation I'm not sure, but she did a good job. The end result was all the original information in a clear and legible form, and for that we must say, "Thank you, Sophie," wherever you are.

Of course, the "Guidebook Wars" then began, but that is another bit of hearsay.

THE DEFILE

Pitch 1: 6a+ (5.10b), 15 meters, 5 quickdraws. This starts at *Mai Pen Rai* and traverses left over the other two routes, belaying at the anchor of *Thank You, Sophi.*

Pitch 2: 7a (5.11d), 15 meters, 11 quickdraws. It then takes off up the main prow of the bigger block.

Pitch 3: 7b (5.12b), 10 meters, 6 quickdraws. The last one is quite dirty, hence the name, and the bolts are in a very bad way.

Descent: You will need two ropes to get down.

5. MAI PEN RAI   6a+ (5.10b), 25 meters, 10 quickdraws★★★★★
F.A. Francois Burnier and Dominique Potard, December 1990
Retrobolted: January 2000

Starting from a boulder at the right side of the wall, this step out can be hard. It's thin at the start, but don't let this stop you. The name is a common expression in Thailand that translates to "no problem" or "don't worry about it." This was perhaps the first rock climb recorded on the Phra Nang Peninsula. At the time of this writing, *"Krabi, Krabi"* shared an anchor with this route.

6. JUNGLE FEVER   5 (5.8), 15 meters, slings for threads, stoppers, Friends★
F.A. Francois Burnier and Dominique Potard, December 1990

A lot of thrashing through viper hangouts! Don't bother. This is to the left of *Mai Pen Rai.*

The Defile Exit

Routes 7–10 are farther through the Defile on a ledge that overlooks the sea. We usually refer to this area as the Defile Exit. A cave, perhaps 20 meters beyond this ledge, was once a Japanese lookout station during WWII. Since then it has served as housing for numerous travelers and, at one time, a number of the local guides. There are routes rising from the ledge, including a 6b and an odd 7a. A multipitch climb that actually went very far up the red wall was put up by Dominique Potard and Francois Burnier in 1990, but it was so dirty and run out that it went largely ignored. Out of respect for the Princess, none of these climbs have been retrobolted and probably never will be. As it turns out, "Defile" is a double entendre!

7. BABOON'S ASS   6b (5.10c), 5 meters, 3 quickdraws
F.A. Frank Dicker and Volker Schoeffl, December 1990

8. MONKEY GONE TO HEAVEN   6b (5.10c), 12 meters, 6 quickdraws
F.A. Sash Nakada and Robbie Williams, January 1995

METEORITES

Thailand's walls are solid, but even the best of rock will come down. One route in particular was voluntarily closed by us climbers due to loose rocks and their landing zone. This was *It's a Boy*, a 7b that reared off the sands of Phra Nang Beach straight out of the shrine. A rock falling from the last pitch would land 45 meters from the base of the wall, so unsuspecting beach bathers regularly were barely escaping with their lives. I saw one stone of roughly the same dimensions as a longtail engine land between two Brits having a conversation. They got up and walked away from their towels and never came back.

9. KHAO PAT GAI   **7a (5.11d), 12 meters, 6 quickdraws**
F.A. Francois Burnier and Dominique Potard, December 1990
This route is different in that it goes up a series of slopers...something Thailand has few of, thankfully. The name means "fried rice with chicken" and represents another first on the peninsula: route names based on last night's dinner!

10. KUM JAI   **7b (5.12b), 15 meters, 7 quickdraws**
F.A. Francois Burnier and Dominique Potard, December 1990
Kum Jai means "to worry," and it's what you will be doing, both about the bolts and the rock quality, if you get on this.

HAPPY ISLAND

Sun exposure: In the dry season, this wall is in the shade almost all day, with early morning being the exception. In the rainy season that time can be shortened, but afternoons are usually cool.

Wall angle and difficulty: The climbs here are gently overhanging with some steep sections (depending on the grade). There is one easy pitch here, but most of the routes fall in the moderate category, with a few being very difficult.

Hazards: As always, some of the bolts are very bad. The bolts on *Happy Project* and *Violent Brain Fever* have never been replaced and are very bad.

Approach: The island is accessed via Phra Nang Beach. To reach Phra Nang, walk down Railay East toward 1, 2, 3 and Muai Thai, then go right and follow the Monkey Bite Trail that goes from one beach to the other between the resort's fence and the rock walls. Walk about halfway down the beach, then either wade over to the island (at low tide) or take a boat.

At the very lowest tides, you can wade to Happy Island; otherwise, you will need to make a short swim or get a boat ride (from either beach at something like 10 baht—US 25 cents—per person...barter). At high tide, routes 1–7 start in the water, so you might want to time the afternoon around the whims of the moon and gravity. Two routes, 11 and 12, are on the block that used to be attached to the main wall. From climber's left to right, you go from extremely good to extremely bad.

A fair number of publications have referred to Phra Nang Beach as "the most beautiful beach on earth." It has been the backdrop for a number of movies and has become somewhat of an icon for Thai vacations. A lot of different sights have to come together to create such enthusiasm, and one of those is Happy Island. This pretty crag, with its own minibeach and jungle, stands in plain view just in front of the middle of Phra Nang. This island was given its name by climbers, but it was originally known as Ko Rung Nok, or Bird's Nest Island. Fortunately for us, the birds grew tired of having their nests made into soup and have flown the coop. If they were still around, we would not be allowed to climb here.

1. WAITING FOR DONKEY KONG 6c (5.11b), 40 meters, 6 quickdraws
F.A. Ian Turnbull, February 1995
Three pitches for the price of one. Pretty sharp in spots and the bolts are the devil's work. I recommend you don't do it.
Pitch 1: 6c (5.11b), 16 meters, 4 quickdraws.
Pitch 2: 6a+ (5.10b), 12 meters, 6 quickdraws.
Pitch 3: 6b+ (5.11a), 12 meters, 4 quickdraws.

2. DON'T WORRY, BE HAPPY 6a+ (5.10b), 25 meters, 9 quickdraws★★★★★
F.A. Mark Hansolman and Will Hair, December 1993
Retrobolted: January 2000
Excellent route, but the start often seems more thuggy than the grade suggests. It starts at the base of the big stalactite system with overhanging moves through the tidal bulge. Boosts are accepted, and spots, even while belaying, are a must.

3. KING FISHER 7a+ (5.12a), 28 meters, 14 quickdraws★★★★★
F.A. Mark Hansolman and Will Hair, December 1993
Retrobolted: January 2000
Don't miss this one. Shares a start with *Don't Worry, Be Happy,* then works its way right.

4. LAND OF SMILES 7b (5.12b), 48 meters, 7 quickdraws★★★★★
F.A. Joe Picalli, December 1992

C-Mac on **King Fisher** *(7a+), Happy Island*

Retrobolted: January 2000

This fine route has an outrageous start, then a serious pump factor. The base is 6 meters right of route 3. Doing it in one pitch makes for a great enduro 7b.

Pitch 1: 7b (5.12b), 24 meters, 7 quickdraws. There is a very difficult move at the start of this pitch. From the hanging stance at the top of pitch 1, there is a heinously difficult variation known as *Coral Soul*. It is rated 8a, but I don't believe it has ever been redpointed (I may be wrong). It was not retrobolted and is thus deadly.

Pitch 2: 7a (5.11d), 24 meters, 7 quickdraws.

Descent: You will need two ropes to rappel from the second anchor of the 7a to reach the ground.

5. HAPPY PROJECT   8 (5.13), 13 meters, 6 quickdraws
F.A. It hasn't had one?!

This is the line of nasty bolts a couple meters right of *Land of Smiles*.

6. VIOLENT BRAIN FEVER   8a+ (5.13c), 25 meters, 12 quickdraws
F.A. Ian Turnbull, February 1995
Retrobolted: February 2005

This climb is quite hard. It starts about 3 meters right of *Happy Project*.

7. HAPPY THAILAND   6b+ (5.10a), 25 meters, 11 quickdraws★★★★★
F.A. Mario Waser and Peter Hachler, December 1997

HAPPY ISLAND, LEFT

Fun climb. This starts on a big chockstone 6 meters above the beach and shares an anchor and last bolt with *Razor Back*.

8. RAZOR BACK   6c+ (5.11c), 20 meters, 7 quickdraws★★★★
F.A. Duncan, February 1994

Pitch 1: 6a (5.10a), 20 meters, 7 quickdraws. The first pitch of this starts at the top of the hill, traverses out a ramp, and continues on to a point 25 meters above the beach. The traverse really gives you an airy experience quickly.

HAPPY ISLAND, RIGHT

Pitch 2: 6c+ (5.11c), 10 meters, 5 quickdraws. The second pitch is pretty poorly bolted and a bit scary. These bolts look pretty good, but they are the same as the ones placed at Duncan's Boot. Read the sidebar "Duncan's Bolts," above.

9. TV ROUTE   7a (5.11d), 38 meters, 10 quickdraws★★★
F.A. Unknown

Rather than traverse out over the beach as you do for *Razor Back*, this starts on the ledge and then goes more or less straight up on the left side of the big stalactite. Sadly, this route has not yet been retrobolted.

Pitch 1: 7a (5.11d), 26 meters, 10 quickdraws. The first pitch is quite fun, but a fall in the crux would put a lot of strain on a very old-looking bolt.

Pitch 2: 6a+ (5.10b), 12 meters, 6 quickdraws.

Descent: You need more than one rope to get down from this, and the first anchor is a bit far out with a standard rope. Wait until it gets retrobolted before you get on it.

10. JUNGLE BOOGIE   6b+ (5.10d), 25 meters, 10 quickdraws★★★★
F.A. Stefan Pisburek and Markus Weisenforth, February 1998

Let's call this extremely grippable or a little porcupinish. Fun climb, with a nice view. It starts 4.5 meters right of *Razor Back*.

11. GALETTE S'ABSTENIR   7a+ (5.12a), 27 meters, 10 quickdraws★★★★★
F.A. Alan Dudoignan, date unknown

This is classic Thai jug pulling, and it has a Buoux-type finish to keep you on your toes.

12. PEE MAI   7a (5.11d), 27 meters, 10 quickdraws
F.A. Pascal Clementi, January 1995

Not recommended. This is the sharpest route in Thailand, making it possibly the sharpest route in the world, but it makes up for it with boring moves and a contrived location. Don't bother. The name, depending on the tone, probably means "Happy New Year."

ESCHER WORLD

Sun exposure: This is really a downside to Escher World. It faces southwest, so in the dry season it gets a lot of sun. You can expect excessive photons from mid- to late morning until dark. The closer you get to the rainy season—i.e., when the sun moves north—the more shade it gets. By June you can climb here for much of the day.

Wall angle and difficulty: Most routes are slightly overhanging, though a few are very steep. Despite the overall angle, the bottoms of many of the routes are low angle and the large holds makes it a good place for beginners.

BABES IN THAILAND

It is impossible, no matter what your age, sex, or marital status, to ignore the abundance of attractive and scantily clad bodies that adorn our beaches. The Phra Nang Peninsula has been this way for longer than there have been climbers, and it will continue for as long as the water is blue and the sand is clean. Celebrities from Kate Moss to Anthony Kedis have been to Phra Nang, but at times they just seem to blend in with all the other hunks and beauties. Even after fifteen years of this constant visual distraction, I occasionally find myself stumbling down the beach for lack of concentration in my steps.

For some climbers, the attraction of the opposite sex takes over a climbing trip. More than a couple of men have come on a romantic trip with their girlfriend or wife and then left alone while she sailed off into the distance with a pirate, and I've known male climbers to carry a small harness and small rock shoes with them wherever they went...just in case. (Admittedly, these were two of the most desperate guys I've ever seen, and the girls could see it plain as day.)

Todd Skinner, thoroughly distracted on the way to Escher World

Hazards: Because of the intense sun this area receives and the onshore winds during the rainy season, it has some of the worst bolts on the peninsula. Failures are normal, and there have been some injuries here. Until this is retrobolted, every route should be considered dangerous.

Approach: The following area is accessed via Phra Nang Beach. To reach Phra Nang Beach, walk down Railay East toward 1, 2, 3 and Muai Thai, then go right and follow the Monkey Bite Trail that goes from one beach to the other between the resort's fence and the rock walls. It's a great little trail, except the macaques often stand guard at the resort and have been known to exact a toll from those on the trail. This trail opens up in Phra Nang Cave about 100 meters from the main shrine honoring the Princess. Walk to the north end of Phra Nang Beach, then look for a good climber's trail going up toward the cliffs.

This area is technically closer to the central part of the peninsula than the southern end, but you have to access it via a southern approach. Traversing the full length of Phra Nang Beach, stumbling through a sea of tan, very fit, thong-clad bodies, makes this one of the most difficult approaches in the area. It's a flat and a pleasant walk, but scenery often makes it hard to maintain focus on the climbing at its end. Don't be steered away from the one true path.

The original Thai name for the area is *Tum Choe,* which, as best as I can tell, translates to "bat man." Apparently there was a man who used to come up to the big cave to collect bat guano, though more than likely he was snatching birds' nests and just telling everyone there was nothing but bat *kee* up there.

A fun way to get home, or to the nearest shady crag, is to go through the Thaiwand. Most folks don't realize this, but these towers are hollow, and the Thaiwand has a cave passage running from one climbing wall to another. You will need your headlamp for a few minutes, and you will need to do a short rappel when you get to the other side. However, it's fairly straightforward. Follow the path in and up through the largest chamber. Ladders and ropes get you over the worst of the steep bits. After about 10 minutes you turn a corner and are looking out at the Tiger Wall. A short rappel off the *Cave Route* anchors, and you are at the base of *Lord of the Thais.*

1. BEST ROUTE IN MINNESOTA   6c (5.11b), 25 meters, 12 quickdraws★★★★
F.A. Todd Skinner and Mike Tupper, January 1993

This is the obvious black arête in the mouth of the big cave. You should stick-clip the first bolt...if it's still there! At the time of this writing, it had not been retrobolted, so the gear is a horror. The anchor is also a pair of these horrors. Until you hear that it is rebolted, stay off.

2. HALF PIPE DREAM   7a+ (5.12a), 20 meters, 10 quickdraws★
F.A. Dary Robinson, January 1995

This route ascends a dirty black corner on threads. As the name implies, it can be a bit wet.

3. HELLO, DALI   7a+ (5.12a), 10 meters, 6 quickdraws★
F.A. Will Hair, February 1994

Though I like the name, the route sucks. Sorry, Will, but in my not-so-humble opinion, it is dirty and contrived. Shares a start with *Goodbye, Salvador,* then forces itself out on the more blank face.

4. GOODBYE, SALVADOR   6a+ (5.10b), 10 meters, 5 quickdraws★★★
F.A. Will Hair, February 1994

Find this route on the main trail in the cleft between a huge boulder and the wall. Follow the direct line to the anchor on the right. It's an improvement over its neighbor, though still a bit loose and dirty. Maybe it will clean up.

5. NASTY   7a (5.11d), 15 meters, 6 quickdraws★
F.A. Wee Changrua, April 1998
This climb starts about 6 meters right of *Goodbye, Salvador.* Its gear has mostly been consumed by the elements.

6. RIBBED FOR HER PLEASURE   6b (5.10c), 13 meters, bad bolts★★★★
F.A. Cyro Glad, January 1993
This is a little over 1 meter left of *Short and Easy* on the other side of the column. Pretty fun, but wait for the titanium replacements. I seem to remember Cyro had a wild girlfriend who really enjoyed this route.

7. SHORT AND EASY   5 (5.8), 13 meters, 6 quickdraws★★★★
F.A. Cyro Glad, January 1993
This is a popular route at this grade. The guides use it a lot as well, so you need to get to it early. Find it on the juggy orange rock next to a wide crack and column near the middle of the wall.

8. DON'T GRAB THE KRABI   7a+ (5.12a), 13 meters, 6 quickdraws★★★
F.A. Will Hair, February 1994
It's sharp but still a fun climb. This route takes the line of pockets 2.5 meters right of *Short and Easy.*

9. CRAZY PENINSULA   7a+ (5.12a), 15 meters, 6 quickdraws★★
F.A. Wee Changrua, March 1998
Yes, it is, Wee. This climbs *Long Doo,* then goes over the bulge and trends left to the anchor for *Don't Grab the Krabi.* The gear on it is highly questionable.

10. LONG DOO   5 (5.8), 12 meters, 5 quickdraws★★★
F.A. Unknown
This is the line of threads just right of *Don't Grab the Krabi.* You might want to carry extra thread material to replace gear that has seen too many UV rays.

11. THE PLAYGROUND   5 (5.8), 12 meters, 5 quickdraws★★★
F.A. Dean Saydom, July 1994
This climb is 6 meters right of *Short and Easy.*

12. NAME UNKNOWN   6c (5.11b), 12 meters, 6 quickdraws★★★
F.A. Unknown

This route starts on a ramp 3 meters right of the *Playground* and is all done with threads. If they look tattered, replace them.

13. NAME UNKNOWN   6c (5.11b), 12 meters, 6 quickdraws★★★
F.A. Unknown

Do this by starting on *Humming a Song* and then trending left on more difficult terrain. It's another all-threads route, so be prepared to replace gear.

14. HUMMING A SONG   6b (5.10c), 15 meters, quickdraws and some   · gear★★★
F.A. Will Hair, February 1994

This route starts in a hold-cluttered dihedral roughly halfway between the Escher Cave and *Short and Easy*. From the ground, the dihedral appears to be leadable on slings, but the threads are not that big and thus may not hold a good fall. Best to take gear or top-rope it.

15. SCORPION   6a+ (5.10b), 15 meters, quickdraws★★★
F.A. Will Hair, February 1994

Starts in the dihedral of *Humming a Song*, then moves right, then back to the anchor. Fun climb on threads.

16. HUMDINGER   7a+ (5.12a), 21 meters, 9 quickdraws★★★★
F.A. Cyro Glad, January 1993

This fun route, which has a lot of threads, is one of the better ones on this wall. However, some of the route is protected by bolts and they appear to be older than the rock they are in. Safe bet is to wait for the rebolt. Find the start to this climb just left of the boulder at the cave entrance.

17. FREEDOM OF A FIEND   7a+ (5.12a), 21 meters, 11 quickdraws★★★★★
F.A. Cyro Glad, January 1993

Sadly, this route is far more bolt-dependent than *Humdinger*. There are a couple of threads, but they probably won't save you. Because it's a classic, it's at the top of the retrobolt list. You start this one from a large block just before the cave.

Escher World Cave

Escher World Cave routes are just down from *Freedom of a Fiend* and then in a cave. They are the original routes at this area and get a lot of shade. Routes 18–20 are on the left or slabby side of the slot; routes 21–24 are on the steep side.

18. NAPALM BABIES   7a (5.11d), 15 meters, 7 quickdraws★★
F.A. Jim Schwalbach, December 1992

ESCHER WORLD

21–24

20
19
18
17
16

trail to
beach

15
14
13
12
11
10
9
8
7
6
5
4
3
2
1

Very bolt-dependent. Shares an anchor with *As Far as Siam*. This route starts on an overhanging arête on the left side of the south-facing slab in the cave. Bad bolts.

19. AS FAR AS SIAM   6a+ (5.10b), 15 meters, 7 quickdraws★★★
F.A. Elizabeth Hendricks and Mike Tupper, January 1993
    This runs up the center of the slab. Fairly fun, but needs bolt help. Shares its anchor with routes *Napalm Babies* and *Mekong Crazy*.

20. MEKONG CRAZY   6a+ (5.10b), 15 meters, 4 quickdraws★★★
F.A. Todd Skinner and Mike Tupper, January 1993
    Has threads. Shares an anchor with route 19.

21. GOOD WITH A MACHETE   7b (5.12b), 15 meters,
7 quickdraws★★★★
F.A. Todd Skinner and Mike Tupper, January 1993
    This pumpy arête, which is a bit contrived, could exist only in Thailand. All the threads are drilled and often need replacing. If they look aged, make sure you do so, because every one of them is protecting you from hitting the back side of the cave. What a strange feature! The name refers to a jungle guide who, while hacking through vines, saw a deadly snake and changed his swing to cut it in two as it struck. His boss's only English praise was the route's name.

22. THE DANGER IN BEAUTY   7c+ (5.13a), 15 meters,
9 quickdraws★★★
F.A. Todd Skinner and Mike Tupper, January 1993
    This goes up the face right of *Good With a Machete*. If I recall, this route name is related to *Sam I'm Not* at Hueco Wall! The belayer must be on his or her toes here because a big fall will bounce you off the back wall.

23. FEVER DREAM   8a+ (5.13c), 15 meters, 11 quickdraws★★★★
F.A. Todd Skinner and Mike Tupper, January 1993
    Start on the first few bolts of *The Danger in Beauty*, then trend slightly right and straight up to an anchor it shares with *The Beauty in Danger*. This route is very bolt-dependent, and if one were to fail you would hit the back wall.

24. THE BEAUTY IN DANGER   7c+ (5.13a), 15 meters,
12 quickdraws★★★
F.A. Todd Skinner and Mike Tupper, January 1993
    Again, start on *The Danger in Beauty*, then hang a hard right going past the line of gear for *Fever Dream*, up, and back to the anchor.

Chapter 9

KRABI'S OUTLYING AREAS

KANAAB NAM

From the boat dock in Krabi Town (see the Krabi town map in Chapter 5, The Phra Nang Peninsula in Southern Thailand), you can look up the river and see a spire that hangs over to its southwest. This is Kanaab Nam, which figures into the legend of the founding of Krabi town. It was also a Japanese fort of sorts during World War II. There are seven routes here, including three that are actually inside the cave. This is an obscure wall, and these routes have not been climbed in years and have never been rebolted. I don't have the topo for them, but do offer the basic information in a written format in case you climb every other route in Thailand and then want to move on to these! You reach it by getting a longtail up the river, then climbing through the spire in a series of caves. Make sure you can get a ride back from here. You don't want to end up swimming the Krabi River like Tup did. It's a glorified sewer.

1. DRY ICE   6a (5.10a), 20 meters, extra slings ...no bolts★★
F.A. Todd Skinner and Mike Tupper, January 1993
Look for the old slings near the cave entrance.

2. SIAMESE TWINS   5 (5.8), 10 meters, gear and slings★★★
F.A. Todd Skinner and Mike Tupper, January 1993
This route is near the middle of the cave.

3. BEGINNER'S REQUEST   6b (5.10c), 12 meters, threads★★
F.A. Todd Skinner and Mike Tupper, January 1993
This route starts off the beach where you enter the cave.

4. HONEY HUNTER   7a+ (5.12a), 25 meters, 6 quickdraws★★
F.A. Todd Skinner and Mike Tupper, January 1993
To find routes 4–7, go out the exit at the far end of the cave. Facing the wall, this route is on the left of the ledge.

5. FREE THE DEAN   7b (5.12b), 10 meters, 4 quickdraws★★
F.A. Todd Skinner and Mike Tupper, January 1993
This is on the lip of the cave entrance.

Koh Ma
Tang Ming

(Sea Gypsy)

Koh Po Da

Chicken Island

Koh Ya
Wa Bon

6. SPANNING THE UNIVERSE   **8a (5.13b), 30 meters,**
                                      12 quickdraws★★★
F.A. Todd Skinner and Mike Tupper, January 1993
   This is on the right.

7. GOD'S OWN 5.11   **7b+ (5.12c), 30 meters, 12 quickdraws and ex-**
                               tra threads★★★★
F.A. Todd Skinner and Mike Tupper, January 1993
   Also on the right. This one would be good if there were even a prayer of one
of the bolts catching a fall.

KOH PO DA

Sun exposure: Paradiso is in the shade most of the day, but Windward goes
into the sun in early afternoon.

   Wall angle and difficulty: Paradiso is short and pretty steep. Windward is very
long and gently overhanging. The climbs on Windward are not for beginners.

   Hazards: Most of the bolts out here are state of the art, but the rock at the
base of the left side of Windward is sketchy. Also, be careful lowering your
partner because some of the routes are longer than standard rope length.

   Approach: To get to Po Da, hire a boat for a day or half-day in Ao Nang or
Railay Beach at the going rate. At the time we went to press, it was about 800
baht per day. Access the Windward Wall from the beach by going over a small
hill above the right side of the beach, dropping down to another rocky beach,
and then going up through the jungle on a faint trail. At high tide it's possible
to just pull straight up onto the rocky beach.

On the west side of Po Da, past the beautiful sweeping wall that is its northwest
corner (I already tried...it's blank!), is a small bay (Paradise Cove) with a tiny
beach. Back in from this bay is Paradiso, a small, shady crag in a pretty setting.
When facing the beach from the mouth of the cove, you can look to the right
and see, up in the jungle, a large wall known as Windward. Two of the climbs
up here are excellent and two are pretty sketchy, although with some cleaning
they will be very nice (the problem is the base of the wall).

Paradiso

1. MAILLOT JEAUNE (PROJECT)

2. LIVESTRONG   **7b (5.12b), 22 meters, 11 quickdraws★★★★**
F.A. Sam Lightner Jr. and Luang Vintsanu, February 2005
   This route is brand new and a bit dirty, but if you like step jug hauls, you
will like it. Find the start on a ledge about 2 meters above the beach. Near the

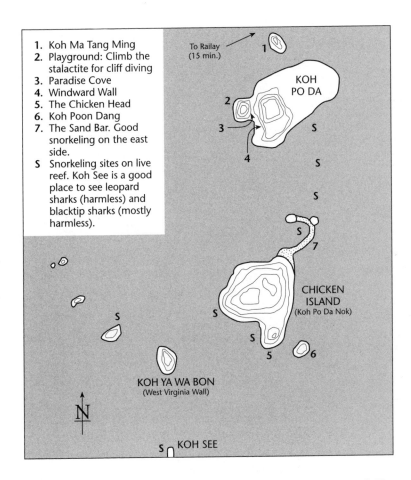

1. Koh Ma Tang Ming
2. Playground: Climb the stalactite for cliff diving
3. Paradise Cove
4. Windward Wall
5. The Chicken Head
6. Koh Poon Dang
7. The Sand Bar. Good snorkeling on the east side.
S Snorkeling sites on live reef. Koh See is a good place to see leopard sharks (harmless) and blacktip sharks (mostly harmless).

To Railay (15 min.)

KOH PO DA

CHICKEN ISLAND
(Koh Po Da Nok)

KOH YA WA BON
(West Virginia Wall)

N

KOH SEE

right side of the steep wall there is a small ramp that leads up to a roof. The start is here.

The route is named in memory of someone who was killed here in the tsunami. While searching for people and gathering their lost effects, Luang and I found a Livestrong T-shirt at the base of the wall. The owner of the bright yellow shirt, a product of Lance Armstrong's cancer victim support foundation, was never found.

I can't think of a more terrifying place to have been on that horrible day than this beautiful little bay.

3. SHAMICK ROUTE 1   6c (5.11b) 20 meters, 8 quickdraws★★★
F.A. Shamick Byszewski and friends, date unknown

This ascends the left side of a pretty tufa system. The start is about 15 meters right of *Livestrong*. It shares an anchor with *Shamick Route 2*.

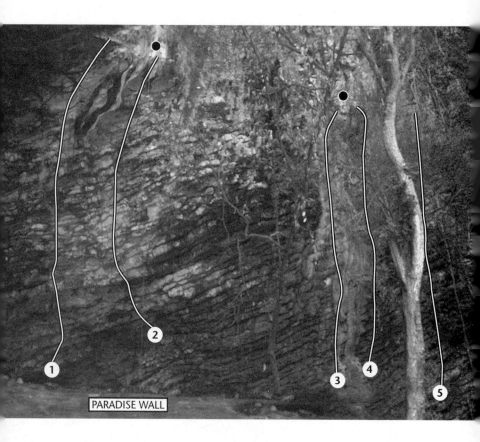

PARADISE WALL

4. SHAMICK ROUTE 2   6b+ (5.11a) 20 meters, 8 quickdraws★★★
F.A. Shamick Byszwski and friends, date unknown

This goes up the right side of the same tufa system to the same anchor as *Shamick Route 1*.

5. SHAMICK ROUTE 3   5+ (5.9) 20 meters, 8 quickdraws
F.A. Shamick Byszwski and friends, date unknown

This route starts about 3 meters right of *Shamick Route 1*.

WINDWARD WALL

1. JUTLAND   7b (5.12b), 30 meters, 12 quickdraws★
F.A. Sam Lightner Jr. and Elaine Catlin, February 2001

This is the leftmost route and the first one you walk under when approaching the Windward Wall. It's dirty and dangerously loose at the bottom but excellent once you get through that band.

WINDWARD
WALL

2. SALAMIS   7b+ (5.12c), 35 meters, 15 quickdraws★
F.A. Sam Lightner Jr. and Elaine Catlin, February 2001

This climb starts 3.5 meters right of *Jutland*. The bottom of this is very nasty, and to be honest, I could not get through to a layer I trusted. Best to avoid it. In the future, a ladder might be established here to give access to the excellent wall above. You need a 70-meter rope to lower off.

3. MIDWAY   7b+ (5.12c), 35 meters, 17 quickdraws★★★★★
F.A. Sam Lightner Jr. and Michelle Garbert, March 2001

Find the start to this one on the right side of the Windward Wall going up steep ground in horizontals. This climb is brilliant. Unfortunately, you may be the first person to get on it in a long time due to its remote location, so it may be a bit dirty at the base.

4. LEYTE   7a+ (5.12a), 25 meters, 12 quickdraws★★★★★
F.A. Sam Lightner Jr. and Michelle Garbert, March 2001

This also begins on the right side of the Windward Wall and has perhaps the cleanest start.

5. REMEMBER THE MAINE   6b+ (5.10d), 20 meters, bad bolts and threads
F.A. Unknown

This has sketchy gear that should not be trusted. Up around to the right, I found this climb, with no written record of its existence. I named it in keeping with the wall's theme, but have no idea who established it.

KOH MA TANG MING
Koh Ma Tang Ming is the big spire that faces the main beach on Po Da. Getting out of the boat here can be a hassle, and the bolts are falling out of the wall.

1. THE SEA GYPSY   8a (5.13b), 50 meters, 14 quickdraws
F.A. Todd Skinner and Mike Tupper, January 1993

This ascends the east-facing wall, skirting the very attractive but severe overhang on the north side of the island.

KOH DO
Dead Calm is a gear route put up by Malcolm Matheson, Glen Tempest, and Greg Caire on Koh Do. Nothing else is known about this.

KOH YA WA BON
Sun exposure: This wall gets afternoon shade.

Wall angle and difficulty: This wall is overhanging but not absurdly so.

The climbing is not too hard, but it is not a beginner's wall.

Hazards: The protection takes a beating out here, so watch for bad hardware. Tom Cecil has even ventured so far as to say that the routes have reached their "expiration date." Also, it is possible that fishermen will steal the ropes that are fixed in place. If so, getting around out here will be quite difficult.

Approach: You need to hire the boat for at least the afternoon for this crag. Each leg of the trip is about 30 minutes. If there is any wind, you might want to blow it off and climb somewhere else. Wind will mean swell, and swell will mean your boat driver might not want to get close enough to the wall to let you get out. Accessing the wall means climbing the fixed lines. They were set up for prusiks or ascenders and are rappellable, but getting out of the boat and staying dry will be one of your cruxes. I think we can dub this fixed pitch "Squeal Like a Pig"! Routes 4–7 are accessed by traversing right along a fixed line that runs across the wall from the top of the vertical fixed lines.

South of Po Da is Chicken Island, and south of that is a karst spire poking out of the sea called Koh Ya Wa Bon. The southeast face of this island, dubbed the West Virginia Wall, has seven climbs on it. The wall goes into the shade in the afternoon, so it might make a nice combination with Windward on Po Da, which goes into the sun in the afternoon. Take a mask and snorkel with you to make sure you have something to do if you can't get on the wall.

1. FRIEND OF THE DEVIL   7a+ (5.12a), 30 meters, 10 quickdraws★★★★★
F.A. Tom Cecil, Mark Miner, Doug Downs, Josh Lyons, and Chaz, December 2003
This is the left-most line starting about 3 meters to the left of the fixed ropes. You get to it by climbing the ropes and then traversing to the base past various bits of fixed hardware.

2. RIPPLE   7a (5.11d), 30 meters, 10 quickdraws★★★★★
F.A. Tom Cecil, Mark Miner, Doug Downs, Josh Lyons, and Chaz, December 2003
This starts 1 meter left of the fixed lines.

3. AMERICAN BEAUTY   6c+ (5.11c), 70 meters, 12 quickdraws★★★★★
F.A. Tom Cecil, Mark Miner, Doug Downs, Josh Lyons, and Chaz, December 2003
This three-pitch climb goes up from the fixed ropes and then straight up the wall. Each pitch is 30 meters or less, so a single 60-meter rope should be enough. You may have to back-clip the second pitch, and you should watch the ends of the rope or tie a knot in it when rappelling.

Pitch 1: 6a+ (5.10a). Climb 30 meters, past a cave to a nice ledge above the rope traverse.

Pitch 2: 6c+ (5.11c). Continue on up and left on steep ground to a cave belay.

KOH YA WA BON

Pitch 3: 6b (5.10b). Climb up and right to an anchor. It is probably easier to clean this via top-rope rather than belay from the high anchor.

4. COUNTRY ROADS   6a (5.10a), 30 meters, 10 quickdraws★★★
F.A. Tom Cecil, Mark Miner, Doug Downs, Josh Lyons, and Chaz, December 2003
   This climb goes out the right side of the cave at the end of the fixed lines. You climb this one to access routes 5–7.

5. CHAMPE   6b+ (5.10d), 30 meters, 10 quickdraws★★★★★
F.A. Tom Cecil, Mark Miner, Doug Downs, Josh Lyons, and Chaz, December 2003
   This climb is found, when climbing *Country Roads,* by going left to an anchor rather than right to the ledge. The climb itself goes up the right side of the giant stalactite.

6. SENECA   7b (5.12b), 30 meters, 12 quickdraws★★★★★
F.A. Tom Cecil, Mark Miner, Doug Downs, Josh Lyons, and Chaz, December 2003
   Climb to the ledge at the top of *Country Roads.* From there, climb straight up a steep wall.

7. NELSON   7a (5.11d), 30 meters, 12 quickdraws★★★★★
F.A. Tom Cecil, Mark Miner, Doug Downs, Josh Lyons, and Chaz, December 2003
   This climb starts near the right side of the ledge at the top of *Country Roads.* A bouldery start leads to easier climbing up and right from the ledge.

KOH HONG GROUP
About 30 kilometers northwest of Phra Nang is the Koh Hong Group of islands (see the Krabi Province map in Chapter 5, The Phra Nang Peninsula in Southern Thailand). For years, climbers have been eyeing these walls, and recently a number of exceptional venues have opened up. Among them is Koh Pak Bia, an island with perhaps a dozen four- and five-star climbs all established by Tom Cecil, Mark Miner, Mike Ho, and company. Unfortunately, a topo does not exist yet because the birds' nest gatherers have asked that we let them control that information. It is possible to climb here, but you will have to check with those guys first. The boys at Cliffsman Climbing Shop and Luang at Hot Rock seem to be up on the access issues here better than anyone.

   I cannot overstate the importance of not climbing on these islands if you do not have permission from the birds' nest gatherers. These men have the right to shoot you for trespassing, and this right has been recently upheld in a Thai court. *Do not climb here if you do not have permission.* Check at the climbing shops. Luang and the boys at Cliffsman are all up to date on the conditions.

Chapter 10

KOH PHI PHI

It's astounding. You can't imagine how beautiful Koh Phi Phi is until you actually see it. As your boat pulls around the cape and enters Tonsai Bay, you will be mesmerized by the walls, some more than 350 meters high, rising out of the deep blue Andaman Sea. The turquoise of the reefs and the white of the sand seem to be designed just to accent each other's brilliance, and the jungle has more shades of green than you can count. It's a paradise, just as it has been portrayed in many a book and movie.

But, as the boat pulls up to the pier on Phi Phi Don, the northern of the two Phi Phi islands, things change.

Like a painting by Monet, the scene is a bit more complex when you view it up close, and not nearly as pretty. You step off the boat and into perhaps the most closely packed pool of humanity in Thailand. The sound of longtail engines and Taiwanese cruise ship horns are drowned out by reggae droning from the discos. Dubious tattoo and massage parlors, self- replicating travel agencies, and dive shops offering the ocean so cheap you have to wonder, all fight for space with hundreds of restaurants, three-star hotels, and majestic coconut palms. The delicious smell of tropical fruit and curry is offset by the odors of rotting garbage and the sewer, and awe-inspiring views are crowded in by sketchy electrical wiring and illegally-built, multi-floored hotels. Phi Phi is at once both Cloud Nine and the Devil's toilet.

Or at least that is how it used to be. Twenty years ago, Phi Phi Town was barely a village with one street, and it grew into a densely crowded, urban mess with 4,000 to 5,000 visitors a day during high season. And now Phi Phi Town has been radically altered once again—this time, by the tsunami that destroyed so much of southern Asia on December 26, 2004.

The wave obliterated Phi Phi Town. All the information we would have given you on where to stay, where to eat, and just how to get around in that densely packed village was rendered useless, because all those places were wiped out, as were the lives of unknown thousands of people. What we present to you here is the climbing information, because it was not altered by the wave. However, at the time of this writing, Phi Phi Town was truly gone, and a plan for its rebirth was not in the works. As a matter of fact, it was even being discussed that the town would never be rebuilt. This is unlikely, but it shows just how completely the island's infrastructure was destroyed. In future editions,

Drinking Wall

Tonsai Tower

Thai Stick

Ao Nui Crag

Oyster Blade

Hin Tak

Fight Club Corner

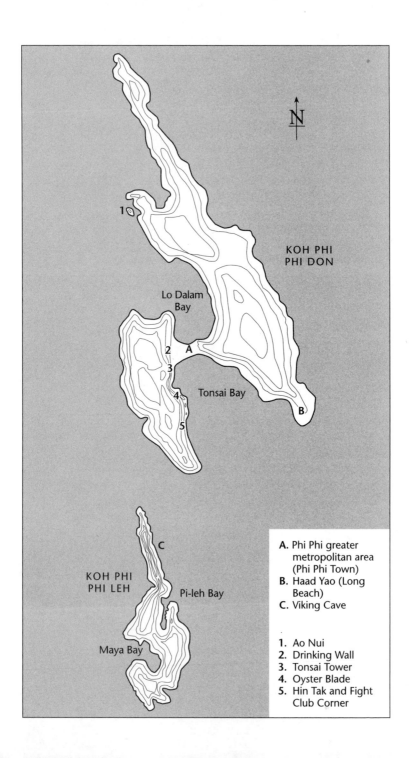

N

KOH PHI
PHI DON

Lo Dalam
Bay

2 A
3
Tonsai Bay
4
5 B

1

KOH PHI
PHI LEH

C

Pi-leh Bay

Maya Bay

A. Phi Phi greater
   metropolitan area
   (Phi Phi Town)
B. Haad Yao (Long
   Beach)
C. Viking Cave

1. Ao Nui
2. Drinking Wall
3. Tonsai Tower
4. Oyster Blade
5. Hin Tak and Fight
   Club Corner

we will include all pertinent information about living on Koh Phi Phi during your climbing trip. But for now, this book only presents the climbing information and a bit of history.

Koh Phi Phi is one of the most beautiful islands in the world, and here you will find some great rock routes. It is the birthplace of climbing in Thailand, and despite the recent destruction, its enduring beauty continues to inspire climbers.

GETTING TO KOH PHI PHI

My recommendation is that you go to Phra Nang first and then make the trip to Phi Phi a day or two later, because it is a simpler trip this way with less "potential" waiting around. Luang at Hot Rock can take you out there in his speedboat. Perhaps, by the time this book is available, there will be other ways of accessing the island, but for now a speedboat is the only way to get there with enough time to do the climbs.

DRINKING WALL

Sun exposure: Like most of the crags on Phi Phi Don, this wall faces east. However, the trees and hanging vegetation tend to give it a lot more morning shade. The best conditions are in the afternoon, but you could climb here in the morning in filtered sunlight.

Wall angle and difficulty: The climbs here are mostly intermediate-level sport routes. However, though they are vertical to slightly overhanging, the compact nature of the rock tends to make each route a bit harder for its given angle. In other words, it can be reachy.

Hazards: This crag had some questionable bolts to begin with. Many of the routes, but certainly not all, have been rebolted. Some routes are only partially rebolted, and even then, some of the retrobolts are showing their age.

Approach: Finding the Drinking Wall requires a short walk and, thanks to the tsunami, a lot of luck. From the pier, walk on the main path along the beach toward Tonsai Tower. After going a couple hundred meters past the (now vanished) medical clinic, you will notice a (mostly destroyed) large grove of coconut palms with only a few bungalows around its eastern perimeter. If you go as far as Tonsai Village (also mostly destroyed), you have gone too far. Walk through the open grove, about 200 meters, at a roughly 45-degree angle from the main path along the beach. At this point you are headed toward the hillside, some employee housing (rickety bungalows), and some very thick secondary jungle. Somewhere on the west side of this coconut grove is a climbers' path going up the steep hill. You get glimpses of the Drinking Wall above, and the path pretty much walks straight toward it. You follow this path for a couple hundred meters up the hill to a level area. It winds around for another hundred

THE DARK AGES

In the late '80s, a few pitches of bolt-protected dagger rock were all that was needed to draw Himalayan mountaineers to Koh Phi Phi for their post-epic thaws. One scantily clad French damsel made a short film about the novelty of scaling walls, and bamboo scaffolding, here on Phi Phi. From time to time, a picture of a tanned body casually pulling down over a white beach would turn up in the photo gallery of a climbing magazine. Then a photo of a climber on Tonsai Tower—yes, there's a Tonsai on Phi Phi, too—pulling hard on clean rock with a white beach and beautiful water below, made the cover of *Rock & Ice*. The next year, there were ten times as many climbers as there had been before, and the climbing scene has never looked back. Thai rock climbing was born on Phi Phi, and for good reason did we take notice.

It all began on Phi Phi and then migrated to Railay. Phi Phi spent the better part of the '90s in relative obscurity. Most of us chose to climb where we could move from sector to sector without a boat and where there were fewer package tours and cruise ships. This meant no one was on Phi Phi to replace the aging bolts, and as a result, many of the routes have fallen into obscurity. Many a wall at Phi Phi has an anchor near its summit but no route, save maybe some white threads flittering in the breeze, to remind us of how that anchor was reached. Even one of the most famous routes, a climb called *Thai Stick* that was a cover shot for *Rock & Ice* magazine in the late '80s, has all but disappeared.

In 1999, with the crowds at Railay peaking, a few climbers began to look south again. Soon there was a migration back, and a breath of life was given to the Phi Phi climbing scene. Groups of climbers began the rebolting process, and before long the old classics were safe for fresh ascents. Phi Phi is the oldest climbing area in Thailand, but it is also the newest.

The climbing at Phi Phi is a bit sharper than that at Railay, because most of the climbs are on vertical, or less than vertical, dagger rock. However, they have a lot of traffic and are thus rubbed down to something your paws can handle.

Also, the fact that Phi Phi's routes fell from use and disintegrated means that many of the routes have been retrobolted in a manner that makes them slightly different than they were originally. Generally, this is a good thing, and despite perhaps a slight variation here and there, the original creator of a route is given credit for it. At times, people have even gone about putting up a new route, ground up, and found themselves clipping in to an old anchor. If you see some tatter blowing in the breeze on a sector of the wall that isn't covered in this book, you can assume that someone has been there. The particulars, other than that shred of evidence, have been lost in time.

meters or so, terminating at the Drinking Wall. This all sounds too vague to pull it off...I know. But it's not that bad. You just have to find the path at the base of the hill. The open coconut grove is the best landmark we have at the time of this writing.

Drinking Wall is an interesting little crag. Most of the rock in Thailand is littered with holds, but Drinking Wall tends to be very smooth in character. Most of the climbs move from large feature to large feature, trying to take advantage of clefts and cracks with the odd hold in between. It's fun climbing and some of the best rock on Koh Phi Phi, but it has some disadvantages.

One is that, like the other crags here, it was left to waste away for many years. A lot of these ancient ruins have been replaced with glue-ins, but not all of them. At times you might find that routes climb partway to their original anchor on new bolts, and then you are forced to use the old relics. Anchors can be sketchy as well, depending on when they were last replaced. You will want to carry extra webbing and such here. Also, some of the original bolts looked like glue-ins but were actually very weak ring bolts. At this crag, don't consider it a glue-in unless you can see the glue.

Most of these routes were established by Michael Hoffman and friends in (I believe) 1994. Great find, Michael.

1. JUP-PHI-PHI   7a+ (5.12a), 20 meters, 10 quickdraws★★★
F.A. Michael Hoffman and friends, 1994
   This is the leftmost route just around the arête. Bad ring bolts.

2. HANGOVER   6b (5.10c), 25 meters, 12 quickdraws★★★
F.A. Michael Hoffman and friends, 1994
   This climb traverses up and left toward the arête and then cuts back. More bad ring bolts.

3. LONG DRINK   7b (5.12b), 30 meters, 14 quickdraws★★★★
F.A. Thomas Bucher, 1997
   A fun route, but it has bad bolts and thus rarely gets climbed. Shares a start with *Driller*.

4. DRILLER   7c (5.12d), 27–22 meters, 14 quickdraws★★★★
F.A. Michael Hoffman and friends, 1994
   Driller is three routes right of the arête going up some flowstone about 3 meters left of the large stalctite that is the start of *Osaptft Is*. *Driller* was rebolted, so after you have done the crux, you traverse over to the anchor for *Osaptft Is*. This has not changed the grade. The original upper bit was fun but was not rebolted due to a lack of funds.

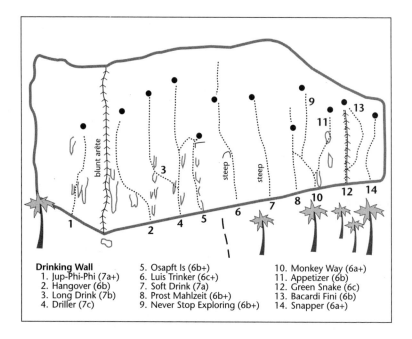

Drinking Wall
1. Jup-Phi-Phi (7a+)
2. Hangover (6b)
3. Long Drink (7b)
4. Driller (7c)

5. Osapft Is (6b+)
6. Luis Trinker (6c+)
7. Soft Drink (7a)
8. Prost Mahlzeit (6b+)
9. Never Stop Exploring (6b+)

10. Monkey Way (6a+)
11. Appetizer (6b)
12. Green Snake (6c)
13. Bacardi Fini (6b)
14. Snapper (6a+)

5. OSAPFT IS   6b+ (5.11a), 22 meters, 8 quickdraws★★★★★
F.A. Michael Hoffman and friends, 1994

A fun climb that starts at the large stalactite just left of where the trail from the beach meets the wall. It was rebolted.

6. LUIS TRINKER   6c+ (5.11c), 25 meters, 9 quickdraws★★★★★
F.A. Michael Hoffman and friends, 1994

One of Phi Phi's best climbs. This route works its way through the overhang near the middle of the wall. This one has been partially rebolted. The upper bit, which is 6b, is still quite a mess, but the lower 25 meters is brilliant, if not a little bit sporty. The bouldery start to this route is just right of where the trail comes to the wall.

7. SOFT DRINK   7a (5.11d), 22 meters, 8 quickdraws★★★
F.A. Thomas Bucher, 1997

I was told this route was rebolted, but I cannot confirm that and sort of doubt it. It goes through the overhangs in a faint dihedral.

8. PROST MAHLZEIT   6b+ (5.11a), 20 meters, 6 quickdraws★★
F.A. Michael Hoffman and friends, 1994

Forest Dramis pulling on the impeccable rock of Luis Trinker *(6c+) at the Drinking Wall on Koh Phi Phi*

This route starts at a faint pink stain to the right of *Soft Drink*. It goes through a bulge to a ledge, then a bit more climbing leads to an anchor shared with *Monkey Way*.

9. NEVER STOP EXPLORING 6b+ (5.11a), 25 meters, 11 quickdraws★★★
F.A. Michael Hoffman and friends, 1994

You climb this by going partway up *Prost Mahlzeit* or *Monkey Way* and then going past a nice glue-in staple to some ugly protection. At this time, the route is not safe.

10. MONKEY WAY   6a+ (5.10b), 20 meters, 8 quickdraws★
F.A. Michael Hoffman and friends, 1994
This route traverses up and left with a crack to join with routes *Never Stop Exploring* and *Prost Mahlzeit*. It was established with good glue-ins by Soley Onbut, but they were put in the wrong place and thus make the route a little sketchy. There is a large stalactite just right of its start.

11. APPETIZER   6b (5.10c), 24 meters, 7 quickdraws★★★
F.A. Michael Hoffman and friends, 1994
Appetizer, as well as the next two routes right, have not been rebolted. Shares a start with *Monkey Way* and then goes right through dirty stalactites.

12. GREEN SNAKE   6c (5.11b), 25 meters, 8 quickdraws★★★
F.A. Michael Hoffman and friends, 1994
This climb has bad bolts. It goes up a bulge in the rock just left of an arête.

13. BACARDI FINI   6b (5.10c), 25 meters, 10 quickdraws★★★
F.A. Michael Hoffman and friends, 1994
Green Snake and this climb share a start, but *Bacardi Fini* follows a crack that can be found about 6 meters up, out to the right and then back left to a shared anchor. It has not been rebolted.

14. SNAPPER   6a+ (5.10b), 22 meters, 10 quickdraws★★★★★
F.A. Michael Hoffman and friends, 1994
The farthest right of the routes, though some tatters can be seen in the vines out right, perhaps from some remnants of the first ascent of this route. This starts with a bit of a boulder problem just right of a fin, then goes up pocketed rock right of the *Bacardi Fini* crack. Excellent climb.

TONSAI

Sun exposure: Like most crags on Phi Phi, this wall comes into the shade in the afternoon. It gathers a lot of heat in the morning, so your best bet is to have an extra cup of coffee and catch up on email before heading out.

Wall angle and difficulty: The routes can overhang, and they can be complete slabs, but somehow the wall averages out to be about vertical. Most of the climbs here are in the easy to moderate category, but a bit of commitment is required for doing the bigger routes. Beginners should not get sucked into something they are not prepared for.

Hazards: Many of the routes are retrobolted, but some vestiges of the past still exist. This wall sees a lot of traffic, so most of the loose rock has been cleared away. However, meteors have been known to cut free from the routes in the middle and the right side of the wall. One other thing; after the tsunami, the area below this wall was used as a giant burn pile. Virtually everything that could be burned, and I think I mean everything, was burned there. Be careful when approaching it.

Approach: This is the one crag you can reach at any tide and regardless of whether you have a boat or not. Just walk to the west end of the beach in Tonsai Bay, step onto the well-worn trail, and hike up for about 60 seconds. You're there.

Tonsai on Railay Beach is what most returning climbers think of as Tonsai, but if you were returning and your last visit was in 1991, Koh Phi Phi's *Tonsai* (Thai for "tower") would be what would come to mind. This is the original Tonsai, and this was the location of the biggest routes in Thailand in the first few years of climbing here. Nowadays it is a very popular place due in part to the number of moderate routes and the fact that it is so easy to access.

The information provided here is given with a couple of caveats. First, you will quickly come to realize that the rush to develop this wall in the last few years has filled in the cliff with so many climbs that it is often difficult to differentiate between them. That is the price we pay for having so many choices. Fortunately, they are all fairly similar in grade and therefore most people will be able to make do.

The second caveat is that there are discrepancies in our information regarding who put each climb up and when they did it. I already mentioned how new climbs have been done on top of old, establishing climbs long after the older fixed anchors had fallen from the wall, but Phi Phi has another problem as well. Like Railay in the early '90s, there is a lot of friction between a number of the locals here, so who did what is often disputed. This has led to one individual, Suchard Sripoh, chopping some of the routes. If you see him, you should ask him why; it's a mystery to me.

We tried to put down the information as we understand it, and we hope that those who established the routes won't be mad if they disagree with our understanding of it. For you, the climber, it really doesn't mean too much because the name of the first ascensionist is probably not going to change whether or not you enjoy the route.

From *Ban Dai* to the right, the information gets sketchy. The quarrels between the locals over who did what first has degraded, on this side of the wall, to the point where some bolts have been chopped. You can assume that most of routes 14–24 are between 6a and 6b+ and that it takes two ropes to get down from the higher anchors. Suffice it to say that there are arguments, but in my opinion Magnus Wiklund did the lion's share of the work.

Oh...the wall is pretty much a grid of bolts and slings, indicating that all the rock is climbable. That being the case, you can consider that there is really not

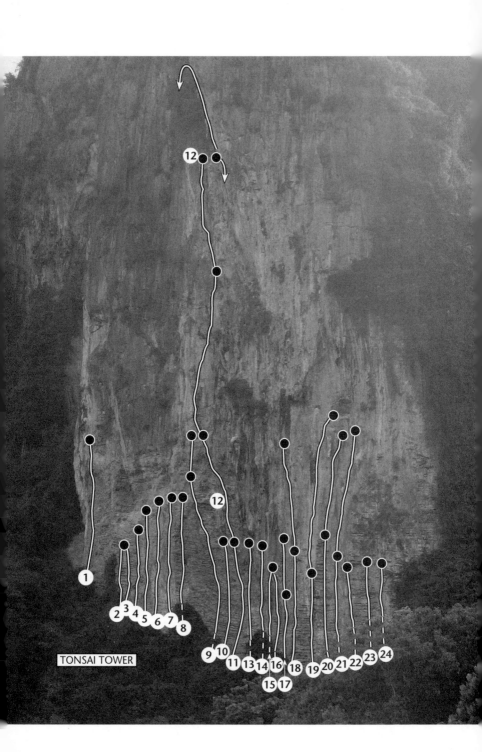

TONSAI TOWER

too much difference in either the difficulty rating or the star rating. The grades change only according to length and whether or not there is a bulge, and they all get three or four stars, depending on your mood when you climb it!

1. SUT YAWD   6a+ (5.10b), 30 meters, 12 quickdraws★★★★
F.A. Suchard Sripoh, July 2001
This climb is found on the very left side of the wall near the white and gray flowstone.

2. BRIAN FAGMAN   5+(5.9), 12 meters, 6 quickdraws★★★
F.A. Soley Onbut and Magnus Wiklund, December 2000
A short climb that starts down and right of *Sut Yawd* just right of the last bits of vine to hang onto the wall.

3. LATITUDE 8   5+ (5.9), 12 meters, 8 quickdraws★★★★
F.A. Dolby Money and Wilfried Colonna, November 1987
Retrobolted: April 2000
This climb, lying just right of *Brian Fagman,* is another strong contender for "first in Thailand." Just for that reason, I'm giving it four stars.

4. BARON VON TOK   6a (5.10a), 18 meters, 7 quickdraws★★★
F.A. Dominique Potard and Francois Burnier, November 1990
Retrobolted: April 2000
An original second pitch to this climb extended it to nearly 30 meters, but I do not think that pitch has been rebolted. Stick with the lower, and better, anchor. It starts a couple meters right of route 3 and passes the right side of a small bush.

5. TRONG PAI   6a+ (5.10b), 20 meters, 8 quickdraws★★★
F.A. Dominique Potard and Francois Burnier, November 1990
Rebolted: April 2000
This route also originally went a way up the wall, above its current anchor. However, the climbing was on dagger rock and was not very pleasant.

6. LOIS LANE   6b (5.10c), 22 meters, 8 quickdraws★★★
F.A. Unknown, but probably the Dutch, 1988
Retrobolted: March 2000
Another route that could continue on sharp climbing higher up the wall but is best not to. The lower pitch is plenty of fun.

7. MR. PHI PHI   6b (5.10c), 25 meters, 12 quickdraws★★★★
F.A. Suchard Sripoh and Pushpong Nomai, December 2000

This climb goes up the smear of flowstone that covers over the horizontals. The left fork of the trail comes out at this route's base.

Starting with roughly *Mr. Phi Phi* and working right, there are discrepancies in first ascent rights for virtually every climb established since 1992. Fortunately, you probably don't care!

8. SEVEN SAMURAI   6b+ (5.10d), 25 meters, 12 quickdraws★★★★
F.A. Shamick Byszewski and Cathy Beloeil, April 2001
This climb is the leftmost of those in the steep, somewhat loose rock in the middle of the wall. It has had a bit of loose rock in the past, but then, so has everything else up here.

9. GLADIATOR   6c (5.11b) 28 meters (35 to second anchor), 16 quickdraws★★★★
F.A. Shamick Byszewski and Cathy Beloeil, April 2001
Starting perhaps 7.5 meters right of *Seven Samurai,* this climb ascends the steepest part of the horizontally broken face on the right side of the most rotten bit. Powerful moves on big holds make it fun. The first anchor will get you safely back to the ground with a 60-meter rope. If you continue on to the second anchor, you will need a 70-meter rope...with stretch. The right fork of the trail comes out at the base of this climb.

10. THREE MUSKETEERS   6b (5.10b), 26 meters, 12 quickdraws
F.A. Shamick Byszewski and Tyt, April 2001
This shares a start with *Gladiator* and then moves up and right to a new anchor next to the original pitch 1 anchor of *Pai Noon Mai.* You can continue on up *Rev de Phi-Phi-Dom* with this as the start.

11. PAI NOON MAI   5 (5.8), 26 meters, 9 quickdraws★★★★
F.A. Dominique Potard and Francois Burnier, January 1991
Retrobolted: March 2000
Find the start to this one on the right side of the steep and broken wall. Dom and Francois decided this would be the line they would push up the wall, but Francois left before they got it finished. Dom was able to scrape up a couple other partners to finish it with.

12. REV DE PHI-PHI-DOM   7b (5.12b), 110 meters, 12 quickdraws, two ropes★★★★★
F.A. Dominique Potard, Francois Burnier, Sam Lightner Jr., and Jacob Valdez, January 1992
The name is applied to the multipitch route that goes *almost* all the way up the

wall. As I understood it in 1992, the first pitch is *Pai Noon Mai* and the continued route was dubbed this name. It all matters not, except that it appeared on the cover of *Rock & Ice* magazine in 1992 under this name, thus sending people looking for its photogenic last pitch, while more recent guidebooks have called it *Pai Noon Mai*. The bolts on the last pitch have never been replaced and are, in a few cases, missing. Don't attempt it until they are shiny and new; even then it will be steep climbing, with some slabby bits in the upper part that are not so fun.

Pitch 1: Climb either route 10 or route 11. If you do not link the first two pitches together, then it is best to belay pitch 1 from the lower anchor (better ledge). You can link pitch 1 to pitch 2 with a 60-meter rope and a few long quickdraws (or skip a couple bolts).

Pitch 2: 6b (5.10c), 18 meters, 8 quickdraws. Continue on from the anchor to a small ledge with a double anchor shared by *Gladiator.*

Pitch 3: 6a+ (5.10b), 25 meters, 10 quickdraws. Continue on up steep, clean rock through a steep cleft to a comfortable belay ledge.

Pitch 4: 6b+ (5.11a), 18 meters, 8 quickdraws. Move up and left on easier ground, then over a difficult block to a belay station on a ledge. The rappel station 3 meters right on the opposing wall is the correct one for descending.

Pitch 5: 7b (5.12b), 25 meters, guts. This pitch ascends the overhanging wall above the rappel anchor. It is also possible to continue to the top of the wall on threads and natural gear by climbing out onto the dagger rock left of the large cleft. Francois and Dominique established this very sharp climb, dubbed *Sortie au Sommet de la Tour*, in 1990 (not in the photo). It was bolted, but those relics have long since wasted away. You will need to take your own gear and slings, and the rappels off the top are known to hold onto ropes.

13. BAN DAI   5 (5.8), 22 meters, 9 quickdraws★★★
F.A. Shamick Byszewski and Eeat Changnarm, April 2001

Climbing just right of *Pai Noon Mai* on the last of the horizontal bands before the prow of flowstone, this climb has had some loose rock. *Ban Dai* means "ladder" in Thai.

14. SCENIC BULIMIC   6a (5.10a), 25 meters, 10 quickdraws ★★★
F.A. Magnus Wiklund, date unknown
Retrobolted: March 2000

This climbs the prow of flowstone to an anchor right of the prow. Staying on the original line makes this climb a bit harder. Most people venture out left onto bigger holds. Far left puts you on loose holds.

15. ANDREA'S SPINE LINE   6b (5.10c), 23 meters, 9 quickdraws★★★
F.A. Magnus Wiklund and friends, January 2002

This shares an anchor with *So People Come, So People Go.*

16. SO PEOPLE COME, SO PEOPLE GO
6a+ (5.10b), 24 meters, 8 quickdraws★★★

F.A. Magnus Wiklund and friends, January 2002

This climb, which was originally done as two very short pitches, shares an anchor with *Andrea's Spine Line*. The name is in reference to the first ascensionists' good friend Ingemaar Isaksson, who died the day it was climbed.

17. HANNA'S GIFT
6a+ (5.10b), 25 meters, 10 quickdraws★★★

F.A. Suchard Sripoh, December 2001

This route might have some missing bolts ....but an extra anchor.

18. COTTON BRAINS OF INFANCY
5 (5.8) to first anchor; 6b+ (5.10d) for entire route, 13 meters to first anchor (35 for entire route), 18 quickdraws★★★★

F.A. Magnus Wiklund, April 2001

Descending from a lower anchor is possible on a 60-meter rope, but doing the whole thing in one pitch means you need to tag along a second rope. The high anchor is a series of threads.

19. WHICH WAY TO THE NEXT WHISKEY BAR
6c (5.11b), 40 meters, 18 quickdraws★★★★

F.A. Magnus Wiklund and Mr. John Daniels, April 2001

This long climb is very good. I believe a lower anchor was added so that you can get down with one rope. Otherwise, you need to rappel to one of the other routes' anchors. It's a bit hard to figure it all out, the gridding of the wall and all....

20. GOLDEN COPULATION
5+ (5.9), 6b (5.10b) to the cave, 24 meters (47 meters), 10 quickdraws★★★★

F.A. Magnus Wiklund and friends, October 2001

This is done as a two-pitch climb—except, of course, that it's done as a no-pitch climb because it has been chopped. The first is 5+ and 24 meters long. The second pitch ascends to the cave and is another 23 meters.

21. STIR FRIED WATER
5+ (5.9), 20 meters, 8 quickdraws★★★★

F.A. Magnus Wiklund and Suchard Sripoh, January 2001

A second pitch (roughly 25 meters) going slightly left has been dubbed *Ride the Snake* (6b). A variation to that is to go right onto *Kiss the Serpent* (6a+), also another 25 meters. If you feel every single pocket on the wall needs to be touched, there is a line in between that is 6b and ends on the right anchor.

22. BRITISH, RUSSIAN, OR NINETEEN   6a (5.10a), 20 meters,
9 quickdraws★★★

F.A. Magnus Wiklund and friends, January 2001

This climb is up and right of *Stir Fried Water* on the horizontally broken rock.

23. MR. VIPER. MR. *PIT* VIPER   6a (5.10a), 20 meters, 8 quickdraws★★★

F.A. Shamick Byszewski and Suchard Sripoh, April 2000

Just right of *British, Russian, or Nineteen.*

24. BIRTHDAY BOY   6a (5.10a), 22 meters, 7 quickdraws★★★

F.A. Shamick Byszewski and Suchard Sripoh, April 2000

The farthest right climb on the wall.

OYSTER BLADE

Sun exposure: Of all the crags on Koh Phi Phi, the Oyster Blade gets the most shade. In the rainy season it gets a lot more sun, but in the dry season you can be there from 10 a.m. until dark.

Wall angle and difficulty: The wall is basically vertical, with easy to moderate climbs. There are some very difficult, tweaky routes to the right of the best climbs, but they have all been erased by time and the elements.

Hazards: Other than the usual warning about sketchy hardware, you need to be wary of the sharpness of the rock high on this wall. A swinging rappel could easily cut a rope. Also, the daggers could catch a rope when you pull it, thus leaving you stranded. Be careful when rappelling here.

Approach: The boatmen can take you on a one-way run for about 40 baht. Make sure you specify that you want to go to Ao Ling. They will know where that is. At high tide, you might have to climb out of the boat, but at all other times it is possible to land in the cove and then traverse under the tidal overhang to a rocky trail through the brush. The wall is about 15 meters from the sea.

I am not certain, but I think the very first rock climbs in Thailand (not including birds' nest gatherers!) are on Oyster Blade. You will find other sources referring to this tower as Ao Ling, though that actually means "Monkey Bay" and refers to the small cove down and right of the rock. The real Ao Ling is a bit of a marine junkyard, a far cry from the pristine bay it was when the Dutch "expedition" first arrived in 1988. Prior to the tsunami, the bay had been filled mostly with plastic water bottles that had drifted in from Phi Phi Town. The wave made it into far more of a mess. This little bay was completely filled with debris from the town and was the final resting place for an untold number of people. Hopefully, by the time you get here, it will have been cleaned up a bit.

The climbing on the Oyster Blade is characterized by vertical edging and

OYSTER BLADE

pockets intermixed with the odd overhang and plenty of sharp daggers. It's prickly, but not so much that you can't pull. Dominique Potard, in Thailand's first climbing guide, described the upper reaches of the wall as "terrorizing at first, [but] it gains in charm, to something akin to a Hindu on his bed of nails."

The pinnacle to the right of the main face has three boring and razor-sharp routes, all established by the Dutch in 1988. *Exit AMC* is on the left at 6a+, *Long Beach Long Beach 10 Baht* is the 6c up the middle (the name tells you something about inflation since 1988), and *Chak Wow Mai Peng* goes up the right side at 6a. All the bolts are relics that can barely hold the weight of a quickdraw.

1. LIGNE DE VIE   6b (5.10c), 80 meters, 13 quickdraws★★★★
F.A. Dolby Monet and Wilfried Colonna, November 1987
Retrobolted: March 2001

Line of Life is a fun climb, but in my opinion the best route to the summit is via *Le Main de Buddha,* to its right. They meet higher up on the wall, and Buddha is the more aesthetic line.

Pitch 1: 6b (5.10c), 20 meters, 8 quickdraws. Find this pitch on the left side of the light gray rock. Climb vertical edges and pockets to a stance at 20 meters.

Pitch 2: 6b (5.10c), 10 meters, 4 quickdraws. This is silly. This pitch should just continue on with pitch 3, and so should you.

Pitch 3: 6a+(5.10b), 20 meters, 9 quickdraws. Climb to a crack, then out on gray dagger rock for exposed moves to a stance with an anchor. This pitch and the anchor are shared by *Hand of Buddha*. At the time of this writing, the anchor was backed with rope knotted in a crack.

Pitch 4: 6a (5.10a), 20 meters, 9 quickdraws. Go pretty much straight up to a decent ledge. A number of variations have been done here, because the featured rock allows just about anything to be climbed. Stick with the straight-up version if you want to keep your hands and feet from being filleted.

Pitch 5: 6a (5.10a), 10 meters, 7 quickdraws. Move up and right, then straight up through wildly shaped chicken heads. Climbing on these things requires a gentle touch, and you want to make sure your rope does not hang up on one (which could cut it). A hanging anchor at the summit, or a belay straddling the summit, is possible. The rappel anchors are down in the cleft between this summit and the main tower. Best to belay each other to reach them.

Descent: Make two long rappels to reach the base of the wall. Rappelling off this and *Le Main de Buddha* is, perhaps, the crux. It can be done in two large raps from the station near the summit, to a station midway on the wall, then to the ground. The key is not getting your rope hung up. I have not gotten my rope hung up, but the number of hooks and daggers on the wall tell me that it is a possible scenario. Rapping with one rope will reach but requires some swinging around very high on the wall. This is not recommended due to the extreme sharpness of the rock up there. You might ask the local shops about a walk-off descent, because supposedly there is a steep gully you can use to get down.

2. LE MAIN DE BUDDHA   6b (5.10c), 80 meters, 12 quickdraws★★★★★
F.A. Bernard Domenech, Wilfried Colonna, and Dolby Monet, November 1987
Retrobolted: April 2001(when rebolted this might have been assumed to be a
   new route and renamed *Red Hawk*)
   This is probably the first rock climb in Thailand. When the Dutch established the *Hand of Buddha,* they did only the first couple of pitches. It seems they decided to go all the way to the summit with the second attempt (*Ligne de Vie*). Perhaps the weather lifted! Of the two, this is the better route and, as it links up to the same anchors as *Ligne de Vie,* it's my recommendation for summitting...if you are so inclined. If so, see descent *for Ligne de Vie.*
   Pitch 1: 6b (5.10c), 20 meters, 8 quickdraws. Climb the line of good bolts to the left of the obvious stalactite 12 meters up the wall and about 6 meters right of *Ligne de Vie.* Belay at a station on top of the stalactite.
   Pitch 2: 6a+ (5.10b), 30 meters, 12 quickdraws. Climb up and left, then join *Ligne de Vie* at a crack. Ascend the dagger rock on exposed climbing to a good stance belay.
   Pitch 3: 6a (5.10a), 20 meters, 9 quickdraws. Go pretty much straight up to a decent ledge. A number of variations have been done here, because the featured rock allows just about anything to be climbed. Stick with the straight-up version if you want to keep your hands and feet from being filleted.
   Pitch 4: 6a (5.10a), 10 meters, 7 quickdraws. Move up and right, then straight up through wildly shaped chicken heads. Climbing on these things requires a gentle touch, and you want to make sure your rope does not hang up on one (which could cut it). A hanging anchor at the summit, or a belay straddling the summit, is possible. The rappel anchors are down in the cleft between this summit and the main tower. Best to belay each other to reach them. Make two long rappels to reach the base of the wall.

3. V. D. RESORT   6b (5.10c), 20 meters, 8 quickdraws★★★★
F.A. The Dutch expedition, January 1988
Retrobolted: March 2001
   While *Le Main de Buddha* ascends the left side of the stalactite, this climb ascends the right side. Start just right of *Le Main de Buddha.* A second pitch of this (7a+) goes up and right from the anchor, but the bolts have rotted off and a fall would most likely put you on the ground. Don't try it.

4. BOULEVARD OF BROKEN FINGERS   Rating unknown, 30 meters★
F.A. The Dutchies, January 1988

I do not think this route has ever been climbed. It was bolted but then not redpointed (as I understood it way back when). It then rotted away, which is more or less where it is today. It would be an easy one to rebolt but a tweaky, evil thing to climb in the heat of Phi Phi.

5. WIWAT   **Rating unknown, 30 meters★**
F.A. The Dutch, January 1988
Not sure if this one was ever done either....It certainly won't be until it gets rebolted.

HIN TAK
Sun exposure: Hin Tak gets blazing sun in the morning. By 12:30 p.m. the routes on the far right side of the buttress are going into shade, with the bigger wall following suit about an hour or so later.

Wall angle and difficulty: *Happy Banana* has a lot of low-angle terrain, but the right side of the wall is tipped back to vertical or just beyond. Between the three different sectors at this crag, you can cover everything from 5 to 7b+.

Hazards: Many of the routes here have been retrobolted, but not all with titanium, so the usual problems persist. The monkeys can be a problem and are not to be taken lightly. Make sure you never look timid to macaques!

Approach: You can be brought out here in about five minutes from the pier. The cost is up to you and the boatman to decide.

Hin Tak means "broken rock" in Thai, perhaps in reference to the Pinnacle, which was obviously attached to the main buttress at one point but now rests comfortably on the beach. The main crag is broken down into three small sectors: Main Buttress, Upper Right, and Lower Right.

You will probably note various tatters and rusty old bolts between these sectors. This was one of the first crags to be developed in Thailand, and many of its routes were never reported to someone keeping tabs on such things. It appears that many climbs simply have not been scaled since the first ascent and thus have died of natural causes.

Hin Tak is a beautiful place to climb, with a clean beach and great snorkeling. However, you won't have it to yourself. This is Phi Phi, and it seems every tourist on the island is being taken to Hin Tak's reef to snorkel. Also, a new tourist activity, monkey feeding, has been dreamed up and put into play here. This is safe for the "feeders," who stay in a speedboat and throw bits of food to the little devils. For you on the beach, it can be unforgiving, because the macaques are being taught that humans equal food. Keep your gear close by or, if you are on a longer route, leave everything but what you are using in the longtail boat that brought you over.

Creating monsters! Tourist taking part in the new activity of monkey feeding on Hin Tak Beach, Koh Phi Phi Don

Main Buttress

This sector is based around the obvious pinnacle in the middle of the beach. You can't miss it. Remnants of routes are out to the left and the right of *Happy Banana* and *Travels with My Aunt*. Off to the left is *Malaria Milkshake* (7a), established by the Dutch, as well as a couple 6as (*Thai Fun* and *Mik, de Mieremuts*). To the right of the Pinnacle, you can see the old anchors of another 6c put up by Francois Burnier and Dominique Potard in 1990. The bolts to these routes have fallen into the sea or are completely useless. I make note of the routes here so that when they do get retrobolted, the information is available.

1. HAPPY BANANA   **6c (5.11b), 101 meters, 12 quickdraws**★★★★
F.A. Wilfried Colonna, Bernard Domenech, and Dolby Monet, November 1987
Retrobolted: March 2000

This climb is sort of the *Humanality* of Phi Phi—or, considering the climbs' relative ages, *Humanality* is the *Happy Banana* of Railay's Tonsai. *Happy Banana* has more than its share of sharp holds, but the setting can't be beat. Climbing steep rock above a perfect beach and beautiful reef are what you came for, right!?!

Pitch 1: 5 (5.8), 10 meters, use a spotter! Find the least sharp-looking holds in the tidal overhang just left of the big pillar and pull up to the start of the real climbing. There may be a thread, but, because the hardest bit is just getting off the sand, you really won't need it.

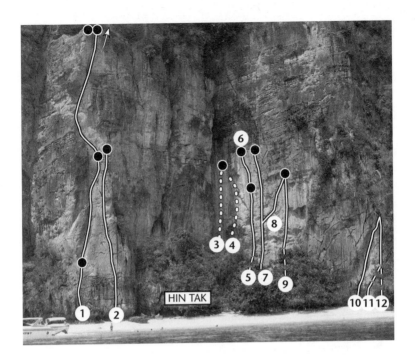

HIN TAK

Pitch 2: 6a (5.10a), 23 meters, 8 quickdraws. Climb the slab left of the pinnacle to an anchor behind the pinnacle. Do not go to the anchor on the pinnacle, which is for *Travels with My Aunt.*

Pitch 3: 6b (5.10c), 18 meters, 8 quickdraws. More delicate climbing out and left of the pinnacle past good bolts leads to a solid belay.

Pitch 4: 6c (5.11b), 30 meters, 12 quickdraws. Climb up and right, following a crack, on steeper ground. There has been some loose rock on this, though most of it has been cleaned off.

Pitch 5: 6a+ (5.10b), 20 meters, 8 quickdraws. This pitch is pretty exposed. Go off the large ledge trending left, then back right. Because of the steepness, it is best to lower the leader back to the belay and then have the second top-rope it. This eliminates having to do an overhanging, back-clipping rappel.

Descent: The route can be rappelled, with some care, on a single 60-meter rope. Tie a knot in the end to make sure, and try to rap straight down (no exploring!) to avoid scraping your cord across Hin Tak's sharper bits of stone.

2. TRAVELS WITH MY AUNT 6a (5.10a), 30 meters, 12 quickdraws★★★
F.A. The Dutch expedition, January 1987
Retrobolted: March 2004

This is some sharp stone, and it holds a lot of heat, but it's in a fun setting and actually goes to a summit! There is an alternative and slightly easier start to this direct route just to its left.

Upper Right

This sector is to the right of the Main Buttress. The easiest way to reach it is to go the right end of the beach, then cut back up into the trees along the wall. A bit of scrambling reaches the cleft in the wall where you find the start of *Powered by Frustration* and *The Glue Gun*.

3. POWERED BY FRUSTRATION   6b+ (5.11a), 25 meters, 10
                                     quickdraws★★★★

F.A. Unknown
Retrobolted: April 2000

   This is an excellent pitch of climbing. The name has been dubbed by the retrobolters and is as good as anything we have, since the route name "Unknown" has already been used quite a bit in this book! If the real first ascensionist will give us the information, we will make note of it. The arête on the edge of the cleft directly behind you as you climb this pitch has not been retrobolted, but I believe it to be a powerful 7b. It is very bolt-dependent and not recommended until it is repaired.

4. THE GLUE GUN   6c (5.11b), 25 meters, 10 quickdraws★★★★★
F.A. Unknown

   This is another great climb; it shares an anchor with *Powered by Frustration*. The story on the route name is the same as for *Frustration*.

5. BARRACUDA   6c+ (5.12a), 20 meters, 8 quickdraws★★★★
F.A. Thierry Renault, Mariele Walch, and Kurt Albert, December 1989
Retrobolted: April 2000

   This route is roughly midway on the wall about 6 meters right of *The Glue Gun*. It is an excellent climb, with a double finish. Most of us end it at the first set of anchors, thus making it the 6c+. It is possible to continue on route 6.

6. NAME UNKNOWN   7b+, 8 meters★★★
F.A. Thierry Renault, Mariele Walch, and Kurt Albert, December 1989
Retrobolted: April 2000

   This route is the second finish to *Barracuda*. It is possible to go on another 8 meters on two bolts. Use your own judgement on gear. It's a very thin 7b+ and would drop *Barracuda* down a star rating if it were the only finish.

7. KARMA   7a+ (5.12a), 30 meters, 13 quickdraws★★★★★
F.A. Thierry Renault, Mariele Walch, and Kurt Albert, December 1989
Retrobolted: June 2000
   This is a beautiful climb just right of *Barracuda*. Keep an eye on the end of
the rope when lowering the leader.

8. SEERIIPHAAP VARIANTE   7a+ (5.12a), 25 meters, 10 quickdraws, the
                              ability not to fall★★
F.A. Francois Burnier and Benoit Loucel, November 1990
   This fun climb is very dangerous, because it has not been rebolted. You
should wait and climb it after the retrofitting! You ascend this by starting up
Karma and then working right to the anchor for *Seeriiphaap*.

9. SEERIIPHAAP   7b (5.12c), 25 meters, 10 quickdraws, the
                          ability not to fall★★
F.A. Francois Burnier and Benoit Loucel, November 1990
   I'd like to offer this one more stars, but I can't because it is barely a climb.
The bolts are just terrible. Again, wait 'til it's fixed...or, better yet, fix it with
titanium bolts for the rest of us. *Seeriiphap* means "liberty" in Thai.

Lower Right
This is the small crag at the far right of the beach, just right of the routes on the
Upper Right sector. A number of short routes *try* to exist just right of *Mai Mii
Panhaa* and *Pu Pui*. They have not been retrobolted and thus are quite dangerous.
The first is *Imkaktus* (6c), established by Hans Christian Hocke in 1992, then *96
Degrees in the Shade* (6b+), established by the now infamous "Unknown," and
finally *Alcoholic* (6a), established by the Dutch expedition on the dagger-rock
pinnacle next to this crag.

10. MAI MII PANHAA   6a (5.10a), 20 meters, 8 quickdraws★★★
F.A. Benoit Loucel and Dominique Potard, October 1990
Retrobolted: March 2000
   Starting on the good rock at the middle of this buttress, this route ascends tufa
stone up and right to a tree anchor. The name means "no problem." A painful
and ugly climb used to exist going up the dagger rock just left of this. Avoid it.

11. PU PUI   5+ (5.9), 20 meters, 8 quickdraws★★★
F.A. Benoit Loucel and Dominique Potard, October 1990
Retrobolted: March 2000
   Climb the easiest ground just right of *Mai Mii Panhaa* to the same anchor.
Pu Pui is a slang term meaning "whore."

12. NAME UNKNOWN   6a (5.9), 20 meters, 8 quickdraws★★★

F.A. Unknown

A direct start about 4.5 meters right of *Mai Mii Panhaa* creates route 12.

FIGHT CLUB CORNER

Sun exposure: This area actually has two aspects. The left wall usually goes out of the shade by late morning; the right side takes a little longer. Both walls are bounded by vegetation that helps to block the sun and keep them cool.

Wall angle and difficulty: The climbs here are a bit harder than most of the other crags on Koh Phi Phi. Unless your name regularly appears in magazines, you will get pumped here.

Hazards: As always, you need to be leery of bolt quality. The climbs on the left were done with glue-in bolts (steel, not titanium). On the right, some were and some weren't.

Approach: Down and right of the pictured crags, you should be able to find a spot where people have accessed the crag. At high tide, you might have to exit the boat directly onto the rock to reach the trail or, better yet, wade a little. At low tide, just a little wading from Hin Tak is necessary to get you to the rock.

Fight Club Corner is a small nook in the seaside walls about 50 meters past Hin Tak. This is one of the newest crags to be developed on Koh Phi Phi, and it is quite popular with moderate-level climbers. The crag's name comes as much from the local scene on Phi Phi as it does the film.

1. EPICMAKER   6c+ (5.11c), 20 meters, 8 quickdraws★★★★

F.A. Sam Lightner Jr., Brian Bergman, and Magnus Wiklund, April 2000

A fun climb on the far left of the wall. As with most climbs on Phi Phi, this one has a bit of sharp stone.

2. P.O.P.   7a (5.11d), 22 meters, 10 quickdraws★★★★

F.A. Sam Lightner Jr., Brian Bergman, and Magnus Wiklund, April 2000

This climb ascends the stripes up the middle of the wall. Of the three on this side of the corner, this is the best. It's steeper than it looks.

3. DEAD MEN WALKING   7a+ (5.12a), 25 meters, 10 quickdraws★★★

F.A. Sam Lightner Jr., Brian Bergman, and Magnus Wiklund, April 2000

This is the first climb you come to on this aspect. Climb up and right to an anchor just below the foliage. The name refers to a drunken threat outside a Phi Phi bar...still here!

4. KID MAAK   6c (5.11b), 15 meters, 6 quickdraws★★★

F.A. Soley Onbut and Magnus Wiklund, March 2000

FIGHT CLUB CORNER

Find the start to this one on the big tufa-column at the left end of the wall. The name means "thinking too much."

5. EQUAL PARTS GASOLINE AND FROZEN ORANGE JUICE CONCENTRATE
6a (5.10a), 18 meters, 6 quickdraws★★★
F.A. Soley Onbut and Magnus Wiklund, March 2000

As you approach the wall from the water, you walk up on a large stalagmite that looks remarkably like an eagle (this may have some ribbon tied around it). *Equal Parts* and *D.O.G.* start on the column behind the eagle. This climb traverses up and left to the anchor of *Kid Maak*.

6. D.O.G. (DIRTY OLD GERMANS)   6b+ (5.10d), 18 meters, 6 quickdraws★★★
F.A. Soley Onbut and Magnus Wiklund, March 2000

This climb goes up the column and then slightly right and past a stalactite.

AO NUI CRAG
Sun exposure: Like so much of Phi Phi, this crag gets early morning sun and afternoon shade.

Wall angle and difficulty: The grades on the routes don't show that this is an advanced area, but it's a steep multipitch crag where you need to have a boat under you when you rappel (or have no problem with getting your rope and gear soaked with seawater). This makes things a bit more difficult than they otherwise might be.

Hazards: Horrid bolts, of course, and the rappel off takes you to the Andaman Sea…not that it's a hazard, but it's hard to do it and keep your gear dry.

Approach: To get here, just hire a boatman to take you to Ao Nui. You want to do this on Phi Phi Charlie's Beach because the longtail will have to take you all the way around Phi Phi Don if you go from the Tonsai Bay side. You need to go ashore at high tide, or at least a higher point in the tide times, because it is otherwise too shallow for a boat to get in here without damaging the coral. You might have to wade a bit to get to the base of the routes from the beach.

This wall is the farthest north of all the climbing on Koh Phi Phi Don. In other guidebooks, it has been referred to as the Monkey Face, a name given to it by climbers due to its slight resemblence from the beach to a macaque. However, this name often confuses the boatmen because there is another formation on Phi Phi with that name. The boatmen all know where Ao Nui is because it is one of the best snorkeling venues on Phi Phi Don. It is in a beautiful setting, in a secluded little bay called, of all things, Ao Nui (translates to "little bay"). The climbing has degraded to such an extent that the wall was unclimbable, but I believe the Über-rebolter fixed up two of the better routes in 2003. Best to check with Luang at Hot Rock on the state of things.

1. DJAMUUK LING	6b (5.10b), 100 meters (revised version: 55 meters), 12 quickdraws, some long slings, two 60-meter ropes★★★★
F.A. Dominique Potard and Francois Burnier, November 1990
Retrobolted: 2003

If your limit is 6b, this is not a climb for you. It is only 6b, but you wouldn't want to fall on much of it because there is a fair bit of traversing and some sharp rock. During the rebolting process, a rope was strung along the traverse to enable a *via ferata*–like approach, but it has seen a lot of UV rays since it was put up there. The original route was 100 meters long and entailed a lot of nasty climbing on dagger rock. The revised version is 55 meters long. The name translates to "monkey's nose." These descriptions lack the gear and pitch length as there were some changes made in the rebolting process and I have not been on them since. Suffice it to say that a dozen quickdraws and an expectation of less than 30 meters per pitch are reasonable.

AO NUI CRAG

Pitch 1: 6b (5.10b). Climb up a small overhanging corner to a newer anchor that probably has a traversing line attached to it. *Kaam Ling,* which is not rebolted, goes straight up from here. I believe *Monsoon* also leaves from this anchor and goes diagonally across the wall to the first independent anchor on *Nai Taa Ling.*

Pitch 2: 6a (5.9). Traverse left, following the fixed line to the next anchor in a large alcove. *Nai Taa Ling* goes up and right from here. If you want to go without the fixed line, there is slightly easier rock a few meters below where the bolts are. Questionable quality.

Pitch 3: 6a+ (5.10a). Climb up and slightly left until reaching the crest of the wall, then climb on the other side. Very sharp.

Pitch 4: 6a (5.9). Continue on sharp rock along the crest of the wall. When you reach the next anchor, the last point that has been rebolted, it is best to head back down with one big rappel. The original route continued on from here, but it was incredibly sharp and not difficult.

2. NAI TAA LING   6c (5.10d), 55 meters, 12 quickdraws, two 60-meter ropes★★★★

F.A. Dominique Potard and Francois Burnier, November 1990

Starting from the anchor at the end of the traverse on *Djamuuk Ling,* this climb takes a line of more resistance up the bulging face of the monkey. This rock is pretty flaky, and anything you use is a bit suspect. You use the same rappel point to get back to the boat. The name translates to "monkey's eye."

Pitch 1: 6b+ (5.10c). From the anchor at end of the traverse (it is possible a second anchor exists in the alcove just for this route), go up and right to another anchor in the middle of the steep face. It's not a long pitch and, with a lot of slings and good rope-drag avoidance, you could push these two pitches into one.

Pitch 2: 6c YDS Go up and left from the anchor, passing some very steep rock and eventually meeting the dagger rock and reaching the rappel anchor shared with *Djamuuk Ling.*

3. KAAM LING   6c (5.10d), 100 meters, guts★

F.A. Dominique Potard and Francois Burnier, November 1990

This goes straight up where the other routes begin to traverse. Lots of dagger rock up high, including a dagger-rock traverse that's dangerous even with good bolts. At the time of this writing, this had not been rebolted and was all but gone. The name means "monkey's cheek."

4. HUA LING   6b+ (5.10c), 70 meters, guts, steel boots★

F.A. Dominique Potard and Francois Burnier, November 1990

This goes up the steep jungle on the right and then onto the face in two pitches. Not fun, and horrid gear. This name means "monkey's ear."

5. MONSOON   **7a (5.11d), 25 meters, 12 quickdraws★★★★**
F.A. Shamick Byszewski and Partner, 2003

This climb went up during the rebolting process, so I have not had the opportunity to climb it. If I understand it correctly, this goes left of the normal start, straight to the anchors for *Djamuuk Ling* and *Nai Taa Ling.* Look for the titanium bolts left of the start for the older routes. It is supposed to be very fun.

PHI PHI LEH

This book is designed to be a climbing guide for currently established rock climbs. As most of the routes are sport climbs and thus bolt-dependent, and as many of those sport climbs have lost their bolts, it follows that they only exist as historical ascents. Yes, you could go out and basically solo them, but you could do that on any stretch of rock. For this guidebook to be a true sport climbing guide it needs to show you how to get on current sport climbs which have protection with a good chance of arresting a fall.

Sadly, none of the sport climbs on Koh Phi Phi Leh (with only a couple of exceptions at Pi-leh Bay) have been kept up to the degree that we can call them "current." For this reason, the entire island of Phi Phi Leh is broken down by crag and then the routes are listed without a star rating, gear requirements, or a written route description. Until the routes are retrobolted, it's a waste of space to show photo after photo with routes drawn on them for climbs that really don't exist as such anymore. If the routes are retrobolted in the future, they will appear in future editions, with the retrobolters getting credit for their efforts. For now, these routes are simply listed minimally here for history's sake.

Maya Bay

At the back of this beautiful bay, just above the beach where the movie *The Beach* was filmed, is a small, picturesque wall with two climbs on it. This wall gets sun most of the day. The routes are listed from right to left.

1. JAPANESE GIRL   **6a+ (5.10b), 10 meters**
F.A. Unknown

2. CULTURE OF PLEASURE   **7b (5.12b), 10 meters**
F.A. Sam Lightner Jr. and Jacob Valdez, January 1992

Maya Bay North

Off a small beach on the north end of Maya Bay are five more climbs on fairly sharp rock. They see very little sun. They're listed here from left to right.

3. LE CRAB AUX PINCES D'OR   6b (5.10c), 12 meters
F.A. Pascal Bourbon, Francois Burnier, Benoit Loucel, and Dominique Potard,
   October 1990

4. LE LOTUS BLEU   7a (5.11d), 10 meters
F.A. Pascal Bourbon, Francois Burnier, Benoit Loucel, and Dominique Potard,
   October 1990

5. THII PHI KOH   6c (5.11b), 15 meters
F.A. Pascal Bourbon, Francois Burnier, Benoit Loucel, and Dominique Potard,
   October 1990

6. LIGNE DE VIE   6a (5.10a), 15 meters
F.A. Pascal Bourbon, Francois Burnier, Benoit Loucel, and Dominique Potard,
   October 1990

The name means "line of life" (somehow we ended up with two routes
with this name).

7. TRAVELING SHOES   5+ (5.9), 15 meters
F.A. Stuart Miller and Pam Andrews, January 1992

Pi-leh Bay
On the east side of Phi Phi Leh is another shallow, pretty bay. At the mouth of
the bay are five climbs that go out a steep tidal overhang to dagger rock. The
routes are listed from left to right.

8. PHI PHI TRIP   6c (5.11b), 20 meters
F.A. Dean Saydom, Somporn Suebhait (King), and Soley Onbut, October 1994

This climb is actually on the wall just around the corner (a bit more into the
bay) from the other four. It may have been rebolted in 2000.

9. SINGHA SEE KU-WAT   6a+ (5.10b), 35 meters
F.A. Pascal Bourbon, Francois Burnier, Benoit Loucel, and Dominique Potard,
   October 1990

Starts on the daggers and then traverses right before going up. The name
means "four bottles of Singha."

10. GLACE PI-LEH   7a+ (5.12a), 50 meters
F.A. Pascal Bourbon, Francois Burnier, Benoit Loucel, and Dominique Potard,
   October 1990

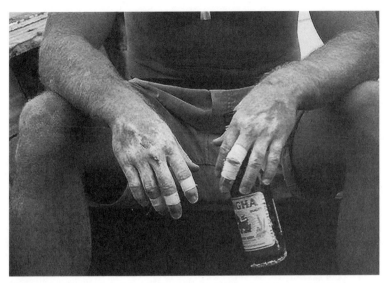

Tired tools of the trade get a welcome cooler on the boat ride home. (Magnus Wiklund)

11. C'EST GRAVE, DOCTEUR   7a (5.11d), 10 meters
F.A. Pascal Bourbon, Francois Burnier, Benoit Loucel, and Dominique Potard, October 1990

12. FACON MAMA   6a (5.10a), 25 meters
F.A. Pascal Bourbon, Francois Burnier, Benoit Loucel, and Dominique Potard, October 1990

The Blue Lagoon
About 200 meters farther into Pi-leh Bay is a sector the French dubbed the Blue Lagoon. Two routes, established by Thierry Renault, Mariele Walch, and Kurt Albert, were established back here. The left is *Calypso* (7b) and the right is *Le Sourire des Crabes* (7a), which means "the crabs' smile."

Chapter 11

LIVE-ABOARD CLIMBING TRIPS
IN THE ANDAMAN SEA

Some of our best adventures in Thailand have been live-aboard climbing trips. You crew the boat, with the captain in command. Sailing lessons come with your berth. If you hate the work, the captain will do it all. His cook looks after your needs in the galley. You eat like a pharaoh, climb like a Sharma, and see some of the world's few uninhabited islands (see the Krabi Province map in Chapter 5, The Phra Nang Peninsula in Southern Thailand).

Of course, there are caveats.

The first is that it isn't cheap. I have the prices all laid out for you below in 2004 U.S. dollars. But to sum it up, if you go with the recommended option, it's going to be about US$150 (most boat operators quote you a price in US Dollars) a day plus your refreshments. (I always travel with a troop of Germans, so we spend about $180 a day because of the beer.)

The second caveat is a bit more complex. As stated in Chapter 2, Climbing in Thailand, under "Access Issues and Local Ethics," the craggy islands of this part of the world are leased from the Thai government by various syndicates that harvest the nests of swifts. It's a very profitable business and they are deadly serious about keeping their private property private. What this means is that just because you see a rock sticking out of a remote reach of the Andaman Sea, it does not mean you can drop anchor and start climbing. You have to get permission, and that is not always easy. Not getting permission will, quite likely, get you killed. The islands are often mined and they are always patrolled. I spent a month in wartorn Cambodia in the early '90s, and I didn't see as many guns there as I did in the armory boat of Koh Petra!

In our experience, the best way to get around all the hassles is to have a boat captain who understands what you want and what the parameters are in southern Thailand. So far, Mr. Nick Band, an expat Brit who lives in Phuket and has been running boat charters in southern Thailand for more than 25 years, has been the best choice. His boat, *Emerald Blue,* is a 14.5-meter ketch that is very comfortable to live on. There are a number of other boats for charter out of western Thailand, but in our experience *Emerald Blue* and Nick Band have been the most adept at understanding our strange needs as climbers. If you are considering this, I suggest you start making your reservations at least six months

Gear Sorting on Emerald Blue. (Bobby Model)

ahead of time. If you want to learn more, go to *www.sail-thailand.com.*

I might add here that if the idea of living on a boat while on your trip to Thailand is cool, but you want to spend the whole time at Railay and Phi Phi, this is possible. Charters between Phi Phi, Pha Nga Bay, and Phra Nang Peninsula are what these boats do most of the time, and you are assured of a comfortable night's rest and a unique vacation, without the hassles of birds' nest harvesters.

KOH PETRA

Koh Petra is the gem of the Andaman Sea. At roughly 1.5 kilometers long, it's really a serrated blade of rock slicing into the blue sky up to 400 meters (twice the height of Thaiwand!). Petra was at one time the largest cash cow in the world for birds' nest gatherers, and the owner of the lease was said to make up to US $5 million a year on just this island. Numerous people were shot or blown up trying to get onto the island, and its reputation with the Thais was something like that of Area 51! The good thing about all this control was that the island was kept in pretty much a pristine state for the wildlife. Hornbills, giant pythons, and civets control the land, while the sea teems with dolphins, lobster,

Dr. Volker Schoeffl getting an escort around Koh Petra

and sharks. It's an amazing place, but not one you can just go visit.

You will need permission, and Nick Band will know how to get that permission, if it's possible. A new company has just started taking tourists, including climbers, to the islands just north of Petra. These islands themselves (Koh Lao Liang) offer a lot of climbing possibilities, and the proprietors of the businesses there probably know what it takes to get onto Petra. They have a website at *www.xsitediving.com/eng/home.asp.*

Sun exposure: The wall we developed faces southwest and thus gets afternoon sun. The longer route stays in the shade a bit longer than the single-pitch climbs.

Wall angle and difficulty: This is classic gently overhanging rock, but the reaches are big so the climbs are all pretty difficult.

Hazards: The birds' nest gatherers covet this island like Fort Knox. It's land-mined, and the guards have high-caliber machine guns that will ruin your day. We saw a lot of snakes here, too.

Approach: About 400 meters from the south tip of the island is a wall facing southwest. You have to climb out of the boat to get over the tidal wall, then go left through the jungle for 50 meters or so to reach the five shorter routes. A four-pitch route was established up to and past the large cave up and right of this wall.

Regarding our routes, we were told *not* to keep a topo of them...advice we enthusiastically heeded. We can tell you that we put up six climbs. All of the single-pitch climbs are between 7a and 7c; the four-pitch route is 7a+ and you rappel the route to get down.

KOH TABON
About 8 nautical kilometers east of Koh Petra is this little island in an uninhabited estuary. It's a pretty place with lots of wildlife. Among other critters, there are giant fruit bats, aka flying foxes, which like to hover about the summit of the

island like a flock of pterodactyls. This estuary could still be home to the *dugong*, or sea cow, a nearly extinct animal that is very similar to the manatee.

Sun exposure: Facing west, this wall gets afternoon sun.

Wall angle and difficulty: This is a gently overhanging wall that is quite pumpy.

Hazards: Ask around for permission from the birds' nest gatherers. When we were there, it was fine, but times change with locations of the rookeries. Only a couple of these routes were established with glue-in bolts, so be prepared for having to rerig everything.

Approach: Getting in here with a sailboat will probably require that you make your move at high tide. There is a spot to drop anchor in about 4.5 meters of water about 100 meters in front of the climbs. The climbs rise off a small rock and sand beach on the west side of the island.

1. EMERALD BLUE   7c+ (5.13a), 25 meters, 10 quickdraws★★★★★
F.A. Volker Schoeffl, Gerd Schoeffl, and Carsten Seidel, March 1999

This climb starts on the ledge at the left side of the wall. It is an excellent route.

2. MUFFENSAUZEN   7a (5.11d), 22 meters, 9 quickdraws★★★
F.A. Matthais Stockmeier, Volker Schoeffl, and Carsten Seidel, March 1999
 A fun pump on a giant flake right of *Emerald Blue.*

3. BAVARIANS ONLY   7c (5.12d), 15 meters, 7 quickdraws★★★★
F.A. Volker Schoeffl, Gerd Schoeffl, and Carsten Seidel, March 1999
 A powerful little thing. As for the name, I consider it a small victory for
the Hun!

4. GLASS OF POISON   7b (5.12b), 25 meters, 10 quickdraws★★★
F.A. Sam Lightner Jr. and Gerd Schoeffl, March 1999
 This ascends somewhat broken rock on the right side of the large stalactite.
It shares an anchor with *Moken.*

5. MOKEN   7a+ (5.12a), 30 meters, 12 quickdraws★★★★
F.A. Sam Lightner Jr. and Gerd Schoeffl, March 1999
 This climb goes out the steep bulge and then up the face to the right of the
large stalactite. The climbing is excellent but very dependent on some small
edges up high. They could break off, and thus the route would be destroyed.

6. MUCKER   6b+ (5.10d), 22 meters, 9 quickdraws★★★
F.A. Matthais Stockmeier and Carsten Seidel, March 1999
 This steep climb can be found on the dark wall 20 meters right of *Moken.*

PHA NGA BAY
Pha Nga Bay is technically the bay created by the island of Phuket and the coast
of mainland Thailand; thus, the Phra Nang Peninsula is technically a part of
Pha Nga Bay. However, most people feel the name refers to the northernmost
reaches of the bay. This area is characterized by large tracts of mangrove and
shallow seawater separating enormous karst spires. For hundreds of years, it
has been a major harvesting area for birds' nests.

JAMES BOND ISLAND
In the early 1970s *The Man with the Golden Gun*, one of the best James Bond
films, was partially shot in Pha Nga Bay. A number of climbing routes have gone
up, some illegally, around James Bond Island, though no technical information
is available. If you want to go looking for said routes, James Bond Island is an
easy place to find because it is very much on the tourist track.

KOH PANYI
King and some of the guides at King Climbers have recently gone about establishing routes on Koh Panyi. This island has been made famous in postcards of

its village which is built almost completely on stilts a couple meters above the water. Not far from here is Koh Batang, with half a dozen routes (see below), and from there it's only a short hop down to the Koh Hong group (see Chapter 9, Krabi's Outlying Areas) and Koh Pak Bia.

KOH BATANG

Koh Batang is located in Pha Nga Bay just off the north tip of Koh Yao Noi. Most of the climbing is quite difficult, though there is room for far more than what we established. The water is quite shallow and murky in this part of the bay, so the snorkeling is rather bland.

Sun exposure: The wall with established routes faces southwest and gets afternoon sun.

Wall angle and difficulty: The wall is slightly overhanging, but the climbs are quite difficult.

Hazards: The bolts here are particularly bad. Also, permission to climb from the birds' nest harvesters is probably called for. This changes regularly, so I have no way of knowing who those gentlemen are. Ask fishermen.

Sleeping with Kryptonite *(7c+) on Koh Batang in Pha Nga Bay.* (Dr. Volker Schoeffl)

KOH BATANG

Approach: It is reachable from Phra Nang in a longtail boat in about 2½ hours. Sailboats can anchor in front of the wall, but there are a lot of sandbars in this area to be leery of.

1. SLEEPING WITH KRYPTONITE
7c+ (5.13a), 35 meters, 14 quickdraws★★★★

F.A. Sam Lightner Jr. and Gerd Schoeffl, March 2001

This climb ascends a steep arête in front of the giant choss cave. Because it's had only a single ascent with limited cleanup time, it was a bit dirty. With time, it should clean up nicely.

2. MYANMAR LOST
8a (5.13b), 25 meters, 9 quickdraws★★★★

F.A. Carsten Seidel, Gerd Schoeffl, and Volker Schoeffl, March 2001

This one is down on the beach about 100 meters right of *Sleeping with Kryptonite*. The others follow lines of rusting bolts right of this route.

3. NO MORE SUNSETS
7c (5.12d), 25 meters, 9 quickdraws★★★★

F.A. Volker Schoeffl, Gerd Schoeffl, and Carsten Seidel, March 2001

4. NIGHT WATCH
7c+ (5.13a), 25 meters, 9 quickdraws★★★★

F.A. Volker Schoeffl, Gerd Schoeffl, and Carsten Seidel, March 2001

5. OPEN PROJECT
8b (5.13 d) 30 meters

Chapter 12

CHIANG MAI

Chiang Mai, the capital of Lan Na (during the era of Sukhothai, AD 1200–1300), is in a region that was first settled by the Tai peoples as they migrated south from China. The city has at times served as a capital to all of northern Thailand, as well as parts of Burma, Laos, and China. Though it was conquered twice by the Burmese and eventually fell into the control of Ayutthaya and Siam, Chiang Mai managed to maintain a lot of autonomy and thus retain its own spirit.

The people of Chiang Mai are almost all Buddhist and tend to be a bit more laid-back about foreigners plodding about than are the folks of the south. Spirit houses are as common as people houses, and monks in saffron robes are as common a sight as tuk-tuks. With more than 300 temples and a population of fewer than 200,000, Chiang Mai has a much more "Thai" feeling than Bangkok, where industry, finance, and the concrete urban sprawl have eroded a lot of its character. Chiang Mai still has some of its ancient cobblestone streets, and a ban on high-rises has been implemented to maintain its older charm (admittedly, a few exceptions have cropped up). Chiang Mai, like all urban centers, tends to sprawl a bit, but by and large the majority of business is conducted in or just outside the more than 200-year-old city walls.

GETTING THERE

Most people fly to Chiang Mai. Thai Air, Bangkok Airways, PB Air, and Air Andaman all operate flights between Bangkok and Chiang Mai. A flight averages around 2,000 baht per leg, so 4,000 baht round trip. Before you leave the airport, or even while you are in the domestic terminal of the Bangkok airport, buy yourself a copy of Nancy Chandler's "Map of Chiang Mai." Yes, she makes one for this city too, and if you used the one she designed for Bangkok, then you know how useful these maps are.

If you choose to go with the budget option, it will cost you some time but not much money. Overnight bunks on the train from Bangkok are around 300 baht and will eat up about 12 hours. Buses run about the same in cost and travel time. Keep in mind that if you are coming up here from the southern climbing areas, you will eat up a minimum of two days traveling, because you will have to travel overnight on the bus from Krabi to Bangkok, wait in Bangkok for the next bus north, and then travel overnight on another bus again. The trip will be more grueling than the international flight over here.

GETTING SITUATED

Chiang Mai is a pretty big city, so I have picked a particular sector for orientation. There are guesthouses and hotels all over the city, and you have many choices, but this book centers its orientation on a quiet neighborhood with all your necessities: just west of the Mae Ping River between the Nawarat and Iron Bridges. There are clean guesthouses, good restaurants, and easy access to the Night Bazaar, and it's only a quick jaunt from here to the sights of the inner city. This is an excellent area for a climber because there are places to rent motorcycles and cars, a necessity if you want to climb on your own schedule, and the drive from here to the crag is as simple as it gets.

EATS

There are so many choices that it almost seems silly to pick out a few. I really liked the food at Antique House. It's authentic northern Thai served in a huge, old teak house brought, piece by piece, from Burma (you can also eat in the house's garden). The food at Riverside is good, but it's better-known for being just a fun hangout. There's live music and the restaurant is terraced over the river. Outside of town, requiring a drive of about 5 kilometers, is Le Grand Lanna Restaurant. It's got excellent food, but you will want to hire a car to get there and back. The drivers all know where it is. On the edge of the inner city is a place called the Frozen Fountain. It's a French/Thai fusion place that leans a bit more to the French side. Finally, for breakfast, there is Café LiBernard. Lonely Planet has said this place has the best coffee in eastern Asia. After visiting every country in the region except North Korea, I would have to agree. The pancakes are excellent too, and this family knows how to carve up a good fruit salad.

ACCOMMODATIONS

Your baht go a fair bit further up here than they do down south. You can expect clean rooms and a friendly staff at all the places, and unlike at Railay, such luxuries as a fan and hot water don't come at a premium. Because Chiang Mai is a city that has been in existence for the better part of the last 1,000 years, things tend to be more stable, development-wise, than they are on Koh Phi Phi and Railay Beach on the Phra Nang Peninsula. Phone numbers, websites, and physical location won't change as much, so if you want to make reservations (advised in high season), this information should be helpful. That said, prices change, places go out of business, and we all know how easy it is for a web page to move to another address.

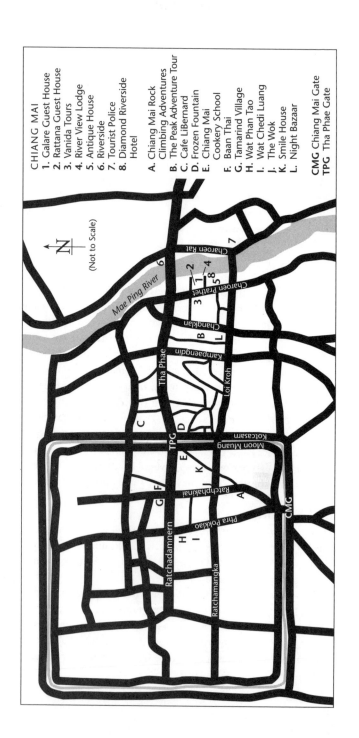

CHIANG MAI

1. Galare Guest House
2. Rattana Guest House
3. Vanida Tours
4. River View Lodge
5. Antique House
6. Riverside
7. Tourist Police
8. Diamond Riverside Hotel

A. Chiang Mai Rock Climbing Adventures
B. The Peak Adventure Tour
C. Cafe LiBernard
D. Frozen Fountain
E. Chiang Mai Cookery School
F. Baan Thai
G. Tamarind Village
H. Wat Phan Tao
I. Wat Chedi Luang
J. The Wok
K. Smile House
L. Night Bazaar

CMG Chiang Mai Gate
TPG Tha Phae Gate

N
(Not to Scale)

Mae Ping River

Charoen Rat

Charoen Prathet

Changklan

Tha Phae

Kampaengdin

Loi Kroh

Kotsasarn

Moon Muang

Ratchaphakinai

Phra Pokklao

Ratchadamnern

Ratchamangka

TPG

CMG

Galare Guest House
www.galare.com
7 Charoen Prathet Road, Soi 2
53-818-887 or 821-011

This is a nice place at the end of Soi ("lane" or "alley"). It has clean rooms with air conditioning for 1,100 baht, a restaurant, and Internet facilities. The family that runs this guesthouse has served as the home of climbers before, so they understand where you want to go if you want to book their driver for the day, for about 1,500 baht. Most of the taxi and tuk-tuk drivers know where Galare is because it is a popular place to stay.

Rattana Guest House
3/5 Charoen Prathet Road
53-272-716

This is the best deal if you are not interested in hanging out on the veranda or watching the boats cruise the river. The clean, brand-new rooms here, with fan or air conditioning and your own shower, start at around 300 baht per night. You can lock up your motorbike, and the staff is very friendly.

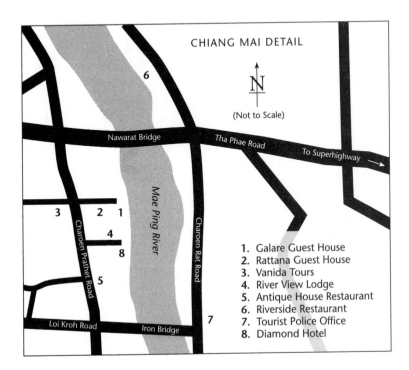

CHIANG MAI DETAIL

N

(Not to Scale)

1. Galare Guest House
2. Rattana Guest House
3. Vanida Tours
4. River View Lodge
5. Antique House Restaurant
6. Riverside Restaurant
7. Tourist Police Office
8. Diamond Hotel

River View Lodge
www.riverviewlodge.com
25 Charoen Prathet Road, Soi 4
53-271-109

This establishment, just a stone's throw away from Galare, has many of the same conveniences at roughly the same price as its neighbor. The rooms are clean and well kept. For an extra few hundred baht, you can get a room overlooking the pool.

Tamarind Village
www.tamarindvillage.com
50/1 Ratchadamnern Road, Sri Poom
53-418-898

If you want to stay in a cool place and are not on a budget, there is really only one worthy place in Chiang Mai. It's not in the area of the other three guesthouses, but all the taxi drivers know it well. The Tamarind is in the old part of the city, so you wake to the chanting of monks and sip drinks by the pool as the evening bells are tolled in the *wats*. The buildings are constructed around a courtyard that highlights a 200-year-old tamarind tree. The food is delicious, the ambiance is relaxing, and the staff caters to your every need. The damage? Low end is about 4,000 baht a night, with suites nearing double that. Also, driving in and out of the old city is lot harder to do (lots of one-way streets) than getting to and from our other places. Of course, the Tamarind can arrange a driver for you.

CLIMBING SHOPS

Chiang Mai Rock Climbing Adventures
www.thailandclimbing.com
55/3 Ratchphakinai Road
53-207-102

If you need any more information on climbing in the Chiang Mai area, this is the place to go. The owners of the place are the primary developers of the crags at Crazy Horse, and no doubt they will have other crags opening soon. The shop has gear, both for sale and for rent. They are located in the southeast corner of the old city near Julie Guest House (150–250 baht per night) and Pha-Thai Guest House (200–300 baht per night). Most tuk-tuk drivers know these places.

The Peak Adventure Tour
www.thepeakadventure.com
28/2 Changklan Road

If you want to climb on an Entreprise Wall in northern Thailand, this is your option. It's 250 baht an hour to scale the 15-meter wall. They have a small shop and can provide some information about Crazy Horse. Just to add to the pleasantness, there is a beer garden at the base of the wall. They are in the Night Bazaar area.

HEALTH CONSIDERATIONS

Prophylactics for the various tropical illnesses of Thailand are perhaps more of a consideration if you are climbing up here. This is especially the case if you are coming in the rainy season. In my experience, there are very few mosquitoes (carriers of malaria and Japanese encephalitis) during the day at Crazy Horse. But then, I have only been there in February, the height of the dry season, and not in times when the rains have left the paddies full.

If you get sick or get hurt, the best hospital in Chiang Mai is Chaing Mai Ram Hospital. It is well known by the taxi drivers.

GETTING AROUND

Getting around Chiang Mai is easy. For much of what you want to see and do, you can just walk. If your dogs are tired, tuk-tuks are cheap and plentiful. Compared to Bangkok, the distances are so much shorter and the speeds so much slower in this city that tuk-tuks are a more comfortable option for getting around.

There are a few options for getting to the climbing area. The first is that you can hire a car and driver for around 1,500 baht per day. They will pick you up at your place of lodging, take you to the climbing area, wait there for you, and bring you home around 6:00 P.M. You can leave gear in the car because the driver will stay with it while you are climbing. Probably the easiest way to find a driver is to step out of your guesthouse and wait for them to come to you. The small *sois* around the guesthouses are where they drum up most of their business.

If no one comes to you and you don't see anyone standing about looking as though they might be an out-of-work driver, then go to one of the local tour operators. Vanida Tours, at the end of Soi 2, is the closest. You can also have the guesthouse call one for you, but chances are, they will just call Vanida and charge you an extra 100 baht for the "arrangement."

The next option is to rent a car or a motorbike and drive yourself. You are probably immediately wanting to dismiss this, because the idea of driving a car in Thailand can be very intimidating. I understand. However, if there were ever a route to a crag that is easy to do on your own, the route to Crazy Horse from this part of Chiang Mai is it (see "Getting to Crazy Horse," below). The tour operators can rent you a car, probably a Suzuki four-wheel-drive or similar, for as low as 700 baht per day. If you're in a group of four or more, that's a pretty good deal.

If you want to get there for a lot cheaper and you don't mind upping the adventure ante, you can rent motorbikes for anywhere from 150 to 250 baht per day. These are usually Honda Dreams or equivalent, so using the clutch and shifting gears is not necessary. You just need to be able to ride a two-wheeler! I feel a need to warn you that riding a motorbike in Thailand is not something the Surgeon General would recommend. I have seen more climbers injured from motorbike accidents than I have from all other possibilities combined. Be careful.

Again, Vanida Tours is the closest place to rent from, although your guest-house may have a motorbike or two you can rent. Make sure you look the bike over thoroughly, and see if you can get the operator to agree to pick up the bike if it breaks down. Ditto for the car.

There is one more option: Chiang Mai Rock Climbing Adventures offers rides to climbers when they are taking guided clients out to the cliff. This, of course, is subject to whether they have space in the van and whether they even have clients, but it does mean fewer hassles for you. Keep in mind you will have to be on their schedule and not on your own.

SEEING THE SIGHTS

The fact is, there are some nice climbs at Crazy Horse, but it's not the huge destination climbing area that Phra Nang is. To highlight a point here, I can say that there are some interesting cultural sights in southern Thailand, but it's not the cultural epicenter of the country. For a good trip to Thailand, for climbers who are also travelers, Chiang Mai is the perfect complement to Railay Beach. I would come up here with the intention of spending 20 percent of my time climbing and 80 percent doing the other things that the north is famous for.

There is so much to do in Chiang Mai that here I give you just the highlights. Remember that this city was one of the country's capitals and that much of Thailand's Buddhist heritage came from the monasteries of this region. If you spend a few days up here, you will get into the groove and find lots to do. In my mind, these are the highlights.

Visiting a few of the various *wats* is a must. Chiang Mai has more than 300 *wats,* and I mention only a couple here (my favorites). Remember that you need to be on your best behavior in these temples. You should cover your shoulders and never point your feet toward a Buddha when sitting down. This is particularly important for women, who should also make sure they don't hug a monk even if they find him really cute and fun...he will have to go through an arduous cleansing process to get rid of all the impure thoughts a female might have caused him.

Wat Chedi Luang

This is one of the larger temple complexes and monasteries in Chiang Mai. It is centered on a Lan Na–style stupa that was built in the 1400s. When General Taksin retook the city from the Burmese in 1775, much of this stupa was

THE CODE OF THE ROAD

The code is more what you'd call guidelines than actual rules.
—*Captain Barbossa*

Before you venture onto the road in northern Thailand, I feel compelled to write a few things about said "road." Great volumes have been written concerning driving in the Third World, so I shall not belabor the subject too much, but a few points should be understood.

First, as P. J. O'Rourke so eloquently put it, "What would be a road hazard anyplace else, in the Third World is probably just the road." If you do much driving in northern Thailand, you will no doubt find yourself face-to-wind-shield with a water buffalo, elephant, or chicken. The worst of these is the chicken, because the locals will take serious offense if you kill the breakfast provider. Elephants and water buffalo can prove hazardous as well, because they always walk to the side of the road you have chosen as your own—so give them a wide berth. Children like to run into the road chasing the chickens, and hitting a child gets you the death penalty from the local village (usually by stoning). Also, the locals have not yet learned to look both ways before they pull out into oncoming traffic.

All of this means you should drive slowly. The problem is that driving slowly will, predictably, end in disaster. The dominant traffic, trucks and buses, drive like Schumacher at Monza. Seeing one of these behemoths overrunning you will necessitate an increase in speed, which will, predict-ably, end in disaster. So the code of the road is, "Don't drive too slowly, but don't drive too fast, either."

And try to stay relaxed. Don't think about the fact that despite one of the highest HIV rates in Asia and a population that smokes enough to make the entire tobacco industry profitable, highway accidents are the leading cause of death in Thailand.

damaged. No one knows exactly what it looked like then, but UNESCO, and I believe the Japanese, are trying to put back a few of the more obvious features. Statues of trumpeting elephants, only one of which survived Taksin's artillery, and huge elephant and Buddha statues looking out over the city from near its summit highlight the stupa. A few of the elephants and Buddhas have been replaced, as have the *naga* guardians to the entrances (very Angkor).

This temple is also a good place to do "monk chat." Monk chat is simply sitting down with a monk and helping him to learn English while you learn what it's like to be a monk. You can find the monks waiting to chat at tables on the north side of the main stupa. This is also a nice temple for dog lovers, because the monks here keep the local pooches—which often get the shaft in Thailand—well fed and (I believe) vaccinated. A very kind woman and her daughter do the feeding in early evening.

Wat Phan Tao

The most amazing thing about this *wat* is its Lan Na–style, all-teak *wihan* (the building where the most sacred Buddha statues are kept and most people go for prayer). The teak pillars supporting this building are enormous, and the multitiered roof is one of the most perfect examples of Lan Na architecture around. Check out the mosaics in the pillars at the entrance—but watch out for the pigeons.

Chiang Mai Night Bazaar

Originally founded when goods were being carried via caravans from China's Yunnan Province to the port in Burma, this is the place to do your gift collecting for the trip. The Night Bazaar could be called the Chatachuk Market of the north, because you can get just about anything you want if you look hard enough. Keep in mind that the folks here plan on bartering the price and that they have been doing it for, like, twenty generations, so you won't get the best deal there is to get. Still, that's part of the charm. The Night Bazaar is on Changklan near its intersection with Loi Kroh. It runs every evening after dark.

Thai Cooking Schools

Want to take something home that will enhance your romantic life and really astound your friends? Take home the ability to cook Thai food. Chiang Mai has a number of cooking schools that offer one-, three-, and five-day classes. Prices vary from 800 to 900 baht per day (discounts for multiday courses) and generally include your own recipe book and the necessary ingredients. You learn how to pick out the ingredients at the market, how to cook the food, and how to properly display it. After that, you get to eat it. To find out when each school is scheduling classes, here are web addresses.

Baan Thai
www.cookinthai.com
Baan Thai is a block up the road from the Tha Pae Gate, next door to Wat Sam Pao.

Chiang Mai Cookery School
www.thaicookeryschool.com
Probably the pick of the litter, this place is one of the originals and has a very good reputation. It has a business connection with The Wok, a pleasant restaurant on the corner of Ratchmangka and Ratchphakinai. The cooking school is located just inside the Tha Pae Gate on Ratchadamnern Road.

Smile House Thai Cookery School
www.smilehousechiangmai.com/cook/index.html
This one is located down Moon Muang Road from Chiang Mai Cookery School on Soi 2. Smile House is also a guesthouse.

Trekking

This is the outdoor activity most people do in northern Thailand. The infamous Golden Triangle, for centuries the main opium-producing region in the world, is the attraction. It's a rugged landscape of karst spires and deep valleys, smothered in jungle or carved into a mosaic of rice-paddy terraces.

There are two major modes of trekking. One is for you to do the work. This entails hiking from one village to the next, having tea, watching people spin

A FEW WORDS ABOUT ELEPHANTS

There is no nobler animal in the world than the Asian elephant. Big enough to thump anything walking, these animals tend more toward a gentle, almost Buddhist-monk disposition. Elephants, or *chang* in Thai, have a long and distinguished history in Thailand. Buddhism's Hindu past, with its worship of Ganesh, set the stage for elephants to be a somewhat religious icon in Thailand. Beyond that, elephants helped defend the country as the first "tanks" during Siam's wars with Burma, and for most of the country's history they were the ultimate beasts of burden.

A full-grown male elephant can lift a peanut with the tip of his trunk or up to three tons with his trunk and tusks (and he produces fertilizer to fortify any field). Anyone who has been around these animals is amazed at their friendliness and pleasant manner, and I can say that I am sure I have never seen an animal, save maybe a dolphin, with the intelligence of an elephant. Elephants have a lifespan like humans', reaching their full development in their teens and dying in their 70s.

Traditionally, a *mahout* (elephant handler) and an elephant bond for life, working and living together as a team. With the end of commercial logging in Thailand (which coincided with the destruction of the last large tracts of forest in Thailand) and the advent of widespread powered tractor use, many elephants can no longer earn their living. The *mahouts* have been forced to take the animals into the cities to beg for food money. If you ate 225 kilos of food a day, think how much money you would need to live on. Even the begging is going by the wayside, because Bangkok has banned the animals from entering the city. Fortunately for them, there are a few agencies that can help with this.

silk and just going about their daily lives. The other is to sit on an elephant and let it do the work. Elephants like to work, and this is one of the only jobs left to them in Thailand, so don't feel like you're offending the animal by hoisting yourself, your family, and all your worldly belongings onto Jumbo's back.

To find out more about the various places you can trek to and the different hill tribes you might meet on various treks, contact our friends at Chiang Mai Rock Climbing Adventures (see "Climbing Schools," above). They lead trips for rock climbing and caving, but trekking is the most common activity they organize.

Friends of the Asian Elephant

This organization (*www.elephant.tnet.co.th*) has established a large hospital and sanctuary for the elephants that are needy in northern Thailand. You can visit the main hospital daily. It shares a large chunk of land, outside of Lampang (about 90 minutes south of Chiang Mai) with a government organization that helps care for elephants as well. In the morning, the government-operated facility puts on an elephant show in which the critters show off their traditional roles in Thai society. An elephant nursery is maintained so that mothers and babies can hang out with tourist folk who might lend a helping dollar or two. Friends of the Asian Elephant also operates a roving veterinary clinic. Weighing six tons, most of the patients require house calls and can't be put on a stretcher and taken to the clinic. All of this costs money...lots of it. By visiting these places and making a donation or just buying a tee shirt, you really are helping those who can't help themselves.

There are elephant centers north of Chiang Mai, but I know little about them. This one is for sure the real deal.

CLIMBING AT CRAZY HORSE

The main climbing area in Chiang Mai is a karst mountain called Crazy Horse. As a climbing venue, it is as different from those in the south as the people of the north are from those of the south. It's still that same Ratburi karst limestone that runs the length of Southeast Asia, but the distance from the ocean and perhaps less rain flowing through the stone make it a different kind of climbing. By and large, it feels a bit more like granite, with larger blocks and dihedrals, lower-angle slabs, and far fewer stalactites. Standing at the crag, which rises over a plain of rice paddies, you are closer to the Yunnan Province of China than you are the Andaman Sea. Coming here, you trade beachside tufa pulling for large, flat edges amid hills that, until recently, grew much of the world's opium.

Getting to Crazy Horse

This is gong to be intimidating as you read it, but trust me, it's not that hard once you get going. The roads are pretty straightforward (ignoring what is said

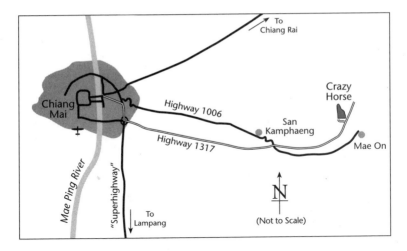

in the sidebar "The Code of the Road"), and it takes only a turn here and there to make it. There are road signs in Western script to follow, and if all else fails, the people are so nice in northern Thailand they will probably help you to and from the crag.

This section is based on the premise that you are starting from the particular block of Chiang Mai that I recommend. Your objective is called Crazy Horse Cliff, but the locals will know the area for the Mae On Cave, which is just east of the town of San Kamphaeng.

The starting point is the bike and car rental place on Charoen Prathet at the end of the small road (Soi 2) on which the Galare and Rattana Guest Houses are located.

From there, drive north on Charoen Prathet to Tha Phae Road and go right. This will take you across the Nawarat Bridge.

Follow this road for a few kilometers and it changes into Charoen Muang. It's a big road and easy to drive on. After a few kilometers, look for a big sign telling you how to go to Lampang. That's your direction...

Take a right onto Highway 1141, commonly called the Superhighway...it's a freeway. Stay on the Superhighway going south for a few kilometers until you reach the "spaghetti junction." This is a set of standard off- and on-ramps for a freeway. Once here, you will exit and take a left onto Highway 1317 going east. This is the road to San Kamphaeng and Mae On. It's a good highway with wide lanes. If you made it here—and you should—then you're golden.

Stay on this road for about 45 kilometers. Watch for a small sign on the left side of the road that says "Muang On Cave." When you see this sign, you will also be able to see the hill with the crag on it on your left. About 100 meters after the "Muang On Cave" sign, a small road goes off to the left. It is just before a tattered bus stop under a tree. Take a left onto this dirt road and follow it about

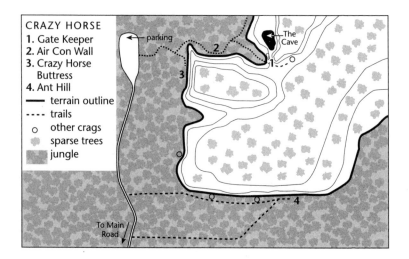

0.75 kilometer uphill to the parking lot. The crag is right there.

To get home, you retrace the route. The only change comes at the very end. Charoen Prathet, the road Vanida Tours is on, is a one-way street. To come up the street in the correct direction, you cross over the Nawarat Bridge, drive past Charoen Prathet to the next street, Chang Klan, and go around the block, returning up Charoen Prathet.

CRAZY HORSE BUTTRESS

Sun exposure: This wall goes into the sun just after noon. Depending on when you are here, this could be a good or bad thing.

Wall angle and difficulty: There is a little of everything here. The majority of the routes are vertical, with the odd bulge here and there. The leftmost routes are quite slabby, whereas the routes at the far end of the crag take on a steep bulge.

Hazards: Although this area is not near the ocean, the bolts still take quite a beating from the elements. Be leery of them. Also, some of the pitches extend your rope to its full length when you're lowering. Finally, watch the ledges and sharp edges.

Approach: It's about a 4-minute walk from the parking area.

This is the first crag you come to when you start hiking up from the parking area. The local climbing shop has done a great job of maintaining the trails and installing comfortable places to belay from. For this, they not only deserve thanks, but also your patronage...let's help those who help us. Along those lines, you should know that the route information given for this area does not cover the entire crag. There are climbs above these routes, and perhaps a few

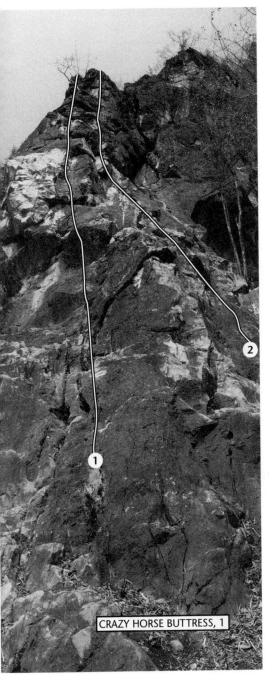

CRAZY HORSE BUTTRESS, 1

other climbs established along the base of the wall. For more information on those climbs, you should stop by Chiang Mai Climbing Adventures back in the city.

1. THE MUPPET SHOW
5 (5.8), 25 meters, 8 quickdraws
★★★

F.A. Francis Haden and Josh Morris, February 2001

Named for one of the pinnacles of Western civilization, this climb is the first one you pass as you come to Crazy Horse. It goes up the low-angle wall at the very left end of the buttress.

2. DING DONG   5 (5.8),
25 meters, 8 quickdraws★★★
F.A. Francis Haden and Josh Morris, February 2001

This climbs the slab just right of *The Muppet Show*. Ding Dongs were my staple as a kid.

3. REINDEER REQUEST
6a+ (5.10b), 25 meters, 8 quickdraws★★★
F.A. Francis Haden and Josh Morris, February 2001

This climbs the weak gray corner just left of the cave.

4. AYAH!   6a (5.10a), 25 meters, 10 quickdraws★★★
F.A. Francis Haden and Josh Morris, February 2001

Find this one's start on white rock 3 meters left of *The Beehouse*.

5. THE BEEHOUSE   6c+ (5.11c), 30 meters, 13 quickdraws★★★
F.A. Kraisak Boonthip, October 1998

This climb starts with a steep bulge of yellow rock, then goes to some gray slabs that are a bit prickly.

6. BLOOD, LOVE, AND STEEL   6c+ (5.11c), 30 meters, 12 quickdraws★★★★

CRAZY HORSE BUTTRESS, 2

F.A. Francis Haden, February 2001

This climb goes up the obvious orange streak in the middle of the buttress. It's the pick of the litter.

7. PROJECT

Looks friggin' hard.

8. DANGEROUS JOY   6c (5.11b), 25 meters, 12 quickdraws★★★★

F.A. Kraisak Boonthip, October 1998
Rebolted: February 2001

At the far end of the wall is a steel ladder that leads into the "arch cave."

CRAZY HORSE BUTTRESS, 3

steel
rung
ladder

CRAZY HORSE BUTTRESS, 4

8

9

10

11

11

This climb goes up the steep bulge 3 meters right of the ladder. A second pitch, *Just Give Me More* (6a+), puts you nearly 50 meters off the deck.

9. THE HORSE KNOWS THE WAY   7c (5.12d), 25 meters, 9 quickdraws★★★★

F.A. Francis Haden, March 2002

This takes the harder line out the bulge.

10. DON'T LOOK A GIFT HORSE IN THE MOUTH   7a (5.11d), 25 meters, 8 quickdraws★★★

F.A. Francis Haden and Josh Morris, February 2001

This goes out the right side of the bulge on the biggest holds; it shares an anchor with *The Horse Knows the Way.*

11. INTO THE SUN   6b (5.10c), 45 meters, 9 quickdraws★★★★

F.A. Francis Haden and Josh Morris, February 2001

This climb goes up the edge of the wall on black rock and is broken into two pitches. The first pitch is only 6a and 20 meters long. Watch out for sharp edges and use some long quickdraws to alleviate rope drag.

AIR CON WALL

Sun exposure: I would say this is the shadiest sector here, but it's not in the shade all day. The sun begins to hit it in midafternoon. It can be diffused by the trees, but it will heat up.

Wall angle and difficulty: These climbs are short, steep, and powerful.

Hazards: The belayer needs to pay attention here because some of the cruxes are fairly close to the ground.

Approach: It's just a couple minutes up the trail past Crazy Horse Buttress.

The Air Con Wall, so named for the cool breezes that can flow from the cave, is a place for burly climbers who like to use their biceps.

1. FREEBLAST   7b+ (5.12c), 13 meters, 6 quickdraws★★★★

F.A. Francis Haden, March 2002

This climb follows the obvious line of pockets just right of the mouth of the cave. It's not quite as long as the lower third of El Cap's *Salathe*, but it's fun.

2. FOAMING AT THE MOUTH   7b (5.12b), 14 meters, 6 quickdraws★★★

F.A. Francis Haden, March 2002

This climb shares a start with *Freeblast* and then moves right onto the gray rock.

AIR CON WALL

3. THE WILD PUMPUS   7b+ (5.12c), 14 meters, 8 quickdraws★★★
F.A. Josh Morris and Francis Haden, March 2002

This climb starts 2 meters right of *Freeblast* in an orange corner. Powerfulus.

4. SPORT SATAY   7a (5.11d), 14 meters, 7 quickdraws★★★
F.A. Francis Haden, March 2002

This powerful start is 3 meters right of *The Wild Pumpus*.

5. AIR CONDITIONER   6b (5.10c), 15 meters, 8 quickdraws★★★
F.A. Josh Morris, Uthit Yodkhaman (Son), Khaetthaleeya Uppakham (Kat), Francis
Haden, and Diana Jew, March 2002

This line, which follows a broken crack and pockets, is 3 meters right of
Sport Satay.

6. SHOW OFF THE POLICE   6b+ (5.11a), 22 meters,
                              6 quickdraws★★★
F.A. Kraisak Boonthip, October 1998

This climb is about 15 meters downhill from *Air Conditioner* (not shown
on the overlay).

GATE KEEPER

GATE KEEPER

Sun exposure: This is a morning crag that comes into the sun around noon.

Wall angle and difficulty: These routes are all roughly vertical, though they have slabby sections and bulges that need to be negotiated.

Hazards: Other than the usual warnings about fixed protection, the one real worry here is getting too lax while hanging out and possibly falling into the cave! It's a long way down.

Approach: To find it, go past Air Con Wall, then go up the steep gully that breaks right off the main trail. There is a bit of 4th-class climbing in this gully that can be belayed if you are uncomfortable. At the top of the gully, this buttress is on your left. The mouth of the cave (really a big sinkhole) is a couple meters beyond the start to these climbs.

The Gate Keeper is at the top of the hill. The first three routes all start in the exact same place, while *All Quiet on the Eastern Front* goes up the rock just a couple meters right. There is also an easy 5th-class pitch on the spire behind you as you face these climbs.

1. THE GATE KEEPER   6b
(5.10c), 25 meters, 10 quick-draws★★★★
F.A. Josh Morris, Kat Uppakham, Francis Haden, Son Yodkhaman, and Steve Coates, March 2002

This route goes hard left on yellow rock, then over a bulge to a small ledge and up a wide crack. You get really exposed really fast.

2. INFERNO   7a+ (5.12a), 30 meters, 12 quickdraws★★★★
F.A. Josh Morris and Francis Haden, March 2002

This goes through a groove in the low bulge, then follows a groove up the steep section of wall. Sustained.

3. UNLEASH THE PHAT PHYSIQUE   7a+ (5.12a), 30 meters, 12 quickdraws★★★★
F.A. Francis Haden and Josh Morris, March 2002

This climb branches off *Inferno*, going toward a small tree. There is a bit of fun in a hand crack on this climb, and it goes straight over the bulge with some big pulls.

4. ALL QUIET ON THE EASTERN FRONT   7a (5.11d), 28 meters, 10 quickdraws★★★★
F.A. Francis Haden and Josh Morris, March 2002

Starting just right of the other routes, this climb works its way up a broken arête to a face, then lowers from an anchor on a ledge that is below and right of the other three climbs.

ANT HILL

Sun exposure: Unlike the other sectors listed above, this wall goes into the shade in the afternoon.

Wall angle and difficulty: The climbs here are tipped back just beyond vertical and are long, pumpy affairs.

Hazards: It's all fixed pro, which looks pretty good but does take a beating from the sun and the rain. Also, if the bees are in the nests, don't climb.

Approach: You find the wall by going back down the dirt road from the parking lot about 100 yards. The trail goes off to the left, trending slightly downhill. The original trail traverses the hill about 30 to 50 yards below the various other buttresses, all of which have climbs that are not quite so inspiring. There is also a newer trail that runs along the base of the wall. Either way, after perhaps 400 yards you should be able to see a white wall up and to the left. That's it.

This is the best of the crags at Crazy Horse. Every climb here is excellent and worth the effort.

1. THE ABSENT-MINDED BOLTER   7b (5.12b), 20 meters, 9 quickdraws★★★★
F.A. Josh Morris and Francis Haden, September 2001

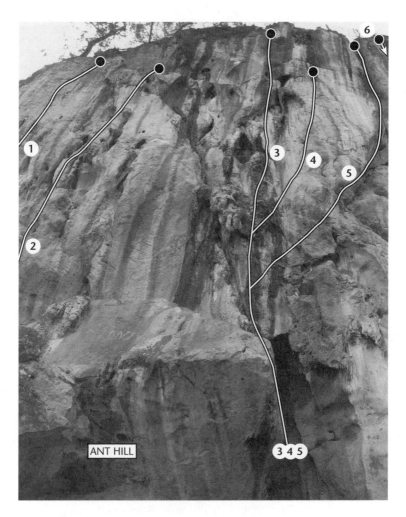

This climb ascends the gray streak in white rock at the left side of the wall. The start is at the base of a ramp that goes up and right.

2. ANTS IN MY PANTS   6c (5.11b), 20 meters, 8 quickdraws★★★★
F.A. Josh Morris and Francis Haden, September 2001

Find this start on top of the ramp. You can belay from the ground. This is juggy fun. It's no finger crack, but it helps if you know how to climb one!

3. THE WASP FACTORY   7a (5.11d), 25 meters, 12 quickdraws★★★★
F.A. Francis Haden, September 2001

This climb shares its start with *Bleachin'* and *Flushed*. At the mouth of a small

The last few moves of Flushed, *a 6c at Ant Hill*

cave, climb a boulder to a ledge, then up over tufas and up a groove with a tufa in it. This is an excellent climb, with big reaches to big holds.

4. BLEACHIN'   7b+ (5.12c), 20 meters, 10 quickdraws★★★★
F.A. Francis Haden, October 2001

Start with *The Wasp Factory*, then move out onto the thin white face. Tweaky.

5. FLUSHED   6c (5.11b), 30 meters, 12 quickdraws★★★★★
F.A. Josh Morris and Francis Haden, September 2001

Start with *The Wasp Factory*, then traverse right, working up toward a half-pipe that could be called "Groove Tube of the North." This is a fun climb with very interesting moves. The anchor is at the top of the tube.

6. INTENSIFY 7b+ (5.12c), 30 meters, 12 quickdraws★★★★★
F.A. Francis Haden, September 2001
This climbs the wall just right of *Flushed* but is started at the mouth of a small cave 7.5 meters right of that route's start. More fun.

7. SEXY BEAST 6c (5.11b), 25 meters, 12 quickdraws★★★
F.A. Josh Morris and Francis Haden, September 2001
This difficult start is at the very right side of the crag (not shown in the photo). Some long slings are recommended in various places to limit drag.

Chapter 13

LAOS

With the surge in popularity of climbing in Thailand, it only makes sense that climbers have looked into the hinterlands of Southeast Asia for that same limestone. The geography of Laos is dominated by mountains, and the country may have more karst formations than Thailand. Though rock runs the entire length of Laos, the formations with established routes that you are allowed to climb is all centered around the town of Vang Vieng.

SAFETY CONSIDERATIONS

However, there is a downside to climbing in Laos. Right here at the start we should point out that this is not the safest country in the world. Ghosts of the country's twentieth-century history, which was dominated by the Second Indochina War (Vietnam War), are still howling. Small groups of the Hmong, a mountain tribe of U.S. allies in the war who were left when the United States pulled out of the battlefield in Southeast Asia, are still hoping for independence from the communist Lao government. Militant uprisings, and a state of low-intensity guerrilla war, were prevalent all through the 1990s.

The karst spires of Vang Vieng from the balcony of your room. (Volker Schoeffl)

In 2003 a bus was attacked just a few kilometers north of Vang Vieng, the town where climbing is legal, and more than a dozen locals and tourists were killed. Vang Vieng itself went from being a bit of a travelers' boomtown to a ghost town. You are taking a risk by being in Laotian backcountry, and you are off the beaten track when you are climbing.

One more unfortunate remnant of the Vietnam War that makes Laos a less-than-ideal, bring-the-whole-family type of tourist destination is all the un-exploded ordnance (UXO) that is lying about the countryside. During the war, more tonnage of bombs was dropped in Laos than was used in all of WWII. Per-haps worse are the landmines left behind by the North Vietnamese Army, because the NVA never mapped their minefields, and all of the unexploded artillery and mortar shells from the ground battles still await victims. The areas covered in this book have, for the most part, been cleared of these problems (if they ever

An undetonated 2000-pound bomb on the Plain of Jars in central Laos

had them). However, traipsing around in the woods looking for new crags could bring you across UXO. It's just one more howling ghost from the war and one more reason to watch your step.

VISAS
Upon your arrival at Luang Prabang, the Friendship Bridge in Vientiane, or Vientiane International Airport, visas issued are good for 14 days. If you want to stay longer, you need to apply for one at a Lao embassy. The website *www. visit-laos.com/before/visas.htm* gives all the information you currently need. The easiest way to get the longer visa is to get your travel agent on Khao San Road in Bangkok to apply for it on your behalf. You just have to give the travel agent your passport for a day or two and pay a nominal fee.

CLIMBING PERMITS AND GUIDES
Wildside Eco Group will be able to tell you right away if there are any hang-ups with climbing at the moment, and then get you to Vang Vieng at a cost comparable to that of any other travel agency (probably less than US$30). If

you are going to Laos specifically to climb, you might want to contact them ahead of time.

Wildside Eco Group
www.wildside-laos.com
info@wildside-asia.com
68 Nokeo Khummane Road (off the Mekong waterfront), Vientiane, Laos
856-0-21-251-563
Fax: 856-0-21-223-741

Wildside also has a sales office in the United States in Seattle, Washington.
Wildside Travel
wildsidetravel@yahoo.com
1-206-390-1201

GETTING TO VANG VIENG, LAOS

Vang Vieng lies about 170 kilometers north of the Laotian capital, Vientiane, on Route 13. You can get there a few different ways.

Via Vientiane

More than likely you will go through Vientiane. Direct flights from Bangkok to Vientiane are available on both Thai Airways and Lao Aviation. From Vientiane, I recommend you go to the Wildside Eco Group office to proceed on to Vang Vieng. It's possible to just hop on a bus or hire a taxi to take you there, but you will have to go to Wildside anyway once you get to Vang Vieng, so you might as well make the contact in Vientiane.

Via Udon Thani

You can also fly from Bangkok to Udon Thani, then take a cab for 45 minutes from there to the town of Nong Khai on the Mekong River. The Friendship Bridge that spans the Mekong (the Mekong forms the border between Thailand and Laos) in Nong Khai is the most commonly used border crossing. Flying through Udon Thani costs about the same as the direct flight to Vientiane, but it is easier to book because the direct flight tends to fill up fast.

It is also possible to get to Udon Thani via train and bus from Bangkok and then catch the taxi to the border.

Via Luang Prabang

A third method is to fly into the town of Luang Prabang, which lies about 200 kilometers north of Vang Vieng, and either ride a public bus or rent a motorcycle to get to Vang Vieng. This is the most scenic way because Luang Prabang is an amazing little city and Route 13 between Luang Prabang and Vang Vieng is staggeringly beautiful. However, the insurgents along the road between the two cities are active from time to time and have been known to target buses.

The bus is cheap, less than a few dollars U.S. Motorcycles, usually Honda Dreams, are for rent for around US$5 per day. You will of course be responsible for any damage done to the bike, and though there are quite a few motorcycle rental agencies in Luang Prabang, only a limited number of them will let you take a bike all the way to Vang Vieng. Shop around. It is possible to hire a driver to take you all the way, depending on the danger level of Route 13, but finding a driver to do it can be rather difficult. In the past this has cost about US$70. The ride from Luang Prabang to Vang Vieng takes about five hours.

VANG VIENG

Vang Vieng is a small town. In the early 1990s, this little town was not much more than a rest stop for buses and trucks before they entered the most treacherous bit of Route 13 between Vientiane and Luang Prabang. However, it took only a few passing travelers to realize what a beautiful gem the town is. The skyline to the west is dominated by karst towers, while the Nam Song River flows through the town and keeps the local rice paddies well irrigated and green.

Eats and Accommodations

At the crossroads of the two main streets, Wildside Eco Group has an office, and from that central point, restaurants and guesthouses extend down either street. You can expect to spend US$3 to $10 per day on your room and far less than that on food. A really nice guesthouse with great views is Xayhoo Riverside. It is across from the hospital and costs around US$18 per night.

Communication and Transportation

Internet cafes are common, and it is possible to use a public phone to call home using calling cards for sale at most shops. Motorcycles can be rented at numerous places (and probably your guesthouse) for about US$5 per day.

Health Considerations

Laos is one of the poorest countries in the world and thus has a very limited health-care system. There is a hospital in Vang Vieng, but it is really just there in spirit and I wouldn't recommend you even get stitches there. If you get hurt or sick, you should try to get to the Lao-Luxembourg Hospital in Phomnemy. Phomnemy can be reached by going back down Route 13 to the town of Pong Hong, then taking the only turn and following that road for about 9 kilometers. It takes about 2 hours. Wildside Eco Group is your best bet for getting a car to take you there. I might add that Dr. Volker Schoeffl spends part of the year in residence at this hospital. If the doctor is in, it is probably the best place in the world for you to go with a climbing injury!

THE FORGOTTEN WARRIORS

The Hmong began their fight against the North Vietnamese before America entered the war and then accepted and requested as much assistance as the United States could give. At one point Laos, which was the main conduit for the Ho Chi Minh Trail, was occupied by more than 70,000 North Vietnamese Army troops. In comparison, the U.S. Central Intelligence Agency had around 100 people in-country then. The real fighters were the Hmong, who numbered as many as 40,000.

The Hmong's general, Vang Pao, was an instinctive leader with an uncanny ability as a guerrilla warrior. He was highly respected by both the North Vietnamese and Americans, and he led the war against the North Vietnamese in the same way they conducted the war in South Vietnam against the United States. Among hundreds of other distinctions, General Vang Pao was, and remains, the only non-American to be allowed to call in B-52 air strikes as he saw fit.

When the United States gave in to world opinion and pulled out of the Second Indochina War, General Vang Pao and his 40,000-strong Hmong army were left up a creek without a paddle. Many fled, making their way to Thailand and then from there to France and the United States. Those who didn't flee found themselves heavily persecuted by the communist forces. Vang Pao and many of his comrades in arms still live in the United States.

A few great books to read on this subject are listed in the References (under Historical) at the back of this book. Reading just a couple of them will probably give you a completely different perspective on the Vietnam War.

THAM NAM THEM

Sun exposure: The wall outside the western end of the cave faces west, and the main amphitheater gets sun for much of the afternoon. However, if it gets too hot, you can go into the cave and climb in there (routes 15–20).

Wall angle and difficulty: There's a little of everything here. The easier routes are very short and not steep. There are some very steep powerfests and long endurance routes.

Hazards: The main wall outside the western entrance of the cave seeps a lot in the rainy season. This means the bolts do get wet, so they are aging faster than you would like. It also means that if you are the first one on the routes for the season, you are probably going to be grabbing a lot of holds that are covered in silt. Perhaps the biggest danger at the time of this writing is the insurgents. This is the very area where the last big attack along Route 13 took place! Also, remember you need a permit and guide from Wildside Eco Group to climb here.

Approach: Take Route 13 north out of Vang Vieng. At about 7 kilometers, a small dirt road veers off to the west (left). Follow it until it ends in rice paddies. Continue on foot toward the mountains. Cross the Nam Song River (it's about knee-deep here) and then follow a small, usually dry streambed on the other side toward the pass in the mountains. This stream goes into the eastern opening of this cave. You walk through the cave, sometimes wading for a short distance in waist-deep water, before arriving in a large room near the western mouth of the cave. You exit the cave at the "the cube," an obvious block of limestone near the center of the main crag. *Barrel Roll* starts on the wall to the right of the cave's western mouth, moving through the roof just above the opening of the cave; *Prince of the Sky* is farther to the right. *Quicky* and *Poppy Seed* are on the cube. Routes 5–11 are on the wall to the left of the cavern's western entrance. Routes 12–14 are on a boulder about 30 meters in front of this wall. Routes 15–20 are on the left-side wall of the room inside the cave, on the right wall from the western entrance (or the left wall as you approach the crag from the other end of the cave)—these routes aren't shown on the topo.

Getting through Tham Nam Them ("Running Water Cave") is a fun little adventure that requires a headlamp. In midafternoon, the sun shines into the cave for about 3 hours. In the morning it can be pretty dark, but once you spend about 10 minutes in here, your eyes are fully adjusted! Many of these climbs are on tufa material and stalactites, so the holds can be sharp. In fact, the wall above the cube (see *Approach*) is a sea of stalactites, and if you are the first one here for the season, you can expect a lot of silt on them. Also, note that I do not mention the number of quickdraws needed for these routes. All are sport climbs, but I can't remember how many bolts there are for each. Use your judgment.

1. PRINCE OF THE SKY   8a+ (5.13c), 30 meters★★★
F.A. Volker Schoeffl and Tina Mueller, February 2002
Sadly, this arête looks better than it is. If it has cleaned up with time, then it should be outstanding. Otherwise, be prepared for dirty holds.

2. BARREL ROLL   8a (5.13b), 14 meters★★★★
F.A. Volker Schoeffl and Sam Lightner Jr., February 2002
This is a fun route, but it often needs to be cleaned. If it were on Tonsai on Railay Beach, there would be permanent quickdraws on it. Find the start down inside the western end of the cave, and climb up to just above the cube.

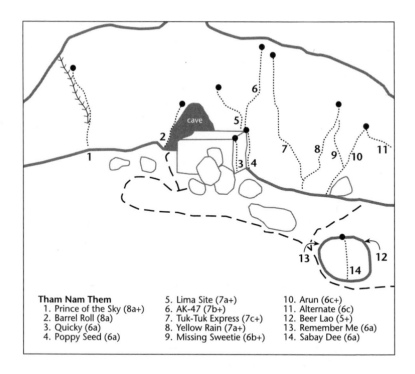

Tham Nam Them
1. Prince of the Sky (8a+)
2. Barrel Roll (8a)
3. Quicky (6a)
4. Poppy Seed (6a)

5. Lima Site (7a+)
6. AK-47 (7b+)
7. Tuk-Tuk Express (7c+)
8. Yellow Rain (7a+)
9. Missing Sweetie (6b+)

10. Arun (6c+)
11. Alternate (6c)
12. Beer Lao (5+)
13. Remember Me (6a)
14. Sabay Dee (6a)

3. QUICKY   6a (5.10a), 8 meters★★
F.A. Gerd Schoeffl, February 2002

Find the start to this one at the base of the cube.

4. POPPY SEED   6a (5.10a), 10 meters★★★
F.A. Radek Capek, February 2002

This starts a couple meters right of *Quicky* and goes to an anchor on the main wall at the right side of the cube.

5. LIMA SITE   7a+ (5.12a), 20 meters★★
F.A. Gerd Schoeffl, February 2002

From the right side of the cube, climb up and left above the mouth of the cave.

6. AK-47   7b+ (5.12c), 30 meters★★★★
F.A. Carsten Seidel, February 2002

This is a fun route up the center of the amphitheater on big holds and stalactites. Good pump.

7. TUK-TUK EXPRESS   7c+ (5.13a), 35 meters★★★★
F.A. Radek Capek, February 2002
A big pump up the middle of the wall. This climb shares a start with *Yellow Rain*. You need a 70-meter rope to safely lower from this route.

8. YELLOW RAIN   7a+ (5.12a), 25 meters★★★★
F.A. Sam Lightner Jr., February 2002
Shares a start with *Tuk-Tuk Express* and then trends up and right to a shared anchor with *Missing Sweetie*.

9. MISSING SWEETIE   6b+ (5.11a), 25 meters★★★★★
F.A. Sam Lightner Jr., February 2002
This starts a couple meters right of *Yellow Rain* and goes up the easier ground to that route's anchor.

10. ARUN   6c+ (5.11c), 25 meters★★
F.A. Somporn Suebhait (King) and Aey, February 2003
This is the connection of *Missing Sweetie* and the anchor for *Alternate*. The name, which means "dawn," also happens to be King's son's name!

11. ALTERNATE   6c (5.11b), 25 meters★★★
F.A. Sam Lightner Jr., February 2002
This climb starts on the far right side of the wall and traverses to your left.

12. BEER LAO   5+ (5.9), 8 meters★★
F.A. Carsten Seidel, February 2002
This is the leftmost climb of the two routes on the boulder that faces the main wall.

13. REMEMBER ME   6a (5.10a), 8 meters★★
F.A. Carsten Seidel, February 2002
This one is on the boulder's right side as you face it from the wall.

14. SABAY DEE   6a (5.10a), 8 meters★★
F.A. Tina Mueller, February 2002
This climb is on the side of the boulder facing away from the main wall.

15. ANOTHER DAY IN PARADISE   8a+ (5.13c), 12 meters★★★★
F.A. Volker Schoeffl and Tina Mueller, January 2003
This is the rightmost route inside the cave. It climbs up and right and is very powerful.

16. FEBRUARY 5   **8a (5.13b), 12 meters, 6 quickdraws★★**
F.A. Dr. Volker Schoefl and Isa, March 2005

The furthest right of the cave routes, this one is named in memory of the people killed on February 5, 2003, ambush by bandits.

17. THE CRITTER   **7a+ (5.12a), 12 meters★★★★**
F.A. Sam Lightner Jr. and Volker Schoeffl, February 2002

A fun climb inside the cave that is steep and powerful.

18. VOLKER'S EISTRAUM   **7b+ (5.12c), 12 meters★★★**
F.A. Volker Schoeffl, February 2004

This climb is left of *The Critter* and goes up and left inside the cave.

19. NAME UNKNOWN

Grade unknown as well; shares the anchor with *Volker's Eistraum.*

20. NAME UNKNOWN

A climb exists on a boulder in this part of the cave. That's all I know.

SLEEPING WALL

Sun exposure: Though this wall faces pretty much south, it creates its own shade with vegetation and its absurd angle. The routes on the outer walls are in such a tight canyon that they also rarely see any sun.

Wall angle and difficulty: The left side of this wall would be the Tonsai of Laos with some very steep roof problems. The right side is not as steep and has moderate routes.

Hazards: Depending on climbing traffic here, the routes can be dirty. Following the rainy season, they may be seeping. Bring lots of bug repellent.

Approach: To reach this area, take Route 13 north out of Vang Vieng for 2 kilometers. Look for a sign that says Tham Non ("Sleeping Cave"). At this sign, take the marked left turn down a small dirt road toward the cave. At the river, you can either wade across, though it's fairly deep, or you can ask the boatmen who are always there to give you a quick ride across (a small tip for this is appreciated). Once on the other side, find a trail that skirts along a dirty wall for 30 meters or so, then hang a right into the tight little canyon. Routes 1–6 are about 50 meters to the left and routes 7-19 are in the canyon on the right. Routes 7–14 are right of the big overhang in the canyon. Climbs 13–17 are just beyond the photo but easy to find. Routes 15 and 16, just beyond what's shown in the photo, share an anchor. Routes 17–19 are on the back wall.

The Sleeping Wall is actually two different areas separated by about 50 meters of jungle. I have only climbed a couple of the routes so most of this information is not first-hand. A special thanks goes to Volker Schoeffl for not only putting

THE ROUTE NAMES

Almost all of the route names for Tham Nam are in reference to the Hmong, the CIA, and their struggle against the North Vietnamese Army in Laos.

The Hmong have a legend that Chao Fa, the Prince of the Sky, would come to protect them in the worst of times (which could be said to be the 1960s and '70s). *Prince of the Sky* refers to Hmong pilot Ly Liu, who was considered by many Americans to be the best and bravest during the Vietnam War. He lived in a house with no electricity and had never ridden in a car when he learned to fly. Ly Liu's abilities as a pilot garnered him this nickname. He was shot down and killed in June 1969 after surviving thousands of successful sorties.

Barrel Roll is a flying maneuver (useful on this route!), but it's also the name of a bombing campaign during the Vietnam War.

Lima Site refers to the CIA and Air America reference for a landing strip for dropping off supplies during the war. The airstrip in Vang Vieng was a CIA-built Lima Site.

Yellow Rain is the name the Hmong gave to the chemical attacks against them by the communist forces between 1975 and 1991. It's probably in reference to mustard gas. Some *Yellow Rain* was used in the Vang Vieng area.

During the war, *Alternate* was the code name for the so-called secret city of Long Tieng in the highlands of Laos (about 97 kilometers from Vang Vieng). This was the Hmong Army's center of operations and the main staging point for Raven pilots (CIA forward air controllers) to work out of against the Vietnamese. Forty thousand people lived in Long Tieng, but it appeared on no map.

The Critter was an animal given to the Raven pilots as a pet by some Hmong children. The Ravens didn't know what this animal was, but we now think it might have been a pangolin (scaly anteater). The Critter flew a number of missions with the Ravens but was eventually blown up while eating its breakfast during a North Vietnamese artillery barrage.

up most of these climbs, but also getting the information to me. Routes 1–6 are very steep; the other routes are in a tight canyon with walls that are near-vertical to just beyond vertical. All of these routes are less than 25 meters long and require no more than 10 quickdraws. However, I don't have specific information for each route.

1. OSCAR   7b+ (5.12c)★★★
F.A. Volker Schoeffl and Christina Mueller, December 2002
This climb starts around the corner and left of *Tina*. Steep and fun.

2. TINA   **7c (5.12d)★★★**
F.A. Volker Schoeffl and Christina Mueller, December 2002
  This roof route works its way from the back of the overhang out through stalactites on the left side of the roof.

3. SPIDER   **7a+ (5.12a)★★★**
F.A. Volker Schoeffl and Christina Mueller, December 2002
  Sharing a start with *Snake Skin,* this climb moves past stalactites right of *Tina.* The anchor just over the lip is also shared with *Snake Skin.*

4. SNAKE SKIN   **7a (5.11d)★★★★**
F.A. Volker Schoeffl and Christina Mueller, December 2002
  Start on *Spider* and then follow large holds out right then back left to the anchor shared with *Spider.*

5. LONELY COWBOY   **6b (5.10c)★★★★**
F.A. Volker Schoeffl, October 2003
  Climb just right of *Snake Skin* to an anchor just over the lip.

6. HATE   **6b (5.10c)★**
F.A. Volker Schoeffl, October 2003
  Climb through the large stalactites right of *Lonely Cowboy* to a shared anchor.

7. WHITE JUNGLE   **6b+ (5.11a)★★★**
F.A. Enrico Ramoth, Gerd Schoeffl, and Volker Schoeffl, October 2003
  This climb is on the right-side wall at the mouth of the small canyon.

8. HAPPY   **6a (5.10a)★★★**
F.A. Sek and Volker Schoeffl, February 2004
  Starting between the two large roots running down the wall, this climb shares an anchor with *Sek Billion.*

9. SEK BILLION   **5 (5.8)★★★**
F.A. Sek and Volker Schoeffl, February 2004
  Sharing a start with *Sam's Dream,* just right of the second large root, this climb then shares an anchor with *Happy.*

10. SAM'S DREAM   **5 (5.8)★★★★**
F.A. Volker Schoeffl and Christina Mueller, December 2002
  Climb the low-angle wall to a shared anchor with *Wildside.*

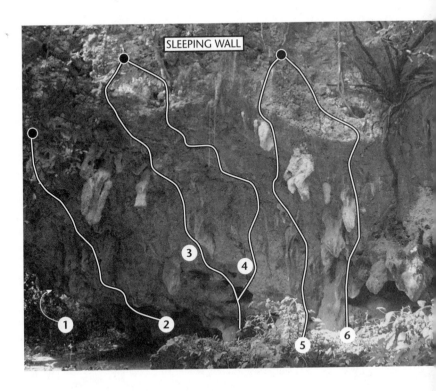

11. WILDSIDE   6b (5.10c)★★

F.A. Volker Schoeffl and Christina Mueller, December 2002

The start of this route is a couple meters right of *Sam's Dream* and shares its start with *Kouky*. The anchor is shared with *Sam's Dream*.

12. KOUKY   6c+ (5.11c)★★★

F.A. Volker Schoeffl and Christina Mueller, December 2002

Climb halfway up *Wildside* and then tend right onto steeper ground to an anchor just below the lip of the wall.

13. SI POU   7b+ (5.12c)★★★★

F.A. Volker Schoeffl and Christina Mueller, December 2002

This climbs the steep wall just past *Kouky*. It shares an anchor with *La*.

14. LA   6c (5.11b)★★★

F.A. Volker Schoeffl and Christina Mueller, December 2002

Find this climb on the easier ground just right of *Si Pou*.

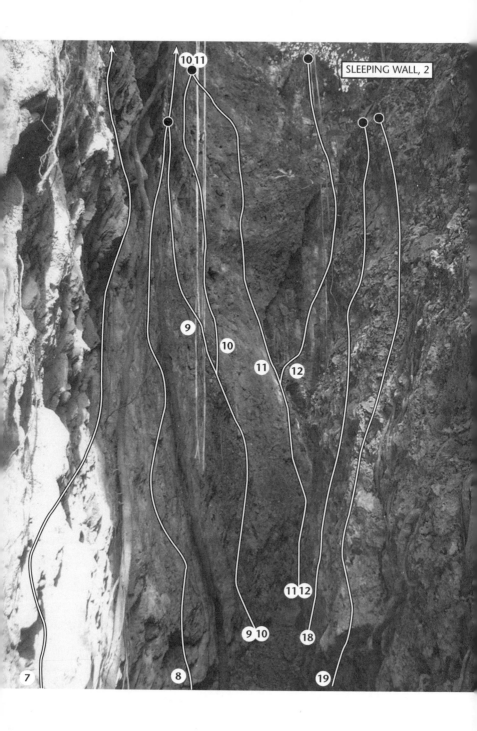

SLEEPING WALL, 2

15. HAPPY TU TU   6c (5.11b)★★★★
F.A. Volker Schoeffl and Christina Mueller, December 2002
> This climb just past *La* shares an anchor with *Give Pizza a Chance.*

16. GIVE PIZZA A CHANCE   6c+ (5.11c)★★★
F.A. Volker Schoeffl and Christina Mueller, December 2002
> This is the last climb near the end of the canyon.

17. NO NAME #1   4 (5.5)★★
F.A. Volker Schoeffl, date unknown
This route is the leftmost of the three on this tower, just across the canyon from *Happy Tu Tu* and *Give Pizza a Chance.*

18. NO NAME #2   5 (5.8)★★
F.A. Volker Schoeffl, date unknown
> This is just across from *Si Pou.*

19. VOLKER'S DREAM   5 (5.8)★
F.A. Volker Schoeffl, date unknown
This dream of Volker's is just across from *Sam's Dream....* Never taunt the author, Herr Doctor!

THAM NON ("SLEEPING CAVE")

Sun exposure: It really is the mouth of a cave, so there is not much sun. If it's a hot day, this is the place to be.

Wall angle and difficulty: These climbs are very steep but juggy and have plenty of rests.

Hazards: Watch where you put your hands in caves...you never know whose home you're climbing through! Also, in November and October there is often standing water at the base of these routes making it nearly impossible to climb here.

Approach: Tham Non, the "Sleeping Cave," is just upstream from Sleeping Wall. Approach it the same as for Sleeping Wall, but once you cross the river, follow the trail and signs to the cave. It's pretty obvious. Routes 1–4 are under the roof to the left of the cave; routes 5–8 are on the left side of the cave as you enter. Routes 9–14 are on the right side of the cave as you enter it. The routes at the back of the cave can be pretty dark.

This crag is the mouth of a cave. The climbs extend into the actual cave as far as you might want to go without wearing a headlamp. Creating a topo for a tube of rock is not easy and is confusing, so I have simply listed the routes on the left and right sides of the cave. The routes are all less than 25 meters in length and require no more than a dozen quickdraws.

1. XAYHOO   7b+ (5.12c)★★★★
F.A. Volker Schoeffl, Carsten Seidel, Gerd Schoeffl, and Enrico Ramoth, February 2004

This is the first climb on the left side of the entrance to the cave.

2. SOK DI PAI MAI   8a (5.13b)★★★★
F.A. Volker Schoeffl, April 2003

This route is just right of *Xayhoo.*

3. BUTTERFLY   8a (5.13b)★★★
F.A. Volker Schoeffl, February 2004

This route begins right of *Sok di Pai Mai* and shares a start with *Tag Am Meer.* It trends up and slightly right, then goes out the roof toward the large stalactite.

4. TAG AM MEER   7c+ (5.13a)★★★
F.A. Volker Schoeffl, February 2004

Start with *Butterfly* but then continue on the line of bolts up and right.

5. JUST HORRIFIED   7a (5.11d)★★★
F.A. Volker Schoeffl, March 2004

The line of bolts right of *Butterfly* and *Tag Am Meer* traverses up and left behind a large stalactite.

6. KARAOKE   7b (5.12b)★★★
F.A. Volker Schoeffl, March 2003

Just right of *Just Horrified,* this climb goes up then traverses hard to the left, ending on the stalactite.

7. FLASH KEKS   6b (5.10c)★★★★
F.A. Volker Schoeffl, March 2003

This route is the line of bolts right of *Karaoke.* The anchor is shared with *Hamilton Powerarm Meets Tyrone Shoelace,* which starts on the other side of the cave.

8. PIN PAH NOI NGUN   5+ (5.9)★
F.A. Volker Schoeffl and Stefan Zenker, March 2003

This climbs the easier ground right of *Flash Keks* to a ledge.

9. CHICKEN SCHNITZEL   7b+ (5.12c)★★★★
F.A. Volker Schoeffl, March 2003
This route is the farthest back in the cave, on the right side.

10. CORNFLAKE   6c (5.11b)★★★
F.A. Volker Schoeffl, Max Felle, Alex Hislop, and Oscar Willemson, March 2003
This one is right of *Chicken Snitzel* and shares an anchor with *Ostkamin*.

11. OSTKAMIN   6a+ (5.10b)★★
F.A. Volker Schoeffl, Max Felle, Alex Hislop, and Oscar Willemson, March 2003
This takes a straighter line on larger holds to the anchor used by *Cornflake*. The name means "east chimney."

12. PUZZLE   6c+ (5.11c)★★★
F.A. Volker Schoeffl, Max Felle, Alex Hislop, and Oscar Willemson, March 2003
Just left of *Hamilton Powerarm Meets Tyrone Shoelace*.

13. HAMILTON POWERARM MEETS TYRONE SHOELACE   6b (5.10c)★★★
F.A. Mark Ryan and Volker Schoeffl, February 2004
This climb is across from *Flash Keks* and shares an anchor with that route.

14. SCARY TUNA   5 (5.8)★★★
F.A. Stefan Zenker and Volker Schoeffl, March 2003
This climb ascends behind and ends on the large stalactite. It uses the same anchor as *Karaoke*.

LESS-VISITED CLIMBING AREAS
IN THAILAND

There are a number of other climbing areas around Thailand that are not covered in this book. I have included here a very brief listing of them with a bit of a description. Very few climbers venture to these places, and often the climbs go months without being scaled. This means that in all likelihood, you will be one of the few, if not the only, *farang* in that general area. It also means that the climbing is probably not as clean and the routes not as well maintained as the areas covered in this book. Keep in mind that getting to these areas is often a good adventure in itself because they are, for the most part, not on the normal tourist track and therefore not supported by the tourist infrastructure of Thailand. Local buses might be what you have to use, but in all likelihood you will end up renting a car or motorcycle. At the time of this writing, the best source of information on these crags is at *www.simonfoley.com/climbing*. Wee and King, on Railay Beach, have also been to a number of these crags and will no doubt be helpful if you stop in at their shops. Good luck.

Khao Yoi

This crag located about an hour and a half south of Bangkok is the most popular climbing venue for Bangkok's climbers. The rock is high-quality Ratburi karst, and there are about twenty sport routes ranging from 6a to 7c+. A topo can be found on the Web.

Khao Jin Lar

Located in the beautiful Lopburi region two hours northeast of Bangkok, this climbing area is also very popular with the Bangkok boys. There are quite a few karsts in this region, but the lion's share of climbing is all done on one 180-meter-tall spire that is somewhat reminiscent of the Thaiwand on the Phra Nang Peninsula. So far, a couple dozen sport routes have been established, all in the 6a to 7a range. There is room for many more climbs in this area, but you cannot just show up and start putting up routes. The crag is a sacred spire, and although the monks that run the local *wat* are getting along with climbers, too much development might make them close the area down to climbing. It's best to talk with the head monk when you pass through the *wat* on the way to the crag to make sure that climbing is still acceptable and to find out what they are willing to accept in the way of new routes.

Langsak

Located in Uthai Thani Province about half a day's drive northwest of Bangkok, this crag sees very few visitors. I have not been here and thus cannot judge for myself, but I have been told that the wall is of excellent rock and there is potential for more routes.

Koh Tao

This is something different for Thailand. Unlike all the other areas, this one is granite and, for the most part, the climbing is less than vertical. It's also a bouldering area and not a sport crag. Another difference between this area and the few listed above is that it is easy to access via tourist transportation because many visitors come to this island to go diving. The website *www.zengecko.com* is an excellent source of information on the climbing of Koh Tao at the time of this writing.

INTERNATIONAL GRADE COMPARISON CHART

UIAA	USA	GB	F	D	AUS
V−	5.5	4a	5a	V	13
V	5.6	4b	5b	VI	14
V+	5.7	4c	5c		
VI−	5.8			VIIa	15
VI	5.9	5a	6a	VIIb	16
VI+	5.10a		6a+	VIIc	
VII−	5.10b	5b	6b	VIIIa	17
VII	5.10c		6b+	VIIIb	18
VII+	5.10d	5c	6c	VIIIc	19
VIII−	5.11a		6c+	IXa	20
	5.11b	6a			21
VIII	5.11c		7a	IXb	22
	5.11d	6b			23
VIII+	5.12a		7a+	IXc	24
IX−	5.12b		7b	Xa	25
	5.12c	6c	7b+		26
IX	5.12d	7a	7c	Xb	27
IX+	5.13a		7c+	Xc	28
X−	5.13b		8a	XIa	29
	5.13c	7b	8a+		30
X	5.13d		8b	XIb	31
X+	5.14a		8b+		32
XI−	5.14b		8c		33
	5.14c		8c+		34
XI	5.14d		9a		

The UIAA encourages the inclusion of information in guidebooks that helps visitors from overseas understand the most important information about local access, grades and emergency procedures. The UIAA also encourages climbers and mountaineers to share knowledge and views on issues such as safety, ethics, and good practice in mountain sports. The UIAA is not responsible for, and accepts no liability for, the technical content or accuracy of the information in this guidebook. Climbing, hill walking and mountaineering are activities with a danger of personal injury and death. Participants should be aware of, understand, and accept these risks and be responsible for their own actions and involvement.

SELECTED REFERENCES

To write this book, I called on information that can be found in all of the books listed below. They are all excellent sources of information, although some are a bit harder to read than others and a couple of them take potshots at rock climbers!

HISTORY AND CULTURE

Castle, Timothy. *One Day Too Long: Top-Secret Site 85 and the Bombing of North Vietnam.* New York: Columbia University Press, 1999.

Hamilton-Merritt, Jane. *Tragic Mountains: The Hmong and the Americans and the Secret Wars for Laos 1942–1992.* Bloomington, Ind.: Indiana University Press, 1999.

Heidhues, Mary Somers. *Southeast Asia: A Concise History.* London: Thames & Hudson, 2000. An easy read on the region's history, but it's a bit dated.

Osborne, Milton. *Southeast Asia: An Introductory History.* New South Wales: Allen & Unwin Pty., Limited, 1998. Covers the entire region and does a good job of explaining how Thailand has fit in with its neighbors.

———. *The Mekong.* New South Wales: Allen & Unwin, 2000. Another book by Milton Osborne; it's a good read, but again it does not focus solely on Thailand.

Robbins, Christopher. *The Ravens: Pilots of the Secret War in Laos.* Bangkok: Asia Books, 1989.

Ruohomaki, Olli Pekka. *Fisherman No More?* Bangkok: White Lotus Press, 1999. Explains how the changes that have come to modern southern Thailand have affected the people. It is difficult to find outside of Thailand.

Seagrave, Sterling. *Lords of the Rim: The Invisible Empire of the Overseas Chinese.* London: Corgi Books, 1996. About the ethnic Chinese who live around the Pacific Rim. Though it's not purely about Thailand, this very interesting book has some excellent information on the Chinese in Thailand.

Warner, Roger. *Back Fire:* The *CIA's Secret War in Laos and Its Link to the War in Vietnam.* New York: Simon & Schuster, 1995.

White, Walter Grainge. *The Sea Gypsies of Malaya.* Bangkok: White Lotus Press, 1997. A difficult read but it gives a good explanation of how people lived in the Krabi region up until very recently. This is difficult to find outside of Thailand.

Wyatt, David K. *Thailand: A Short History.* New Haven, Conn.: Yale University Press, 1984. A good, concise history, though a bit dry. It's the standard on the subject of Thai history.

GENERAL TRAVEL

O'Rourke, P. J. *Holidays in Hell.* New York: Grove/Atlantic, Inc., 1998. No trip abroad should be started without reading this. It's not set in Thailand, but it's a fun read about roaming the Third World.

Cummings, Joe et. al. *Thailand*. Oakland, CA: Lonely Planet, 1993. This publisher's best work. They update it pretty much every year. If you are going to be hitting only the sand and sea, then Lonely Planet's *Thailand's Islands and Beaches* will be enough for you. However, I recommend the big tome, because it covers Bangkok and Chiang Mai more thoroughly than any other publication.

ECOLOGY

Henley, Thom. *Krabi Caught in the Spell: A Guide to Thailand's Enchanted Province*. Bangkok: Asia Books, 2003. Calls itself a guide to the province but is more of an explanation of how the people, the animals, and the environment all get along (or don't). It covers a lot of the information found in *Reefs to Rainforests, Mangroves to Mountains* as well. This is an excellent book to read while you are staying on the Phra Nang Peninsula.

———. *Reefs to Rainforests, Mangroves to Mountains*. Bangkok: Asia Books, 1999. An excellent book for understanding the flora and fauna of southern Thailand. Henley is not much of a fan of rock climbing and unfairly labels us as one of the major hammers on the environment of southern Thailand, but he understands the ecology of the region and does an excellent job of explaining it.

INFORMAL CLIMBING GUIDES TO THAILAND

Changrua, Wee, and Elke Schmitz. *Rock Climbing in Thailand*. Krabi, Thailand: Self-published, 2004. Kept current with the latest routes. Available directly from the shops on Phra Nang and Koh Phi Phi.

Morris, Josh, and Khaetthaleeya Uppkham. *Rock Climbing in Northern Thailand*. Chiang Mai, Thailand: Nopburee Press, 2004. Covers the areas around Chiang Mai. Available at Chiang Mai Rock Climbing Adventures.

Suebhait, Somporn. *King Climbers Route Guide Book*. Krabi, Thailand: King Climbers, 2003. Kept current with the latest routes. Available directly from the shops on Phra Nang and Koh Phi Phi.

FICTION

Aylwen, Axel. *The Falcon of Siam*. London: Methuen, 1989. The one great historical novel about Thailand is sort of the *Shogun* of Thailand. It's a great read.

Hoskin, John. *Falcon in the Court of Siam*. Bangkok: Asia Books, 2003. As the preceding title was such a success, another author has written a similar book...I haven't read this one.

INDEX

ABOUT THE AUTHOR

Sam Lightner's life changed in 1990 when the longtail boat he was traveling in rounded the Phra Nang Peninsula and he saw the steep cliffs rising off Phra Nang Beach. Since then Sam has made Railay Beach his winter home and spent the last 15 years exploring its towers, caverns, walls, beaches and jungles. He has established many routes on the Phra Nang Peninsula, graded from 5 to 8b, and spearheaded the rebolting of its numerous crags, a project which is close to his heart and is ongoing. This has led to the publishing of this guide book; which is the accumulation of information and knowledge about Thailand that Sam has acquired over his years spent in Railay. Reared in Jackson, Wyoming,

Sam Lightner Jr.

Sam's dedication to adventure runs deep, with many months spent exploring the jungles of Borneo, ice climbing in the Canadian Rockies, crack climbing in the Utah Desert, and establishing new and challenging routes all over southern Thailand. Sam now splits his time between his house on Railay Beach and Jackson, Wyoming.

Sam is the author of *All Elevations Unknown: An Adventure in the Heart of Borneo, Exotic Rock: The Travel Guide for Rock Climbers* and the editor of *One Move too Many.... How to Understand the Injuries and Overuse Syndromes of Rock Climbing.*

THE MOUNTAINEERS, founded in 1906, is a nonprofit outdoor activity and conservation club, whose mission is "to explore, study, preserve, and enjoy the natural beauty of the outdoors...." Based in Seattle, Washington, the club is now the third-largest such organization in the United States, with seven branches throughout Washington State.

The Mountaineers sponsors both classes and year-round outdoor activities in the Pacific Northwest, which include hiking, mountain climbing, ski-touring, snowshoeing, bicycling, camping, kayaking, nature study, sailing, and adventure travel. The club's conservation division supports environmental causes through educational activities, sponsoring legislation, and presenting informational programs.

All club activities are led by skilled, experienced instructors, who are dedicated to promoting safe and responsible enjoyment and preservation of the outdoors.

If you would like to participate in these organized outdoor activities or the club's programs, consider a membership in The Mountaineers. For information and an application, write or call The Mountaineers, Club Headquarters, 300 Third Avenue West, Seattle, WA 98119; 206-284-6310. You can also visit the club's website at *www.mountaineers.org* or contact The Mountaineers via email at *clubmail@mountaineers.org*.

The Mountaineers Books, an active, nonprofit publishing program of the club, produces guidebooks, instructional texts, historical works, natural history guides, and works on environmental conservation. All books produced by The Mountaineers Books fulfill the club's mission.

 Send or call for our catalog of more than 500 outdoor titles:
The Mountaineers Books
1001 SW Klickitat Way, Suite 201
Seattle, WA 98134
800-553-4453
mbooks@mountaineersbooks.org
www.mountaineersbooks.org

 The Mountaineers Books is proud to be a corporate sponsor of The Leave No Trace Center for Outdoor Ethics, whose mission is to promote and inspire responsible outdoor recreation through education, research, and partnerships. The Leave No Trace program is focused specifically on human-powered (nonmotorized) recreation.

Leave No Trace strives to educate visitors about the nature of their recreational impacts, as well as offer techniques to prevent and minimize such impacts. Leave No Trace is best understood as an educational and ethical program, not as a set of rules and regulations.

For more information, visit *www.LNT.org*, or call 800-332-4100.

OTHER TITLES YOU MIGHT ENJOY
FROM THE MOUNTAINEERS BOOKS

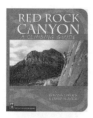

Red Rock Canyon: A Climbing Guide
The most comprehensive guidebook
to the area.

Classic Dolomite Climbs
More than 100 of the
best rock climbs in the
Italian Dolomites.

Bugaboo Rock: A Climbing Guide, 2nd Edition
200 routes in Canada's most famous climbing
destination.

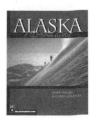

Alaska: A Climbing Guide
Local guides show you climbs not
found anywhere else.

Aconcagua: A Climbing Guide, 2nd Edition
Both the popular and less traveled routes
are included.

Ecuador: A Climbing Guide
Includes all the major peaks
in the country.

*A Climber's Guide to the Teton Range,
3rd Edition*
800 routes on more than 200 peaks.

*Mountaineering: Freedom of the Hills,
7th Edition*
"If the mountains are my church,
then *Freedom* is my Bible."
- Will Gadd, author of *Ice and Mixed
Climbing: Modern Technique*

Available at fine bookstores and outdoor stores, by phone
at 800-553-4453 or on the Web at *www.mountaineersbooks.org*

THE MOUNTAINEERS BOOKS